Nobel
Universal
Graphical Language

Nobel
Universal
Graphical Language

Milan Randić

Library of Congress Control Number: 2009908257
ISBN: Hardcover   978-1-4415-6362-0
                  Softcover   978-1-4415-6361-3

To order additional copies of this book, contact:
Xlibris Corporation
1-888-795-4274
www.Xlibris.com
Orders@Xlibris.com
59977

Contents

PART 3

PART 4

PART 5

To my wife

Dr. Mirjana Randić
and
the whole medical profession
for their dedication to help people,
to reduce human suffering and agony of pain,
to eliminate the scourge of epidemics from the globe,
to improve health and quality of life, and to prolong our lives.

Foreword

*N*obel: *Universal Graphical Language*, by Professor Milan Randić, one of the leading experts in the field of computational chemistry with great international experience, is a carefully structured description of a universal pictographic language designed to contribute to simpler and more effective human communication. The design of any artificial language is a complex task encompassing a multitude of intricate issues, which need to be resolved in order for the language to function efficiently. The development of Nobel and its description is the result of undeniable enthusiasm and many years of dedicated effort: the language is presented in the form of a thorough and systematic manuscript dealing with the linguistic as well as philosophical issues.

The book covers all aspects of Nobel: from the basic signs and arrows, to their combinations and the particulars of the more complex semantic units, as well as the grammar of this constructed language. An illustration of the use of Nobel is provided by the translation of one hundred Chinese proverbs from English into Nobel.

Some of the features of Nobel make it particularly accessible to wider audiences; these include the relatively small number of its basic signs (approximately 120), its fairly simple grammar, the nature of the design of the individual signs (they are designed in such a way that they are easy to identify and reproduce) and the fact that in addition to new signs, conventional (mathematical) symbols are also included. A further characteristic of Nobel, which is intended to ease the recognition and memorization of the signs, is that the design of the signs relies on mental associations and etymology. The limitation of the possible combinations of signs to a maximum of three signs makes the language even more transparent and accessible.

On the whole, Nobel is constructed following both the principles of linguistics and the method of the hard sciences: the vocabulary, syntax, semantics, and even discourse features of the language reflect an efficient and logical approach used in the process of its structuring.

The use of pictograms has been a fixture of human communication since the first written records; the earliest writing systems (Mesopotamian, Sumerian, early Egyptian, early Chinese) were in fact at least in part based on pictography and even in nonliterate societies, some form of pictographic tradition was often present. In contemporary Western societies, the presence of pictograms is ubiquitous (labels, public signs, instructions) although its importance is often overlooked. Nobel is a systematic attempt to organize and present the pictograms in the form of a standardized language.

The manuscript presents a brave, serious, and enthusiastic attempt to develop a universal pictographic language, the aim of which is to be available to each and every representative of contemporary civilization. This puts the author in the ranks of great philosophers, such as Ramon Lull and Gottfried Leibniz, who undertook similar tasks. The dedication and seriousness of the enterprise has already been noted, among others by Umberto Eco who, in his book *The Search for the Perfect Language,* mentions Nobel and its author. In his discussion of the visual alphabets of the present day, Eco observes that many of these are not true languages because they lack a grammatical component. Yet, as Eco points out, Milan Randić's *Nobel* is different in the sense that it entails two sets of conventions: those governing the meanings of the basic signs and those governing the meanings of combinations.

It is difficult or even impossible to speculate about the chances of any constructed universal language to reach wider audiences and in fact fulfill the task it was designed for, i.e., to ease communication, since there are many factors which may influence the turn of events. The fact that Nobel is a pictographic language makes it more accessible, and it is interesting that the author himself points out several potential uses of Nobel which have been suggested to him (including such diverse uses as an aid in the process of the recovery of post-stroke patients who temporarily lost knowledge of writing and communication, or as a form of shorthand used in conference interpreting). It is clear, however, that regardless of whether the language achieves wider diffusion or not, the complexity of the work presented in the manuscript, the methodological approach used, and the international recognition it has already received all testify to the importance of this undertaking.

Agnes Pisanski Peterlin, Ph.D.
Department of Translation and Interpreting
Faculty of Arts
University of Ljubljana
Slovenia

About Nobel

Nobel is a pictographic language based on some 120 basic signs and many arrows of different shape that are mutually combined. It is named after Alfred Nobel (1833-1896), Swedish chemist and industrialist, inventor of dynamite, who left most of his fortune to a foundation that annually gives awards to individuals whose work is characterized as "greatest benefit to mankind," known as Nobel Prizes. Besides the awards for sciences and literature significantly, Alfred Nobel included, among others, a prize for peace (that besides individuals, also organizations may obtain). Although it would be utopian to believe that human conflicts could be avoided if communication tools would improve, the emergence of universal languages certainly cannot make the situation worse!

Universal languages are a communication tool, which makes it possible for people of no common language to communicate. They are graphic, but they should be distinguished from picture writings, which only passively offer information on some event or give messages. Universal languages have more similarity with the sign languages that are used for people who lost hearing or the sign language of American Plains Indians, who spoke different languages and could communicate by sign language that they developed. However, written language has some advantages over hand sign languages in that one can communicate at a great distance, particularly today in the age of fax and computer communications, and that one can leave messages for posterity.

This is not the place to argue for or against the promise of written sign languages. Graphic (written) sign languages exist today, and the best known are Chinese characters used in China and Japan. The problem with Chinese characters is that there are too many characters and it is difficult to learn so many. It takes years for children in China and Japan to learn so many different characters, and the task would be even harder for grown people to learn if they have not done this when young. Nobel is designed to remove this difficulty and is based on the following requirements:

1. SMALL NUMBER OF BASIC SIGNS
2. SIGNS SHOULD BE EASY TO RECOGNIZE
3. SIGNS SHOULD BE EASY TO REPRODUCE
4. COMBINATIONS LIMITED TO THREE SIGNS
5. COMPLEMENTARY

We have already mentioned that Nobel uses about 120 basic signs, which can be viewed as a small number, particularly in view of over 100 signs of Nobel that are so obvious that they can be easily absorbed. The other requirements are also very important. There are many signs that can be easily recognized, but in order to be acceptable for Nobel, they also need to be easily reproduced, because that will facilitate communication. Also, when making combinations of signs, one has to make some restriction in order to maintain clarity, so we decided to have no more than three signs combined into single word. Finally, the last requirement, that of complementarities, needs some explanation. Besides having signs that one can easily recognize and easily draw, one needs some *structure* to be embedded into composition of signs that facilitates one to remember and learn signs easily. We refer to this structure as complementary or, broadly speaking, associational, and what it implies is that words and objects that are related should have related signs. Thus, for example, pairs of words like man-woman, cat-dog, coffee-tea, good-bad, love-hate, etc., should have signs that are in some opposition, while words like smoke-flame-fire, tree-wood-forest, water-sea-ocean, good-better-best should have signs that are in competition.

With this in mind when one sees and learns the basic signs, the meaning of many combinations of signs can be in advance anticipated. This helps one to learn Nobel rather fast; not months, not weeks, perhaps not even days, but a couple of hours may suffice that one may learn hundreds and hundreds of words.

In this respect, Nobel may be unique among languages written, spoken of, gesticulated. Soon you will have an opportunity to see for yourself whether this author is exaggerating or not in the promotion of Nobel. We may add also that for artificial languages, whether spoken (like Esperanto, Interlingua, and such) or written (like Nobel and Blissymbolic), the major difficulty is to build sizable vocabulary, while grammar usually represents a minor task—Nobel is not an exception. Sizable vocabulary is essential if one is interested in communications that go beyond concerns of mere survival—or, as Ukrainian writer Vladimir Dmitriyevich Dudintsev (1918-1998) entitled his book, if one aspiration is *Not by Bread Alone.*

About the Author

Milan Randić is Professor Emeritus of Drake University, Des Moines, Iowa, where he was Ellis and Nelle Levitt Professor in the Department of Mathematics and Computer Science during 1980-2000. He studied theoretical physics at University of Zagreb, Croatia, and got a Ph.D. degree at Cambridge University in England in 1958. His research interest has been theoretical chemistry. He founded the Group for Theoretical Chemistry at the Institute Rudjer Bošković, Zagreb, Croatia. He came to the USA in 1970, where he continued research in theoretical chemistry and soon entered the field of mathematical chemistry and recently of bioinformatics. He published over 450 scientific papers. He received in 1995 the Iowa Governor's Science Award and in 1996 the Skolnik Award of the American Chemical Society. He is a member of the Croatian Academy of Science and Arts since 1998. In 2005, he founded the International Academy of Mathematical Chemistry with the seat in the old town on Adriatic, Dubrovnik. In 2007, he was elected as honorary fellow of the International Academy of Mathematical Chemistry and honorary member of the National Institute of Chemistry, Ljubljana, Slovenia. Twenty-five years ago, he was visiting for several weeks in China and spent several weeks in Japan and became intrigued by Chinese characters and Japan's kanji. Already during this brief visit to Japan, he started to explore possibility to develop graphic universal signs, the distinct feature of which is to be simplicity in contrast to apparent complexity of Chinese characters. Before returning to the USA, he already came up with about one hundred signs, which is the number of kanji that children in Japan have

17

to learn in their first year in school. On return to the USA, he continued to expand sign language, which gradually grew to encompass some twenty thousand words.

———

Introduction

From prehistoric times, humans have been leaving messages in written form, either as cave paintings or petroglyphs. With passage of time, these graphic signs multiplied and have eventually led to picture writings that were perfected by ancient Egyptians in hieroglyphic messages and hieroglyphic "alphabets" in the time of pharaohs. Similarly, more involved and at first sight more cumbersome hieroglyphs of Maya have similarly evolved in a phonetic alphabet, which is clearly more efficient way for keeping records of past events than picture writing. Thus, in both cases at vast distances over the globe, hieroglyphic writing eventually reduced to hieroglyphic script. On the other hand, American Indians continued to use picture writing till modern times. One may speculate that this may be not only due to lacking a script of their own but also because of continuing contacts with people of different tongues. Similarly none of people of hundreds of dispersed Polynesian islands, speaking different languages, have script of their own with exception of Easter Islanders, who have writings using some two thousand different mysterious rongorongo glyphs. Not long ago, Steven Roger Fischer, German scholar now heading the Institute for Polynesian Languages in Auckland, New Zealand, succeeded not only to decode these glyphs but also to trace possible origin of writing on Easter Island to a brief disembarkation of Spaniards in the 1700s on that island. Spaniards asked native chiefs to put signs on a Spanish document that proclaimed the island a part of Spanish empire. Having no script of their own and requested for a written signature, native chiefs thus invented some

19

signs of their own, which eventually may have been the seeds for construction of two thousand rongorongo glyphs.

Universal language as a system of signs for the communication today exists in the form of Chinese characters that essentially have not changed over four thousand years. This is, however, not the only living universal language. We should mention Tompa, an interesting and little-known pictographic language used by people in the mountain regions of Yunnan Province of China, not far from the general area of Tibet, Thailand, Laos, Vietnam, and Myanmar (Burma).

We should also mention attempts by several scholars in seventeenth and eighteenth centuries to develop artificial universal languages, which were of two different basic types: (1) based on abstract signs under influence and imitating in spirit Chinese characters but trying to arrive at some simplified versions thereof and (2) based on classification and subclassification of all things to which numerical values were attached. In this case, communication would be based on writing numbers that could be decoded with a list of codes, which would be written for different languages. Among these, we would like to specially mention briefly the approach of Leibniz, a great German philosopher and mathematician. Leibniz had first separated integers into the prime and the composite. The prime numbers are 2, 3, 5, 7, 11, 13, etc., each of which are divisible only by itself or by one if the division is to give as the answer an integer. The composite number may have several additional divisors. Thus, nonprime numbers are first all even numbers like 4, 6, 8, 10, etc., and then any number that can be divided by an integer to give integer as the answer. For instance $21 = 3 \times 7$, or $57 = 3 \times 19$, hence both are composite. Notice that zero and one are neither prime nor composite; you may say they are special! According to Leibniz, prime numbers should be assigned to important concepts (words) while composite numbers are assigned to less important, derived concepts. So here are suggestions of Leibniz:

0   Void
1   God
2   Life
3   Reason

Now since $2 \times 3 = 6$, Leibniz assigned 6 to human person, which is a life with reasoning potential. Unfortunately, Leibniz started his work on his universal language near the end of his life and never developed it much further.

We should end this brief overview of universal languages by mentioning Bliss, an Austrian Jew who was fortunate to escape from Austria in 1940 when Nazi occupation started and moved to Australia. There for twenty years, Bliss was developing his universal language, which became later known as Blissymbolic. Bliss designed a relatively simple set of pictographic symbols that can be combined and used for everyday communications. We have neither time nor space to expand on any of the above-mentioned universal and pictographic sign systems, but collectively, they show that it is possible to have universal graphic language and that one can express most of one's ideas into such graphic forms that ought to be comprehended by people of different language backgrounds.

We selected few books for further reading for those who want to pursue the above topics at greater length.

Bibliography

Bliss, Charles K. *Semantography*, third enlarged edition. 1978, Library of Congress Catalog card 58-41205.

Fischer, Steven Roger. *Glyph-Breaker*. New York: Copernicus, Springer-Verlag, 1997.

Mallery, Garrick. *Picture-Writing of the American Indians*. Toronto: General Publishing Company, Ltd., and Dover edition, 1972.

Morley, Sylvanus Griswold. *An Introduction to the Study of the Maya Hieroglyphs*. New York: Dover Publications, 1975.

Wang Chao-Ying. *Tompa Characters: Living Hieroglyphs*. Printed in Japan, 1996, ISBN 4-8373-0414-1.

PART 1

BASIC SIGNS

Basic Signs—Obvious

Let us start by depicting the first sixty basic signs of Nobel. We have ordered signs alphabetically. First thing we want to point out is that one should observe the simple nature of signs, which consist of few simple strokes, circles, or curves, which anyone should be able to reproduce. The next thing to observe is that if you would be presented with the same list of sixty words and asked to draw the corresponding signs, then probably more than half of the signs that you draw will be the same as those listed on the next pages. There may be a few signs for which slightly different diagrams are possible; the one adopted in Nobel aimed at utmost simplicity.

The signs on the next two pages represent approximately half of the signs of Nobel. Later we will show another sixty signs that constitute the other half of the basic signs of Nobel. The signs selected here have simple characteristics: they are easy to be recognized, hence the title of this section, "Basic Signs—Obvious," which was the only criterion used at this early stage of exposition of Nobel. Clearly not all the sixty words shown are equally important, or important at all. This could be said of BUTTON, CLAW, DIAMOND (unless you are a girl to be married soon!), GATE (except for those visiting the Western-style bars, or watching Western movies), and SOMBRERO (again except for people of Mexico, of course).

Few signs are associated with double interpretation, the first is pictographic or literal and the second is ideographic or figurative, based on one of the dominant properties of the shown sign. Thus ANCHOR symbolizes *safety*, particularly for ships; BALANCE is a symbol of *justice* as many courthouses display; BUTTON symbolizes something that is *automatic*; from the early medieval times CROWN has been the symbol of *authority*; DIAMOND is the *hardest* natural substance; FENCE stands for *keep*; FLOWER is very *delicate*; HEART is a symbol of love or *liking* something; PIPE & VENT allow one to *control* (a flow, or people, work, etc.); ROOF suggests *domestic* environment; SCISSORS imply *cutting*; SOMBRERO gives good *shade* (which is the literal English translation from the Spanish); STAR may also symbolize *decoration*; UMBRELLA is supposed to *protect* one (from rain); while WATCH measures *time*, of course. Thus to the sixty depicted words, we have to add fifteen ideographic interpretations, which slightly increase our vocabulary.

To learn sixty words or more of a new language is not much, but to learn it in fifteen minutes illustrates the important quality of Nobel—very close relationship, either pictographic or ideographic, between the signs and their meaning. If by now you think that all that you accomplished is to become acquainted without much effort with sixty words of Nobel or, to be precise, seventy-five words, when we allow double interpretation of few signs, this is an understatement because one can combine the sixty basic words and one can arrive at many additional words of Nobel, as illustrated on the pages that follow.

ANCHOR	APPLE	BALANCE	BALL	BASKET
BED	BIRD	BODY	BUTTON	CHAIR
CLAW	CLOUD	CROWN	DIAMOND	DIRECTION

DOOR	EYE	FACTORY	FENCE	FISH
FLOWER	FOLDING TABLE	FOOD	GATE	GRASS
HAIR	HAT	HEART	HOOK	HOUSE
LEGS	LETTER	MONEY	MOUNTAIN	PATH
PICTURE	PIPE & VENT	PLATE	PODIUM	POSTER
PRISON	ROOF	SCALE	SCISSORS	SHIP
SMOKE	SNAKE	SNOW	SOMBRERO	STAR
STEP	SUITCASE	TABLE	TARGET	TIME WATCH
TREE	UMBRELLA	WATER	WHEEL	WINEGLASS

W = 60

Below we have listed, with appropriate comments, combinations of signs. The combinations are listed in the alphabetical order.

ACCOUNT—PATH of MONEY (money trail)

ADDICT—BODY that is HOOKED (on drugs)

ADMIRE—HEART on a PODIUM

AIM—EYE over TARGET (goal)

AIR MAIL—LETTER and BIRD

ALCOHOLIC—HOOKED on a GLASS

ALREADY—TIME has COME

ANACONDA—"emperor" snake (the largest snake), hence two crowns above a snake

APPLE PIE—APPLE BASIC CAKE

APPOINTMENT—OFFICIAL (hence crown) TIME

 AQUARELLE—PICTURE with WATERCOLORS

 ASPIRATION—too many goals (targets)

 ATTRACTIVE—LOVELY BODY

 AWARD—DECORATION by JUDGMENT

 BATH—BODY in WATER suggests having a bath

 BEDRIDDEN—HOOKED to the BED

 BEER—DRINK (wineglass) with SMOKE (i.e., air bubbles) inside

 BIRD OF PREY—BIRD with a CLAW

 BLOOD—LIQUID (water) of HEART

BLOOD MONEY—MONEY (coin) associated with BLOOD

 BLOOM—FLOWER of a plant (TREE)

 BLUE BLOOD—royal blood, hence CROWN and BLOOD

 BONE—HARD (diamond) INSIDE a BODY

 BREAD—basic food

 BRILLIANT—CUT DIAMOND

 CAKE—SWEET FOOD

 CANDID—HEART on a TABLE so everybody can see what is inside!

 CENSORSHIP—CUTTING (CONTENT OF A) LETTER (as was the case during WWII, under German and Italian occupation)

 CESAREAN—CUTTING PREGNANT woman

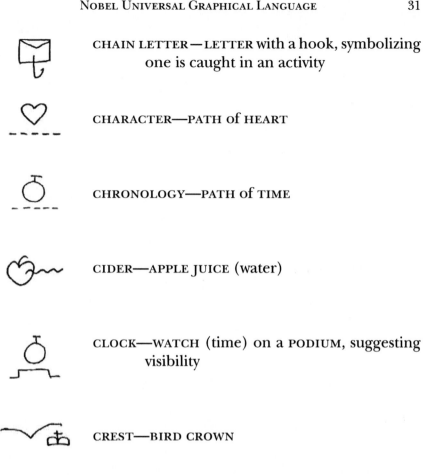

CHAIN LETTER—LETTER with a hook, symbolizing one is caught in an activity

CHARACTER—PATH of HEART

CHRONOLOGY—PATH of TIME

CIDER—APPLE JUICE (water)

CLOCK—WATCH (time) on a PODIUM, suggesting visibility

CREST—BIRD CROWN

DEEP—WALKING under WATER suggests depth

DIAMOND—HARD and very valuable (which is suggested by CROWN)

EAGLE—MOUNTAIN BIRD. There are many birds in mountains, but eagle is most visible!

FICTION—something hooked in a cloud, which means that it does not have a firm basis

 FISHING—HOOK and FISH

 FLOAT—SHIP over WATER

 FOOTBALL—legs and a ball (represented by tennis ball for a better recognition, though it represents any ball)

 FOOTPRINT—PATH behind LEGS

 FRONT—part of BODY that EYE can see

 FUTURE—time in front of us, hence TIME ahead of LEGS

 GLUE—a LIQUID (water) with a HOOK

 GOAL—a BALL in a DOOR

GOODBYE—FRIENDLY LEAVING

 HAIRCUT—CUTTING HAIR

 HARDHAT—HARD HAT

 HARDSHIP—HARD (diamond) TIME

 HEART SURGERY—CUTTING (scissors) HEART

 HEDGE—TREE FENCE

 HUNTING—HOOK follows a PATH

 IMPEACHMENT—AUTHORITY (crown) under JUSTICE

 IN LOVE—heart that is caught in love, hence HOOKED HEART

 LODESTONE—(magnetic) stone, stone that catches metal things, hence stone with a hook

LOYAL—person who LOVES (heart) AUTHORITY

 MARIJUANA—GRASS and SMOKE

 MARSH—WATER over GRASS

 MEAL—TIME FOR FOOD

 METHOD—a PATH to reach a GOAL

 MIRACLE—walking on water, hence legs over water (biblical story)

 MISER—person HOOKED on MONEY

 MOW—CUTTING GRASS

 NEST—a HOUSE of a BIRD

 OBESE—HOOKED ON FOOD

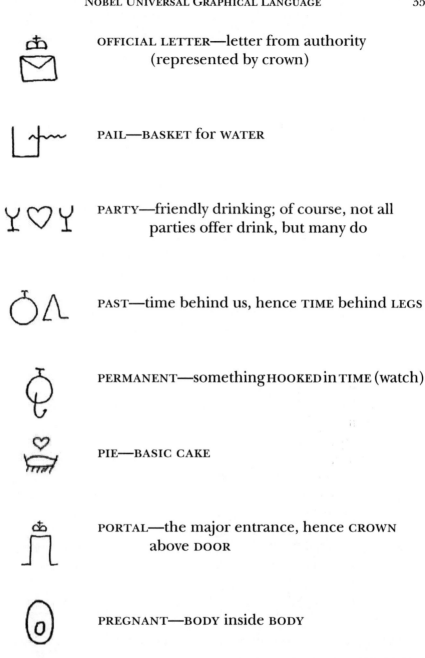

OFFICIAL LETTER—letter from authority (represented by crown)

PAIL—BASKET for WATER

PARTY—friendly drinking; of course, not all parties offer drink, but many do

PAST—time behind us, hence TIME behind LEGS

PERMANENT—something HOOKED in TIME (watch)

PIE—BASIC CAKE

PORTAL—the major entrance, hence CROWN above DOOR

PREGNANT—BODY inside BODY

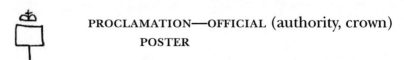

PROCLAMATION—OFFICIAL (authority, crown) POSTER

PROJECT—goal ahead, hence GOAL in front of LEGS

 PUBLIC KNOWLEDGE—letter on a podium, hence public, available to anyone to see

 PUZZLE—PICTURE that is CUT

 RECEPTION—official drinking; of course, not all receptions offer drink but most do

 SCRATCH—CLAW PATH

 SEAM—PATH of SCISSORS

 SENSITIVE—balance over a heart, suggesting continuing weighing responses

 SHALLOW—walking in water that is below knees, suggesting shallow water

 SOUP—LIQUID in a PLATE

STANDARD—SCALE on PODIUM (i.e., public)

 SUCCESS—goal achieved, hence GOAL behind LEGS

 SURGERY—CUTTING (hence, scissors) a BODY

 TEAR—WATER under an EYE

 THRONE—royal chair, hence CROWN above a CHAIR

 TRADITION—FUTURE follows the PAST

 TWINS—TWO BODIES inside a BODY

 VACATION—TRAVEL (suitcase) we LOVE (heart)

 VALUE—time and money are very valuable, hence they are combined into a single sign

WAKE—SHIP PATH (trace)

  WATER LILY—FLOWER of WATER

  WELCOME—FRIENDLY (heart) COMING (legs)

⊚Λ WINNING STRATEGY—PATH of SUCCESS

We proceed with outline of several basic constructive steps that allow growth of the vocabulary of Nobel, doubling the already doubled number of initial basic sign words. In continuing, we want to emphasis the educational merits of Nobel, which is not to promote ignorance, superstition, bigotry, and arrogance. The basic constructive operations include OVERLAP of signs, DOUBLING of signs, TRIPLING the signs, signs INVERSION, CROSSING of signs, construction of RECIPROCAL and FRACTIONS, and MODIFICATIONS of a selection of signs. To this repertoire of operations, we have to add a set of various ARROWS that are combined with signs to add novel interpretation to signs. Then we will introduce another sixty signs that need some introductory comments. They will also be found to have a close pictographic connection or ideographic connection with signs used, and it will not require much effort to learn them. To this list of some 120 signs, we will add some twenty traditional signs, including the question mark "?" that are widely used even if a few, taken from mathematics, may not be known to everybody. Finally, we will introduce *half a dozen* signs that may have a less apparent connection with the content they represent—but half a dozen new signs are not a tall order by any standard.

Overlap of Signs

Double Overlap

By making overlap of signs, we have opportunity to expand the original meaning of a sign to a related concept that corresponds to overlap of the corresponding object literally or figuratively as is illustrated below:

 ADAMANT—overlap of *diamond* (hard)

 BENCH—*chairs* that are overlapping form a bench

 BOUQUET—*crossing flowers*

 CLOUDY—overlap of *clouds*

 CONNECTION—overlap of *hooks*

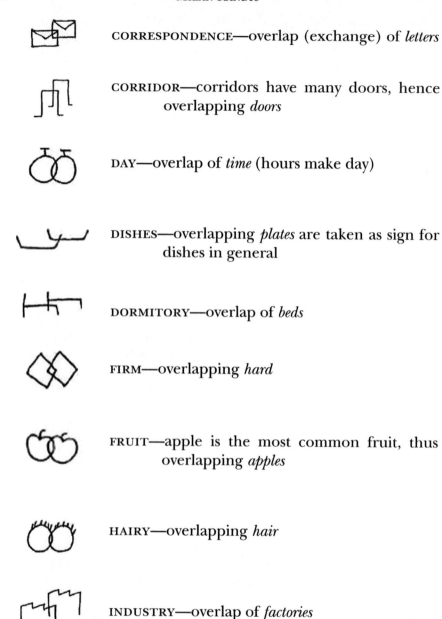

CORRESPONDENCE—overlap (exchange) of *letters*

CORRIDOR—corridors have many doors, hence overlapping *doors*

DAY—overlap of *time* (hours make day)

DISHES—overlapping *plates* are taken as sign for dishes in general

DORMITORY—overlap of *beds*

FIRM—overlapping *hard*

FRUIT—apple is the most common fruit, thus overlapping *apples*

HAIRY—overlapping *hair*

INDUSTRY—overlap of *factories*

INSTRUCTIONS—numerous (overlapping) *directions*

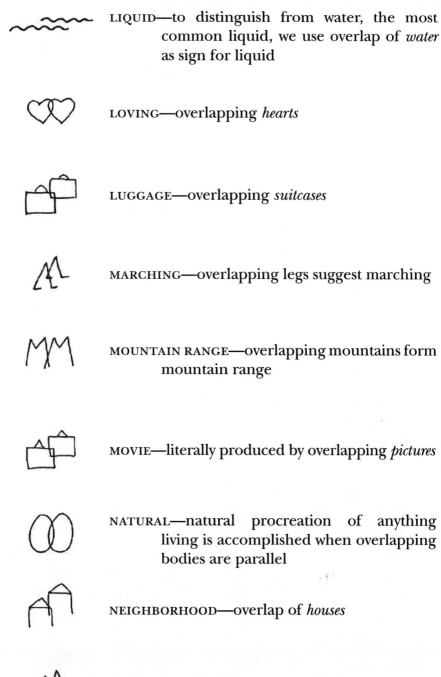

LIQUID—to distinguish from water, the most common liquid, we use overlap of *water* as sign for liquid

LOVING—overlapping *hearts*

LUGGAGE—overlapping *suitcases*

MARCHING—overlapping legs suggest marching

MOUNTAIN RANGE—overlapping mountains form mountain range

MOVIE—literally produced by overlapping *pictures*

NATURAL—natural procreation of anything living is accomplished when overlapping bodies are parallel

NEIGHBORHOOD—overlap of *houses*

PARK—overlap of *trees*. Parks have a mixture of trees and plants

PROTECTION—umbrella protects against rain, overlapping umbrellas suggest more general protection

 SHELTER—overlapping *roof* over head offers shelter

 SIMULTANEOUS—overlapping in time suggests something happening the same time

 SKELETON—overlap of *bones*

Triple Overlap

Constructions based on overlap of already overlapping signs offer additional signs illustrated below:

 ABUNDANCE—lot of fruits, overlap of *fruits* means abundance

 ARBORETUM—various parts of arboretum can be viewed as park, hence arboretum represents overlap of parks.

 INDUSTRIAL ZONE—overlapping *industry*

NETWORK—overlapping connections, i.e., many connections make a network

 OVERCAST—very *cloudy*

 WEEK—overlapping of *days* makes a week.

Exceptions: Quadruple Overlap

There is a saying that every rule has an exception. The rule for construction of combinations of signs in Nobel is that no more than three signs are combined into a new sign representing a novel concept. We will try to respect that rule, avoiding thus construction of cumbersome signs combinations that may be confusing. In addition, construction of such signs may also be time consuming and take unnecessary efforts. However, rules may have exceptions and one such exception is illustrated below:

 GLUT—overlapping *abundance*

Touching of Signs

Double

We have already seen how overlap of signs allows construction of signs for words that are related to the parent sign. In addition positioning of overlapping signs allows further expansion of vocabulary. Thus, as we have seen, the signs of overlapping TIME lead to sign for *day* (horizontal overlap) or sign for *simultaneous* (vertical overlap). To this we may add *touching of time* to mean *contemporary*, which means *at the same time* but not necessarily *simultaneously*. Similarly, by *doubling the sign of house* we obtain a sign for *village, overlapping of the signs of house* stands for *neighborhood*, while touching of the signs of house stands for *duplex*, a house that is divided in two parts, having two separate entrances and offering dwelling for two families. In the case of the sign of house, touching of houses results in fusion of two houses. Duplex houses may be more common to towns rather than villages, where houses tend to be isolated, at least in agricultural areas. However, duplex houses and even larger agglomerations of houses are not uncommon along the villages along the Adriatic coast. Thus my own grandparent's house was duplex, which later became 1¼ : ¾-plex, when my grandmother started to support her neighbor, after her son disappeared (as a seaman) somewhere on Atlantic and neighbor gave her one room of her house. Thus our house was increased by one room, while the house of our neighbor shrank. After our neighbor died, she left her house to my grandmother, which was the end of the duplex. Later my brother, who was an architect, transformed the duplex into a single house.

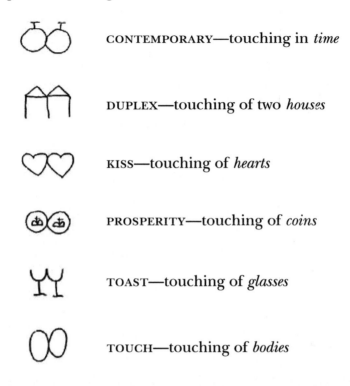

CONTEMPORARY—touching in *time*

DUPLEX—touching of two *houses*

KISS—touching of *hearts*

PROSPERITY—touching of *coins*

TOAST—touching of *glasses*

TOUCH—touching of *bodies*

Before continuing, let us comment on the sign for *prosperity*, shown as *touching money*. Before we have seen the sign for *prosper* shown as being *very successful*, that is, having many successes (goals behind). The two signs have similar meaning, but as one can find in many dictionaries "prosper" has two meanings: (1) to flourish, thrive, do well; and (2) to succeed financially, economically. Hence the two variants for "prosper" in Nobel.

Triple

Finally, not often we can have three signs touching one another as illustrated below:

TOWNHOUSE—contiguous touching of houses

W = 200

We have been counting words for which we have signs, and at this point, which is an early stage in presenting the vocabulary of Nobel, we already have about two hundred words (W = 200). As we continue, we will from time to time report on the word counts, merely to indicate the growth of the vocabulary. However, we should be fully aware that many words that will be presented may not be words widely used in daily conversations. Typically knowing about thousand words of any language (with also knowing minimal grammar) may suffice for most of common conversations. This is not going to be with the first thousand and perhaps two thousand words of Nobel. As we come to those hallmarks one will realize that a number of "important" words (that is, words that may often be needed in communications) may still be missing. Language experts may object to such rather unusual, to say the least, approach to teach a language, but from our point of view, at this early stage in becoming acquainted with Nobel, it seems more important to catch "the spirit" of Nobel and discern the "hidden logic" of the language than to offer a platform for *common* conversations. We hope that in this way, without much effort, one will eventually learn to write messages and communicate in this graphical language. At the beginning, admittedly, the messages may be limited, but the burden of memorizing the signs will be minimal, as we try to provide sufficient background information for the signs introduced. Moreover, we may add to those who would like to arrive as fast as possible at a minimal load of *common words* for *common conversations* that we are not in the business of the construction of a *common language*, but a *language* that will allow communication at different levels.

I recall how many years back while spending three months in Tokyo, I decided to start learning kanji, the Chinese characters that have been used in Japan since the time of their introduction in Japan about thousand years ago. The lovely book *Read Japanese Today* by Len Walsh (published by Charles E. Tuttle Co., Rutland, Vermont, 1969) was very helpful. I may have learned about five hundred Chinese characters, which is about half of signs needed to be able to read newspapers (except of course that in Japan one would also have to learn forty-six hiragana and forty-six katakana syllable letters that are used for grammatical endings and foreign names, respectively). Then I met an Australian scholar who was also interested in learning Chinese characters, who asked me how many I had mastered. I said, "Around five hundred." To this he replied, "This is the maximum that you will ever learn." I was puzzled and asked how would that be possible? He then explained himself, "When you learn additional fifty kanji, you will forget fifty, so you will still know five hundred."

He was right in the sense that after initial few hundred Chinese characters, which one can often see as signs over buildings, shops, streets, etc., one comes across characters that one does not see frequently, so they tend to be forgotten meanwhile. Here we have a sharp contrast between Chinese writings, which represent a universal language, and Nobel, the novel universal language. In Nobel, learning new signs and new combinations of signs reinforces the knowledge of the signs already learned. So after learning five hundred Nobel signs, not only can one easily learn another fifty, but for half of them, one may guess the meaning even before one is told!

For some readers, this book may be a kind of entertainment; some may take it more seriously. Be as it may, as we progress one will see not two hundred but few thousand signs, which one will be able to recognize and even memorize. Umberto Eco, the Italian writer best known for his book *The Name of the Rose,* in the book *The Search for the Perfect Language,* on half a page briefly mentioned Nobel and stated it as having twenty thousand word sign combinations. This is about ten times more than one needs for daily communication. I would dare to say that one may expect to learn easily not five hundred but five thousand—and the Nobel dictionary of twenty thousand (which is in preparation) is a mere effort to show that one can arrive at relatively huge vocabulary starting initially with some one hundred twenty basic signs and some sixty arrows. We will, as we progress, introduce in later sections of this book all the signs and all the arrows or, perhaps to be more correct, almost all one hundred twenty signs and almost all sixty arrows; but just as one cannot climb top of high mountains in a single day, so we will also need a couple of days to reach the top, but we will get there!

We will continue now with illustrations of combinations of overlap of double and triple signs with the already introduced signs.

Combinations Using Overlap of Signs

 AGE—*time scale*

 BLOSSOM—*fruit flower*

 BULLETIN—daily poster (information), hence *day & poster*

 CHRISTMAS—*day* of *decorated tree*

 CONDOR—*bird* of *mountain range* (Andes)

 GRAPE—*fruit* that makes *wine*

IMAGINATION—overlap of *fiction*

 MAKE LOVE—parallel bodies with love (heart), too much attraction

 RIPE—*fruit* on a *plate* (if not ripe, it would not be on a plate)

 SAINT VALENTINE'S DAY—day of love (February 14, the anniversary of beheading of Saint Valentine by Romans)

Doubling of Signs

In spoken language, a word follows a word, forming a sequential string of words. Graphical sign language has an advantage in that it can utilize two-dimensional space and place signs not only sequentially but also one above another or at an angle and thus create additional modification for the meaning of the original sign, as we have already seen with overlapping signs (e.g., simultaneous time and day time). We will see how use of two-dimensional space will enrich our vocabulary when constructing signs obtained by doubling. The same signs can be placed one next to the other or one above the other, i.e., in a *horizontal* or *vertical* mode. Of course, often it would be the matter or convention to assign comparable meanings of the parent sign to the vertical or horizontal combination. In Nobel, doubling of a sign is generally interpreted as meaning "much of," "any of," or "lot of." We have ordered the signs alphabetically.

ADVERTISE—lot of *posters*

AMBITION—*goal* over *goal*

BARRICADE—lot of *fences* one above other

BARRIER—lot of *fences*

BLOODSHED—*blood* over *blood*

CAPITAL—*money* over *money*

CAREFUL—lot of *weighing* (balance)

CELEBRATION—lot of *glasses* (wine)

CONSTELLATION—lot of *stars*

CONVOY—lot of *ships*

DECORATION—lot of *stars* (*star* over *star*)

ENTHUSIASTIC—*heart* above *heart*

FLAME—lot of smoke (reflecting folk saying: where there is smoke, there is a fire)

FLOCK—lot of *birds*

GALLERY—lot of *pictures*

GOVERNMENT—lot of *authority* (authority = crown)

INFLUENCE—lot of connections (connection = overlapping hooks)

LOVE—lot of *liking* (like = heart)

ORDER—lot of *directions*

PASTURE—lot of *grass*

PENITENTIARY—lot of *prisons*

PROCESSION—lot of *legs*

RESTRICT—lot of control (control = pipe and vent, hence a pipe with two vents

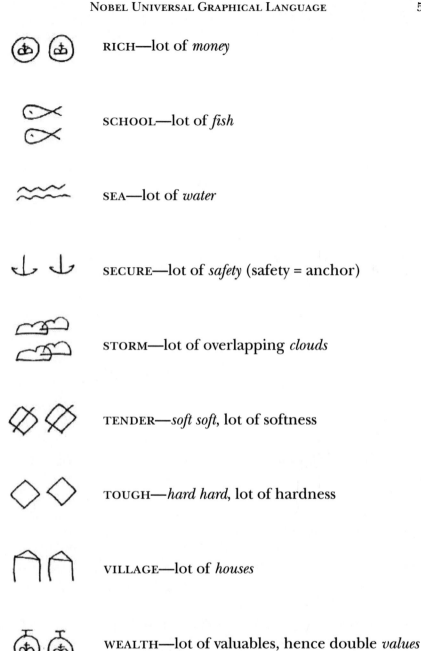

RICH—lot of *money*

SCHOOL—lot of *fish*

SEA—lot of *water*

SECURE—lot of *safety* (safety = anchor)

STORM—lot of overlapping *clouds*

TENDER—*soft soft*, lot of softness

TOUGH—*hard hard*, lot of hardness

VILLAGE—lot of *houses*

WEALTH—lot of valuables, hence double *values*

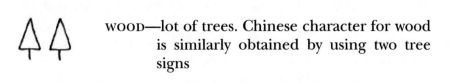

WOOD—lot of trees. Chinese character for wood is similarly obtained by using two tree signs

Challenges and Temptations

Combinations of signs form new words that are closely related to signs used. Challenges in creation of Nobel are words for which there are no obvious signs or combinations of signs that would offer useful characterization for such words. On the other hand, one may be tempted to combine various signs, creating words of Nobel for which there is no clear interpretation. Let us illustrate this on two rather common signs, that of a wheel and flower:

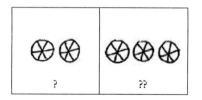   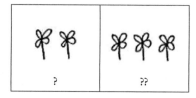

In the first case, we have "lot of wheels" and "lot of lot of wheels," and in the second case, we have "lot of flowers" and "lot of lot of flowers." The question is, what useful concepts can the above signs stand for?

One could for instance interpret "lots of wheels" as a train, and then "lot of lot of wheels," which is tantamount to "lots of trains" as a railway. In a similar fashion, one can interpret "lot of flowers" as flower garden and perhaps "lot of lot of flowers" as flower park. However, there are "lot of flowers" in florist shop and "lot of lot of flowers" in gardens of those who supply florists with flowers. In situation like this, when an outcome is not very clear and obvious, the best is to postpone the decision as introduction of additional signs may yield better solutions. Let illustrate this on another temptation, the signs show below at the left:

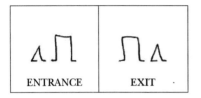

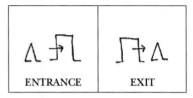

In view of the fact that in Nobel the *left* stands for PAST and the *right* for the FUTURE, it is understood that legs at the left of the door have not yet entered, while legs at the right of the door, having the door "behind" are exiting. Hence, there are no ambiguities, and the two simple combinations of legs and door can represent entrance and exit. On the other hand, if we only add simple arrow as shown in the alternative representations of ENTRANCE and EXIT on the right-hand side of the above figure, we obtain better and more convincing representations for the same concepts. Moreover, by crossing the sign of legs, we can arrive at simple signs for NO ENTRANCE and NO EXIT, as well as a sign for CLOSED and OPEN as shown below:

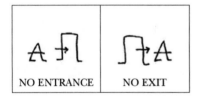

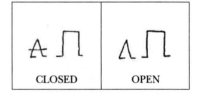

The above discussion only announces what is to come in the remaining pages of this book. The essence of the message is, be patient, we have only started to expose sign operations that arise in Nobel, which will allow better constructions for numerous signs.

Let us end this outline of challenges and temptations with a brief mentions of design of a sign for CHILD, assuming that we already have a sign for PERSON. Where to start? How can we relate and possibly use or modify the sign for a grown-up person in order to arrive at the sign for a child? My initial attempt was to view "child" as "small person" but there are small persons who are not children. Another thought was to connect (or disconnect) sign for PERSON and sign for SEX, associating a mature person with sex and a child, as immature, as being "without sex." However, there are grown-up people who are "devoid" of sex (such as a eunuch, who is a castrated person). Finally, a good ten years later, I came upon the simple solution: child is a person that grows! Thus combining signs for person and growth, one immediately obtains as a combination the sign for child. Moreover, as a bonus, the same recipe when applied to the sign for child leads to a sign for baby, as a "child that grows."

Combinations Using Doubling of Signs

 ADORE—*enthusiastically admire*

 BANQUET—lot of *food* and *drinks*

 BATHE—*body* in *sea*

 BLEEDING—lot of *blood*

 BREWERY—lot of *beer*

 FERVENT—*enthusiastically* inflamed

 FESTIVITY—lot of *party*

FIESTA—*day* of *celebration* (celebration = lot of wine)

 FLAMINGO—*bird* having a color of *flame*

 HARBOR—*security* at *sea*

 HEART INFLAMMATION—*inflammation* of *heart*

 HIVE—*house* for *honey*

 HONEY—very sweet (hence *love*) liquid (*water* sign)

 INFLAMMATION—*flame inside body*

 JIGSAW PUZZLE—*cut cut picture*

 JUICE—*fruit liquid* (water)

MUTILATE — *cut cut body*

 PARADE — lot of *procession* and *celebration*

 PEARL — "*diamond*" of the *sea*

 POULTRY — *domestic birds*

 PROSPER — have many *successes* behinds

 SEAGULL — most common *sea bird*

 SEASCAPE — *picture* of *sea*

 SEASHELL — *hard* under *sea*

SUNK—*ship* under *sea*

WEEP—*eye* and *lot of water*

WINE—drink(wineglass) of *flame*. Wine does warm a person somewhat

WINERY—lot of *wine*

Tripling of Signs

In Nobel, at most, a sign can be repeated three times, or at most, three different signs are combined into a single word unit. We have collected combinations of three signs, which we show in combinations with the sign itself and its doubling form. At the end, we will make brief comments for some of the new signs shown here.

AUTHORITY	GOVERNMENT	DICTATORSHIP
BEER	WINE	BRANDY
BLOOD	BLEEDING	HEMORRHAGE
BREWERY	WINERY	DISTILLERY

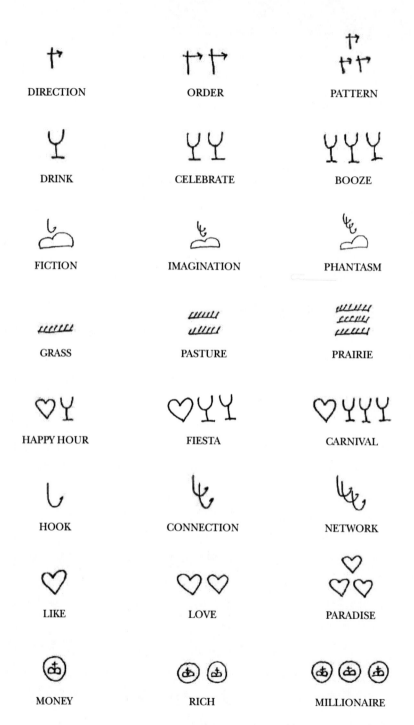

DIRECTION

ORDER

PATTERN

DRINK

CELEBRATE

BOOZE

FICTION

IMAGINATION

PHANTASM

GRASS

PASTURE

PRAIRIE

HAPPY HOUR

FIESTA

CARNIVAL

HOOK

CONNECTION

NETWORK

LIKE

LOVE

PARADISE

MONEY

RICH

MILLIONAIRE

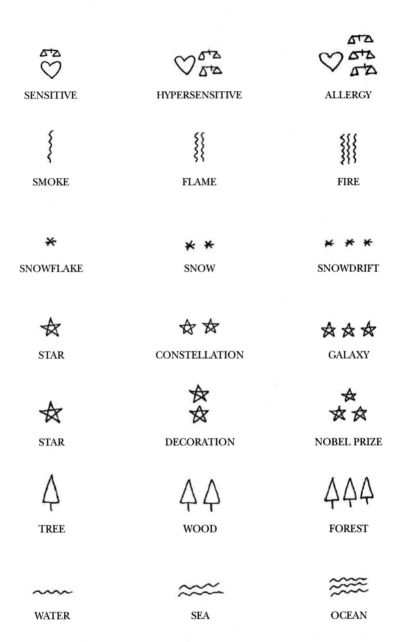

SENSITIVE	HYPERSENSITIVE	ALLERGY
SMOKE	FLAME	FIRE
SNOWFLAKE	SNOW	SNOWDRIFT
STAR	CONSTELLATION	GALAXY
STAR	DECORATION	NOBEL PRIZE
TREE	WOOD	FOREST
WATER	SEA	OCEAN

Most of the sign combinations are self-evident. As one can see, we differentiate among alcoholic drinks using smoke, flame, and fire signs that correspond to increased alcoholic content of the corresponding drinks: beer, wine, and brandy or whiskey, respectively. At one time Tennessee had age restrictions of sixteen, eighteen, and twenty-one years for drinking beer, wine and hard drinks, which parallels our approach to alcoholic drinks to a degree. One can interpret the "triple" sign as a "lot of" whatever stands for the double sign. So a lot of *sea* symbolizes *ocean*, which in the terminology of science, is an order of magnitude larger than sea. Similarly, *snow drift* is a lot of *snow*, *dictatorship* is too much of *government*, *prairie* is too much *meadow*, and too much *fruit* points to *abundance*. Along such line of thought, one can view a *pattern* to reflect a lot of *order*, *allergy* to be result of too much of *hypersensitivity*, and finally *paradise* to be a place of too much of *love*.

Doubling of Combinations

WILDFIRE—*fire fire*, a lot of fire

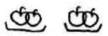

MELLOW—*ripe ripe*, a lot of ripeness

Inversion of Signs

By inverting a sign, that is, writing it upside down, we can convey an opposite meaning to the sign. So the sign of heart that symbolizes to like, to love, became, when inverted, the sign for dislike, hate. Those who have been sailing know that along coast there may come across an upside-down sign of an anchor, which tells, "do not drop anchor here," as the site has undersea cable or other installations that can be damaged. Thus inverting the sign to get an opposite meaning is not an invention of Nobel, but it will be used in Nobel when possible. We have to emphasize "when possible" to draw attention of readers to the fact that by inverting a sign many inverted signs need not be immediately recognized or apparent, particularly when one does not know if such a sign is an inverted sign or perhaps a new sign. This is the case with signs shown below:

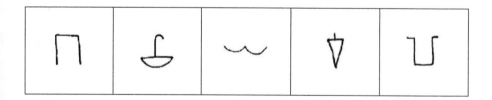

The signs that represent inverted basket, umbrella, bird, tree, and door, may be recognized once we describe them, but an unsuspecting reader not told of their inversion may be somewhat confused. For example, the inverted door looks just as another basket, inverted tree looks like a carrot. There is no simple interpretation for such inverted signs, except perhaps for an inverted umbrella, which does happen sometimes on a windy rainy day. If we are to accept such signs, we would betray our basic requests on signs that they are easy to be recognized—and we certainly do not wish to betray the basic principles of Nobel. Hence the above and many other similar constructions of inverted signs have not been adopted and are viewed as unacceptable.

We will list below ten inverted signs that we consider acceptable, which can be readily recognized as being inverted pictures of already-known signs:

MONEY	LIKE	AUTHORITY	PODIUM	CONTROL
FAKE	HATE	IMPOSTER	PIT	UNCON-TROLLED
SAFETY	MOUNTAIN	DOMESTIC	SNAKE	BODY
UNSAFE	VALLEY	WILD	VIPER	MIND

We have included here also the signs for snake-viper and body-mind, which strictly speaking are not complete inversion, but are constructed in the same spirit. Later we will meet a few additional inversions for signs: above-below, male-female, electricity-transmission. It is tempting to use inverted signs more often, but it is more important to maintain clarity and avoid ambiguities that inversion of signs may introduce. Thus in Nobel, we use inversion rather rarely. Below we show a few signs that are obtained using inverted signs in combination with other signs:

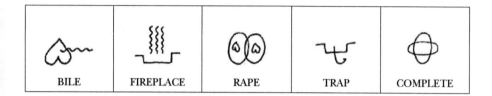

| BILE | FIREPLACE | RAPE | TRAP | COMPLETE |

The sign for COMPLETE may appear unusual, but there is a brief story behind it. The vertical oval, half of the sign, can be recognized as representing BODY, while the other half, the horizontal oval, stands for MIND. Thus COMPLETE in Nobel is overlapping of BODY and MIND. When I was in the elementary school in a small village of four hundred people on the northern Adriatic coast, the school had but a single room and single teacher for four classes of elementary education. Each two rows represented another class, and it was not easy for the teacher to keep all us busy all the time. So while the teacher was more occupied with the senior classes, we in junior classes would occasionally watch through windows birds flying. The teacher would scold us, saying that we are present in the class only with our bodies but not with our minds. Thus we were not complete persons by her account!

Before continuing with the additional operation for construction of opposite signs, let us illustrate few signs that use the sign of COMPLETE:

| SATISFACTION | GRATIFICATION | IDENTICAL | UNIQUE | ENTIRE |
| INDULGE | | | | |

One may argue that SATISFACTION is a peace or happiness of body and mind, which may explain the sign. GRATIFICATION is just upscale satisfaction, hence doubling of heart. Similarly, if something is completely equal to something else, the two are then IDENTICAL, or as ordinary folk would say, they are eggs, even though many, if not most eggs, can be differentiated, except for identical eggs, which give rise to identical twins! Similarly, if something is completely different from everything else, being the only one, it is UNIQUE.

Let us now continue with construction of antonyms.

Crossing of Signs

Another natural way to indicate opposite meaning of a sign is to simply cross it. For example, by crossing *eye* we immediately suggest BLIND person, and by crossing *diamond* or *hard* we obtain a sign for SOFT, as indicated on the next page. However, there are two problems with wide use of crossing of signs: (1) Many signs are not of a suitable form to allow crossing; and (2) Some signs when crossed may suggest an interpretation that is not opposite to the initial meaning of the sign. To illustrate the first point, let us consider crossing the signs of water, bird, fish, chair, or bed, to mention a few, illustrated below:

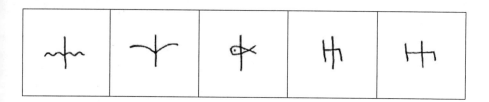

They simply do not look "right," they do not carry a clear visual message, and therefore will not be used in Nobel. Among the initial sixty basic signs we selected only three: EYE, HARD (diamond), and LEGS (walk), which, after crossing, still represent simple and clear signs. Later we will see a few additional signs obtained by crossing. For example, one can obtain the sign for "gradual" by crossing the sign for "sudden," the sign for "not have" by crossing the sign for "have," the sign for "health" by crossing the sign for "ill," and the sign for "abortion" by crossing the sign for "birth." In the case of the sign for legs, as illustrated below, one can use multiple crossing without reducing clarity of the sign. In this way, we have constructed signs for STAND, SIT and LIE DOWN:

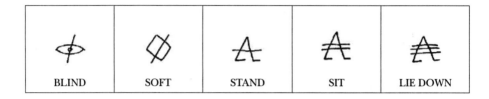

| BLIND | SOFT | STAND | SIT | LIE DOWN |

LEGS suggest *walk* so by crossing legs we obtain the sign for STAND. It was Sir Winston Churchill, the prime minister of the UK during WWII, who said, "*Don't stand if you can sit, don't sit if you can lie down.*" We took advantage of this well-spoken advice of Churchill, and thus, by additional crossing from the sign for STAND, we obtain the sign for SIT, and by crossing the sign for SIT, we obtain the sign for LIE DOWN. Below we show several combinations involving crossed signs:

| SOFTBALL *soft ball* | SOFA *soft bench* | CARTILAGE *soft bone* | SOFT DRINK *soft drink* | BLIND ALLEY *blind road* |
| BACK *body not seen* | NIGHT *not day* | INEDIBLE *not food* | | RICKETS |

Most of the above constructions are self-evident, sofa being soft bench, back being part of body we can't see, night is crossed day, and inedible is crossed food. The sign for cartilage perhaps needs comment, because cartilage is not a bone, though in some fishes, e.g., sharks and rays, including stingrays, it forms skeleton. Literally, "soft bone" would stand for rickets (rachitis), a disease caused by deficiency of vitamin D. Rickets was once not uncommon, particularly in England, because of the climate, which brings a lot of rain and little of sun, which help build up of vitamin D, but today rickets is practically nonexistent. It would be, therefore, a waste to use a simple combination of signs for something that is so rare. So we will use the simpler combination "soft bone" for CARTILAGE and combination "soft" and "bone" for RICKETS.

As illustration of signs that after being crossed change their apparent interpretation, we will mention MOUNTAIN and VALLEY:

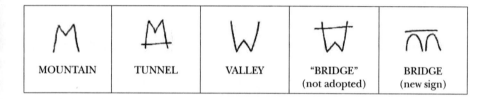

By inverting the "mountain," we obtain "valley," but by inverting the sign for "tunnel," one would obtain a sign for "bridge" as an opposite concept. However, most bridges are over rivers and at best gorges, but not valleys. So the *inverted tunnel* as a sign in Nobel for BRIDGE is abandoned and instead a simple *basic* sign for bridge introduced, which bears more similarity with bridges that one is likely to cross. The sign depicts a bridge with two arches and may be viewed as a fraction of Roman aqueducts and other bridges having many arches. It was Romans who invented and mastered building bridges with arches, in the center of which is keystone—that keeps bridge from collapsing. In contrast, the Inca and Maya, who also left rich architectural heritage, did not discover arch and used instead stone slabs to construct passages, which could span only short range.

By having a sign for BRIDGE, we can *modify* it and obtain sign for AQUEDUCT, as shown below. It is not that this sign will be widely used by most people, but on one side, it is in dictionaries and thus we should consider it, and on the other side, it offers us an opportunity to pay respect to ancient Romans and reminds us of their accomplishments. In addition, this sign points to a useful technique, on which we will later fully elaborate, in how by minor and often obvious modifications we can arrive at novel signs.

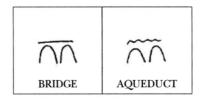

Finally by crossing the sign for DOOR, we obtain a sign that one can interpret as CLOSED (CLOSED DOOR), which, strictly speaking, is opposite of OPEN DOOR, (not DOOR), the sign that has yet to be invented.

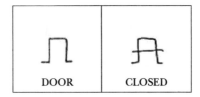

Besides the already-shown double crossing of signs where crossing lines are parallel, we may have double crossing of signs with two lines that are not parallel but perpendicular as illustrated below for the signs of PRIVACY and FORBIDDEN, the latter of which coincides with the traffic sign for streets and roads where stopping and parking is forbidden:

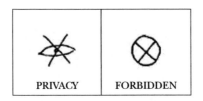

Later, after we introduce additional basic signs of Nobel, we will meet few additional signs obtained by crossing. As we see, *inversion* and *crossing* as methods to derive signs for opposites (antonyms) have rather limited use. We need a more practical and a more general procedure to construct signs representing the opposite of the signs that have been already inducted into Nobel. Bliss, in his *Blissymbolic* universal language, has solved this problem by introducing a separate sign that indicates the "opposite" meaning. As we will see in the next section, Nobel also has an alternative approach for constructing opposites that has its roots in mathematics.

Opposites as Reciprocals

As most readers will know, reciprocal in algebra represents inverse or opposite of a number. Thus "double" and "half," which represent outcome of opposite mathematical operations, multiplication and division, are shown as 2 and 1/2, which is reciprocal of 2. We will use the same recipe, reciprocal 1/x, to construct opposite of x.

BALANCE	IMBALANCE	CLOSED	AJAR
CLOUD	CLEAR	CONNECT	DISCONNECT
CUT	PASTE	DAY	NIGHT
DECORATION	STIGMA	DELICATE	ROBUST

DRINK	ABSENTEE		ENTHUSIASM	MELANCHOLY
FAKE	GENUINE		FOOD	FAST
GOVERNMENT	OPPOSITION		KISS	FRIGID
LIKE	DISLIKE		LOVE	ENMITY
LOYAL	DISLOYAL		NATURAL	UNNUTARAL
ORDER	DISORDER		PERMANENT	TEMPORARY
RIPE	RAW		RICH	POOR
SAFE	UNSAFE		SECURE	PRECARIOUS

SENSITIVE	INSENSITIVE	SUCCESS	FAILURE
SWEET	BITTER	VALUE	TRIFLE

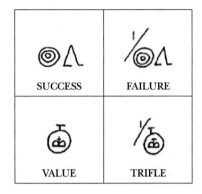

To the above collection of opposites, we may add two additional combinations, which also appear as fractions but do not correspond to objects of opposite meaning. A sign and its fraction form a pair of words, which we used for construction of antonyms, but we can be more liberal and use the same mode of construction for a pair of words that are in close association and need not be opposites, such as:

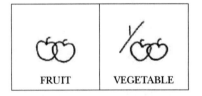

FRUIT	VEGETABLE

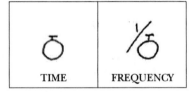

TIME	FREQUENCY

The first case, the pair fruit-vegetable are clearly not a pair of words having opposite meanings but a pair of words that one can associate one with another. In fact there are some plant products, tomato being perhaps the best known, which some people (and in some countries) consider as fruit and in other as vegetable. Already in the introduction, we have mentioned examples of pairs of words like man-woman, cat-dog, coffee-tea, good-bad, love-hate, etc., which tend to have strong association. The list of words that are closely associated is long; fruits-vegetable is just one example:

    all-none
    beautiful-ugly
    body-mind
    child-adult

coffee-tea
day-night
emotion-apathy
extinct-exist
God-Satan
guilty-innocent
infinite-finite
medication-poison
music-noise
poem-prose
question-answer
remember-forget
strong-weak
true-false
war-peace
work-play
yes-no

As we will see in continuation, all the above duals are expressed in Nobel as reciprocals of one another, maintaining thus associations of those words that facilitate understanding of Nobel.

The pair of signs TIME-FREQUENCY relates to physics, rather than linguistics. The concept of frequency in physics is related to the reciprocal of the time, but one need not be student of physics to understand this relationship. The more often (or more frequently) you do something, it takes less time in between, so time and frequency are inversely related. For example, if you go once a month to McDonald's for french fries, that takes thirty days between two such visits, but if you go once a week, so you increased your frequency, it takes seven days in between; and if you go every day, you increased your frequency thirty times and cut the time "distance" of your visits thirty days! While this represents simple mathematical problem, your medical problems may be more serious, unless McDonald's in your neighborhood is using non-digestive oils. Incidentally french fries have nothing to do with France, but got their name from Mr. French from New York, who was the first to make them and attract business.

By now we have already seen about 365 signs of Nobel, one sign for each day of a year! But you need at most a full day, not a full year, to become familiar with all the 365 signs.

Signs as Fractions

W e will take advantage of the mathematical notation of reciprocals to introduce signs in a form of fraction in which we place a sign in the numerator (the upper part) and in the denominator (the lower part) of a fraction. Such signs describe a concept that combines the meanings of the sign and its opposite. For example, SWEET and BITTER, which are opposites with BITTER being shown as *reciprocal* of SWEET, when the two signs are combined, the resulting sign represents SWEET-BITTER, which we have interpreted to be the sign that stands for TASTE, which of course, can be sweet or bitter. To this, we may add also TOMATO, for which we just mentioned that some view it as a fruit and some consider it as vegetable, so in a way TOMATO is both fruit and vegetable, of which Nobel took advantage to arrive at simple sign for tomato. As one continues learning Nobel, one will find out that signs for plants, and to a lesser degree for animals, are a challenge of a kind—not easy to introduce. Below we show additional combinations of signs in the form of a fraction, which often combines opposite qualities into a single sign:

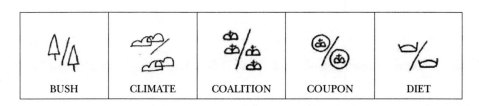

| BUSH | CLIMATE | COALITION | COUPON | DIET |

EQUILIBRIUM	ESTIMATE	FALSE ALARM	GLASS SNAKE	GRIN
HESITATE	HILL	HOUSE ARREST	INSTANT	INSURANCE
LOVE-HATE	MEND	MIDDLE CLASS	MODERATE	MOLLUSK
PLANET	STEAM	TASTE	TOMATO	VEHICLE
WEATHER				24 HOURS

We have assigned to the combination cloud and no-cloud the meaning WEATHER, while overlapping "weather" became a sign for CLIMATE. The sign for COALITION is obtained by fusing the signs for government and opposition. Similarly, the sign for time and no-time stands for INSTANT, something that need be done in no-time! The sign for FALSE ALARM is that of fire and no-fire just as HESITATE is shown as going and not-going, leaving thus some ambiguity at the outcome. The sign for DIET is self-evident: diet is a matter of food (eating) and no-food (fasting), because your body weight only depends on how much food (energy) you consume and how much energy you spend (working or in exercise). When one is to ESTIMATE something, one is suggesting a *measure* (scale) but one is *not measuring*, while EQUILIBRIUM is shown by combining balance and imbalance (a state is in equilibrium when balance replaces imbalance). The sign for MEND, mending, is shown as cut and paste, which are operations often used in mending, whether one is mending some clothes or revising manuscripts. MIDDLE CLASS is shown as people who are rich and are not rich. They have money (hence they are rich) but not enough to put aside (so they are also poor). MODERATE is shown as drink (drinking is implied by wineglass) and not drinking (abstain). COUPON is shown as money and not money, because coupons if used for the occasions offered are equivalent money, that is, they save you money, even if they are not money.

The combination SNAKE / NO SNAKE stands for GLASS SNAKE, which appears as snake, but is in fact a lizard; their legs have so deteriorated that in most cases they are not visible outside its body. Later we will come across the combination VIPER / NO VIPER to stand for common water snake, the bite of which is not venomous, but the bite of the snake will cause putrefaction (decay of tissue). In contrast to the signs SNAKE / NO SNAKE and VIPER / NO VIPER, which are correct characterizations of glass snake and common water snake, the sign FISH / NO FISH for WHALE, if taken in Nobel, would perpetuate incorrect perception, because whale is not a fish, although some three hundred years ago people believed that it is a fish. Thus in the seventeenth century, whales were incorrectly classified, and record on this comes also from early attempts to construct artificial universal languages by using tables of numbers to represent different words. Such tables classified all objects and concepts in various groups, like plants, fruits, vegetables, animals, mammals, lizards, snakes, birds, fish, minerals, precious stones, etc. Because common people know better today than experts knew three hundred years ago, the sign FISH / NO FISH, which is good as a sign, needs in Nobel a novel interpretation, and we took that it stands for MOLLUSKS, animals like snails, slugs, cuttlefish, squid, and octopus, most of which are aquatic invertebrates living in sea. A similar situation is the interpretation of STAR / NO STAR as PLANET. There are a number of celestial objects that are not stars, including meteorites, asteroids, comets, and nebulas (the one in the constellation Orion being the only one visible to the naked eye), that could be candidates for the sign STAR / NO STAR, and we selected PLANET, in view of planets looking like stars to the naked eye. The sign SMOKE / NO SMOKE stands for STEAM, which appears as smoke (very visible as such in cold winter days) but is not smoke—and does not contribute to air pollution. This fact anyone can observe by watching steam leaving chimneys and disappearing after short distance—while smoke stays on. Let us also comment on SMILE / NO SMILE. Technically GRIN is a smile, but there is something artificial about it; it is not a normal smile, which justifies our composition. One can smile by showing teeth, but one can also smile but not show teeth, as is the case with the mysterious smile of *Mona Lisa*, of Leonardo da Vinci. Actually, today the smile of *Mona Lisa* is less mysterious than it used to be only dozens years ago, because study of the remains of La Gioconda (which was the real name of *Mona Lisa*) were excavated and tested for not uncommon gum illness, when gum is shrinking, showing teeth (the so-called horse teeth illness). So here are good reasons why Mona Lisa, and others suffering from the same disease, was not opening her mouth in public. The last sign, 24 HOURS, is shown as day and night, which comprise 24 hours, just as frequently used abbreviation 24/7 stands for day and night, seven days a week.

By minor modifications of a few signs involving fraction, we can further increase the vocabulary of Nobel. Thus the sign for HESITATE can be generalized to signs for SURPRISE and DISAPPOINTMENT by doubling the signs for legs in the numerator (the upper part of the fraction) and denominator (the lower part of the fraction), respectively. The interpretation of such modifications is as follows: HESITATE is shown as indecision between going and not going but can also be interpreted as something is coming and may not be coming. By doubling the sign of legs in the upper part of the fraction we are indicating that what was possibly not coming is coming, hence it comes unexpectedly and represents a surprise. Similarly, the opposite, when we double legs in the denominator, can be interpreted as DISAPPOINTMENT: something that was expected but could have happened is definitely not to happen. Interpretation of the signs for the UPPER MIDDLE CLASS and the LOWER MIDDLE CLASS is perhaps more obvious: the upper middle class is LESS POOR than middle class and lower middle class is LESS RICH than middle class.

SURPRISE	DISAPPOINT		LOWER MIDDLE CLASS	UPPER MIDDLE CLASS

Finally we have few signs that look as fraction but the slash sign is to be interpreted as "by." One such sign is for the word PROOF, which is shown as STEP by STEP, because the task of proving something requires attention at each step of the process. The sign for STEP, which we have not used much, is shown as a simple single step:

STEP *basic sign*	PROOF *step by step*			

Summary of Basic Operations of Nobel

We introduced sixty basic signs of Nobel, which is about half of the basic signs, and by combining these signs using operations such as overlap, doubling, tripling, and touching, then inversion, crossing, reciprocal, and fractions, we arrived at about seven times more signs than we started with. It is true that some of the words that we presented are rather uncommon, while at the same time many common and daily used words are missing. Our effort here was not to introduce the most important words, which we will do later, but to introduce the basic operations of Nobel that allow considerable enrichment of the vocabulary at minimal cost, that is, requiring some learning efforts but relatively small, thus not placing great burden on the memory of readers.

We have not constructed all conceivable combinations of the sixty signs that can have adequate interpretation, and readers may come up with a few suggestions. Apparently, there are two ways to arrive at new signs: (1) Browse through dictionaries and hit upon a word that can be expressed with the available signs, or (2) Construct combinations of signs and then consider what such combination can represent. Both of these approaches have been used to arrive at some four hundred words. More efficient way of constructing novel sign combinations is to screen dictionaries. Reading dictionaries is quite an entertainment that many may have not suspected. Abraham Lincoln, the president of the USA that saved the Union, was known to enjoy reading dictionaries. However, reading dictionaries and having Nobel graphical language in mind may not only be entertaining but also creative!

To illustrate the challenges associated with the approach in which one first constructs various combinations of signs and then worries what they represent, we show below five signs not hitherto considered using CROWN (authority, and also related to crown, that is, king):

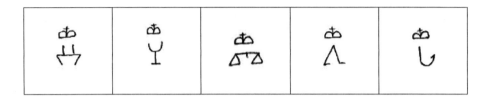

Can we arrive at plausible interpretation of these signs? Well, one may look here at the CROWN as the sign signifying *royalty*, in which case the combination of crown and ship would represent we have royal ship, and the remaining combinations involving CROWN would stand for royal cup, royal balance, royal legs, and royal hook. *Royal ship* can stand for YACHT, which is very acceptable, because yachts are top-of-the-line when it comes to luxury. We can view royal cup, royal balance, and royal legs as signs for royal measures for liquids, weight, and length, which are PINT, POUND, and FOOT. In fact, it was King Henry I who is historically said to have standardized measurements of length, though whose foot was selected as the standard of length is unknown. But what about the last sign, the combination of crown and hook, what it can possibly represent? We leave this as a challenge to readers. We can add to our vocabulary four signs.

YACHT	PINT	POUND	FOOT	?

$W = 420$

Having a vocabulary of over 400 words (in fact, about 420) is a good start in learning a new language even if a number of words may not be words of daily use. By adding sixty additional basic signs, we may more than double our vocabulary and may reach not 800 but perhaps 1,600 or even 2,000 words—but we will not reach 20,000. It is not so vital for most of us to have at disposal 20,000 words, but what is important and what will become clear as we continue to explore Nobel, among those 1,600-2,000 sign combinations, which could appear as a sufficient number of words, there will still be many ordinary words missing. Consider words like

> active-inactive
> arrival-departure
> before-after
> big-small
> come-go
> dry-wet
> early-late
> easy-difficult
> extinct-exist
> fine-crude
> fresh-stale
> good-bad
> hit-miss
> income-spending
> indoors-outdoors
> illness-health
> inside-outside
> lead-follow
> left-right
> look-see
> make-break
> new-old
> please-thanks
> sin-virtue

Most of these words are associated with some action or require some action and may be characterized as implying some dynamics, in contrast with most of the words that we have hitherto seen which represented a situation, a static moment. As we will see on coming pages, Nobel includes a sizable number of arrows of various kinds that suggest often an activity. The inclusion of arrows combined with sixty signs already introduced leads to an explosion of possibilities for construction of novel words, a fraction of which we will consider in this book. Before introducing arrows, we will introduce thirty additional basic signs of Nobel and will also present twenty-five conventional signs that have been adopted in Nobel.

Conventional Signs Used in Nobel

There are many signs widely known and frequently used by many people and therefore one may be tempted to adopt many of such signs in Nobel. However, we should resist such attempts in order to maintain the pictographic and ideographic character of Nobel as much as possible. Besides symbols from mathematics, almost any branch of science and technology has developed numerous graphical symbols of their own. Some of these symbols may have pictographic elements, but nevertheless we will try to avoid them in order to discourage users from contaminating Nobel with signs that may be familiar to some users but are unknown to others. When one examines a catalogue of the existing symbols from various disciplines of science, technology and also pseudoscience, such as alchemy and astrology, one can find a sign for almost anything! We decided therefore to put aside physics, chemistry, biology, etc., and keep only a small selection of mathematical symbols, starting with sign of plus (+), which has been in use over five hundred years, and the sign equal (=), which is also of long duration. Even if a person is not necessarily mathematically informed, one has probably seen above two elementary mathematical symbols, which one can find even on keyboards of typewriters and computers! If one crosses the sign for "equal," one obtains the mathematical sign for "different" ($\neq$), that is, *not equal.* The last of elementary mathematical signs that we have adopted is the sign for multiplication ($\times$). Two geometrical symbols that may be widely known are $\parallel$ and $\perp$ that stand for "parallel" and "perpendicular." We use these signs to indicate "agree" (that is, being parallel with) and "disagree or be against." The following two mathematical signs (∞) and (ø), which represent the concepts of "infinite" and "empty," the first looking like a horizontal number eight and the second is zero that is crossed, may be lesser known to a general public, but we find them useful as signs to measure vastness and emptiness, respectively. The last two mathematical signs that we will use are the Greek capital letter sigma (Σ), which we use, just as is used in mathematics, for summation, and the sign (>), which indicates "greater" and which we use to represent "big."

The nonmathematical conventional signs used in Nobel include the question sign (?), the musical note sign to represent "tone" (♫), the crossed letter R as the sign that doctors and pharmacists use for prescribing medication, the crossed swords as the sign that indicates "battle," the zigzag arrow sign for the electricity, the Greek letter theta, used in printing to indicate "delete" or "eliminate" when correcting printed matter. In Nobel, Greek letter theta is used for "without," because parts of a text so indicated should be deleted, that is the resulting text should be *without* parts so indicated. For the "ground" and the "basis," "basic," or "base," we use the sign which is familiar to radio amateurs and can be seen on electrical networks plans. Two additional signs that many know and for sure those using plastic money (that is, credit cards) and loan money from banks is the sign for percentage (%) and the sign for an item or number (#), both of which can be found on most typing keyboards. Finally we use for God (or gods) the traditional sign "eye in a triangle," which can be seen in many churches and on every one-dollar bill. Below we summarize all mentioned signs with their interpretation in Nobel.

Mathematical Signs

=	+	≠	×	‖
EQUAL	PLUS	DIFFERENT	MULTIPLY	PARALLEL

⊥	∞	∅	Σ	>
PERPEN-DICULAR	INFINITE	EMPTY	SUM	BIG

Traditional Signs

?	♫	℞	✗	⚡
QUESTION	TONE	MEDICATION	BATTLE	ELECTRICITY
∿	⏛	%	#	△
WITHOUT	GROUND	PERCENT	NUMBER	GOD

By using the sign operations (overlap, doubling, tripling, reciprocal, and fractions) we can immediately generate well over sixty additional signs:

⫽=	⫽==	=⫽	==⫽==	==
ERROR	MISTAKE	ROUGHLY	APPROXIMATE	PRECISE
++	⫽∞	%∞	∅∅	≠≠
ADD	INFINITESIMAL	CALCULUS	VACUUM	DIVERSE
ΣΣ	Σ̄Σ	≫	⋙	⫸
TOTAL	COLLECTION	VERY BIG	HUGE	VAST

SMALL	TINY	MINIATURE	QUESTION	ANSWER
NOISE	SOUND	CONCERT	SYMPHONY	JAZZ
ANTIBIOTIC	PANACEA	POISON	DRUGS	HEROIN
ANTIDOTE	LIGHTNING	ELIMINATE	DESTROY	TIME CONFLICT
WAR	ARMISTICE TRUCE	PEACE	WORLD WAR	WORLD PEACE
SATAN	REGARDLESS	CEASE-FIRE	ALLAH	BUDDHA
BACCHUS	VULCAN	BUZZ	TOLERATE	

Before we consider combinations of mathematical and traditional signs with basic signs of Nobel, we have to comment on several of the signs shown above that may be less transparent. The sign for INFINITESIMAL as opposite of INFINITE is clear, particularly to those with firm mathematical knowledge. When the two are combined, we obtain the part of mathematics known as CALCULUS, which deals with such processes and quantities. The sign for FOR is obtained as "against against" in analogy with "enemy of enemy is a friend," thus being against of what we are against counts as to be "for." In reality, such simplistic premise is questionable, but it serves the purpose of introducing novel signs without taxing our memory excessively. Similarly, we interpret the operation of doubling of a sign as a device to add novel *quality* to the sign. This would be in agreement with Friedrich Engels' maxim, "Accumulation of quantity brings novel quality" (which was subsequently exploited by Karl Marx for promoting his political dogmatism). Thus, medications are useful for illness, but antibiotics are more useful (when applicable) than traditional drugs, thus doubling crossed R signifies ANTIBIOTICS. Musical note stands for TONE (MUSIC), and its opposite is NOISE, while tone and noise combined form sign for SOUND. Lots of music we hear at a CONCERT but also at a SYMPHONY performance, which we distinguish by placing signs next to each other or one above the other.

Additional signs that may need comment include

TOLERATE—being *parallel* (i.e., accepting) those who are *against* (perpendicular)

DRUGS—we view street drugs more than poison, hence *poison poison.*

PANACEA—cure for all diseases in reality does not exist, but the word exists, so it is shown as a more potent medication than antibiotics, which are more potent than ordinary drugs

HEROIN—among drugs, heroin is among the worst poisons, hence *poison poison poison*

WORLD WAR—lot of *battles*, lot of *wars*

WORLD PEACE—*opposite* (reciprocal) of *world war*. This may well be the new word combination not to be found in any dictionary yet! It is not among some 150 thousand words of *Webster's New Twentieth Century Dictionary Unabridged* (second edition), but hopefully it may emerge in *Webster's New Twenty-first Century Dictionary* unless world peace continues to be considered unrealistic, utopian.

TIME CONFLICT—*battle* between *times*

With these introductory comments, we present now combinations of novel signs with those already considered. There is no significance in the order in which signs are listed, although we tried to group signs having common elements together.

TRUE	FALSE	PARADOX	AXIOM	HONEST
OATH	SWEAR	HUNGRY	STARVE	BALD
WORTHLESS	BROKE	CRUEL	GHOUST	HAUNTED
SILENCE	SLIP	BUSY	DESERT	DRY
THUNDER-STORM	THUNDER	ELECTRIC CHAIR	EEL	BATTERY
FACT	DATA	FOG	CLEAR	BASEBALL
STONE	ROCK	JEWEL	ISLAND	LAKE

MUD	DANCE	BALLET	DISCO	ORCHESTRA
OPERA	MUSICAL	POLYGRAPH	SCREEN	INDEED
WHEN	WHERE	EQUINOX	DATE	MIST
PIE	HARMONY	DISHARMONY	HARMONY	DISHARMONY
QUIZ	DEHYDRATED	VANISH	SONGBIRD	NIGHTINGALE

The meanings of about half of the signs shown are rather apparent but about half of the signs need a comment to explain how they should be interpreted. Let us start with signs the meanings of which are not difficult to understand:

BALD—*without hair*
BALLET—dance over podium, hence *legs* with *music* over *podium*
BROKE—*without money*
CLEAR—opposite of *fog*, hence *reciprocal* fog
CRUEL—*without heart*; indeed, person without heart tends to be cruel
DANCE—*legs* with *music*
DEHYDRATED—*without water*

DESERT—*land without,* implying without use, without life, without water, though even a desert has some life and some water and some use (or misuse like exploding bombs)

DRY—*without water*

EEL—*electric fish*

ELECTRIC CHAIR—*electric chair*

EQUINOX—*day equal night*

FOG—*ground cloud*

GHOST—*without body,* as ghosts are generally perceived

HAUNTED—is shown as a *house* with a *ghost* inside

HUNGRY—*empty body,* that is, empty stomach

MUD—*water* above *ground*

PIE—*basic cake* (at least in the USA)

SILENCE—*without sound*

SLIP—*legs without sound,* which is walking without making noise

STARVE—is shown as *hungry hungry,* thus we have *empty empty body*

THUNDER—*sound* of *thunderstorm*

THUNDERSTORM—*cloud* with *lightning,* i.e., cloud with a *lot of electricity*

WORTHLESS—*without value* (value is shown as *time & money*)

Many of the remaining signs can also be easily understood once few key signs have been explained. Consider the first sign, *equal* sign overlapping *heart.* What could this represent? We assign to this combination the meaning TRUE, TRUTH. This is based on analogy with people putting their hand over heart when making allegiance and when wishing to emphasize that they speak truth.

By knowing now the sign for TRUE, we can immediately interpret several other signs that involve heart with equal sign.

AXIOM—*basic truth*

FALSE—*not true,* hence *reciprocal* to *true*

HONEST—*path* of *truth,* honest person leaves only truth behind

INDEED—*true true*

OATH—*official truth,* that is truth stated at an official occasion

PARADOX—*true and not true,* that is a statement that appears untrue but is true

POLYGRAPH—measuring true and false statements, hence *true/false* and *scale*

SWEAR—judicial truth, that is, truth stated at in court or similar
     occasions, hence *balance* and *truth*
TRUE—*equal heart* (ideograph)
TRUELOVE—*true love* (signs are combined)

There are a few signs that involve the GROUND sign, besides the
obvious above-mentioned sign for FOG as ground cloud:

BASEBALL—*base* (ground) and *ball.* Pretty obvious, except for those
     who do not know what baseball is (like recent European
     immigrants and some not so recent). So this is the only
     reason for not placing baseball in the class of obvious signs
DATA—*lot of facts*
DATE—*basic day*
FACT—something that has firm basis, hence *hook* in *ground*
ISLAND—land with water around
JEWEL—valuable stone, hence *crown* inserted *inside* the *diamond*
LAKE—water with land around
ROCK—big stone, hence *stone stone*
STONE—*hard* on the *ground*

We are left with few not-yet-explained signs, which we list
below:

DISCO—*lot of dancing*
DISHARMONY—*musical notes against (perpendicular to)* each other
DISHARMONY—*hearts against* each other
HARMONY—*musical notes agree (parallel)* with each other
HARMONY—*hearts agree (parallel)* with each other
JAZZ—is shown as a lot of *sound*
MUSICAL—*lot of music* on *podium*
OPERA—*lot of music on podium*

Both signs have the same description, as was the case with
concert and symphony. The signs are differentiated by placing
musical notes above one another for opera and symphony and
side by side for concert and musical. The vertical and horizontal
placements suggest *quality* and *quantity* respectively in a broad

sense of interpretation. As we know, some popular concerts lasted days, while the longest operas last at most few hours.

ORCHESTRA—*music* in a *pit*, where orchestra is during musicals and operas

QUIZ—*questions / answers*

NIGHTINGALE—*night songbird*

MIST—is shown as *thin fog*

SONGBIRD—*musical bird*

VANISH—disappear without trace, therefore we have disappear *without path*

WHEN—*time* to be *answered*

WHERE—*question* to the *path with direction*

Observe that we have two variants for the same pair of words, the signs for HARMONY and DISHARMONY. We offer these variations occasionally in Nobel, when words are general enough to apply to different situations. Clearly, if we speak of music, then we will use the signs with musical notes. However, if we speak about harmony (or lack of it) among people, appropriately we will use the signs involving hearts.

We will end with gathering together signs combining the signs for HOOK, GROUND and CLOUD. In table 1, we have collected such signs, which illustrate the relationship between the corresponding signs, and related parallelism of their interpretation. If we are comparing the words in the first two columns, we see that just as *overlap of hooks* suggests *connection,* so does *overlap of fact* represent *information, overlap of fiction imagination,* and *overlap of speculation* leads to *hypothesis.* SPECULATION itself is shown as something *hooked into fog,* which may turn out to be a fact but may also turn out to be a fiction, hence speculation. Now if we compare words in the second and third columns, we see again similar relationship. Thus just as *overlap of connections* represents *network,* so *overlap of information* leads to *knowledge, overlap of imagination* represents *phantasm,* and *overlap of hypothesis* builds a *theory.*

Most likely, we have not exhausted all possible combinations of signs hitherto considered, and it is not to be a surprise if a reader comes with one or two novel combinations that have simple interpretation. It may also be true that we have here and there overextended our imagination and that some of the signs shown may not be so straightforward representations of the pictographic or ideographic content of the sign. It is possible that an alternative sign better depicts the content than an already selected sign. If that happens, we should discard the less "friendly" sign and adopt new sign. In this respect, we will follow the advice of Abraham Lincoln (1809-1865): "*I shall try to correct errors where shown to be errors, and shall adopt new views as fast as they appear to be true views.*"

Table 1

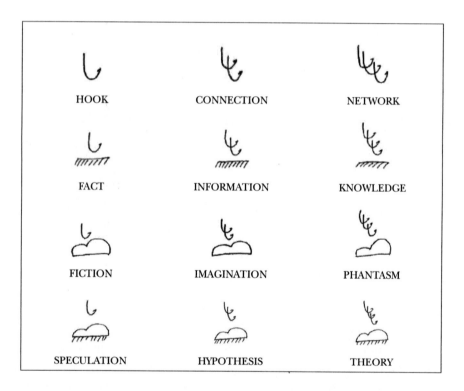

Languages live and are not frozen entities, so the same will be true of Nobel. We may mention here in passing that the fate of Esperanto, one of the most widely successful and known artificial spoken language, composed by Polish doctor Zamenhof, was at one time in very critical situation, losing ground, because Zamenhof was so inflexible in adopting suggestions from others that it was only after his death that Esperanto began to revive. There are no reasons to be inflexible with Nobel, providing the novelties follow the general spirit of Nobel, the signs to be easy to reproduce, easy to recognize, and easy to interpret.

With the set of sixty basic signs and twenty conventional signs, we constructed so far about 550 words of Nobel (in fact, 555).

$$W = 550$$

Additional Basic Signs

We follow with thirty additional basic signs, which include some very important words, words of high frequency of usage like ANIMAL, BOOK, BRAIN, FACE, KNIFE, words, with exception of BOOK, which may have been frequently used by cavemen in the Stone Age. In addition, we included here more sophisticated words, words of modern time, like ATOM, CELL, COMPASS, MAGNIFYING GLASS, and SIGNAL. Finally, here appears the sign for SMILE, which we do not know how much was used in the Stone Age, but we are aware that our times are for the most part not the times of smile, when you think of all the problems that are threatening our planet, humanity, and future generations: global warming, widespread starvation, warring, AIDS, malaria, global pollution, shrinking of wildlife, increasing illiteracy, child abuse, women abuse, animal abuse, limited recycling, shrinking rain forests, overfishing, whale protection, overexploitation of natural resources, corporate greed, to mention few.

ABOVE	ALPHABET	ANIMAL	ATOM	AWAKE
BELLY	BELOW	BETWEEN	BOOK	BRAIN

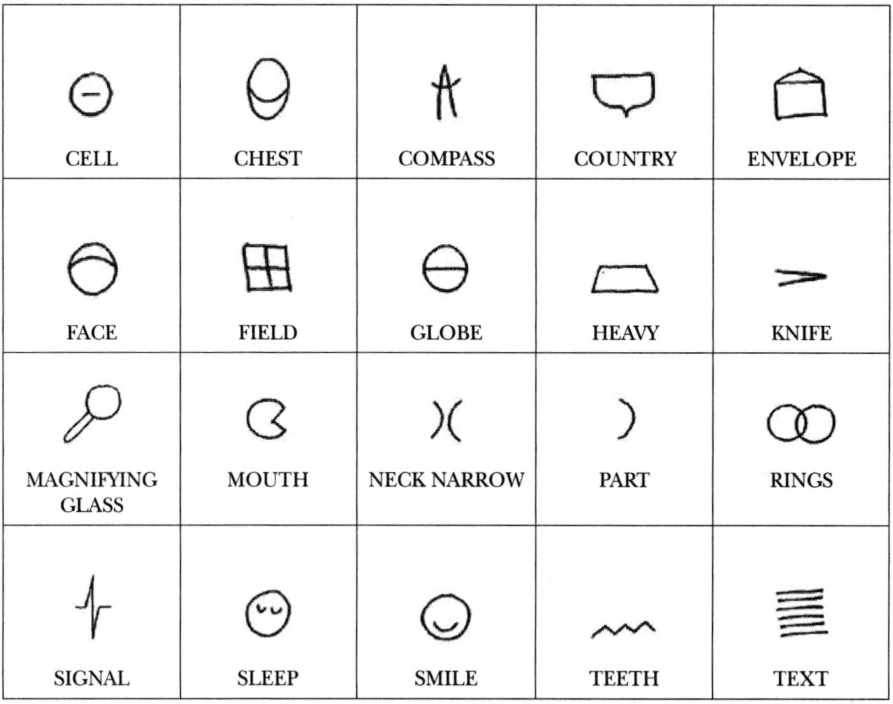
CELL
CHEST
COMPASS
COUNTRY
ENVELOPE
FACE
FIELD
GLOBE
HEAVY
KNIFE
MAGNIFYING GLASS
MOUTH
NECK NARROW
PART
RINGS
SIGNAL
SLEEP
SMILE
TEETH
TEXT

Some of the listed signs can be easily recognized. Such is the sign for SMILE, which is so common and so widespread that it is almost impossible to trace its origin. Often the sign is depicted with two dots for the eyes, but we do not need such perfection: in Nobel, simplicity overrules perfection! Other signs that can be easily recognized include the sign for magnifying glass, the sign for compass (at least to those who have used it to draw circles), perhaps the sign for teeth and mouth (the latter resembling Pac-Man, of an earlier computer game, though the mouth of Pac-Man was somewhat exaggerated), and possibly the sign for text, shown as many lines. Even though all the signs have strong connection to concepts they represent and there will be no difficulty to remember them, they need introduction the first time when shown.

The signs for ABOVE and BELOW, shown as semicircles open up and down, respectively, are also rather obvious. Such signs have been used in corrections of typed manuscript to indicate superscripts and subscripts. When the two signs are combined with a circle, the resulting signs signify BRAIN and FACE, the former being in the upper part of head and the latter indicating lower

part of a head. The same two signs when combined with the
sign for body lead to the signs for CHEST and BELLY respectively.
The sign for SHIELD, besides its literal interpretation (which is
not a word with a high frequency of occurrence), in Nobel also
represents the sign for COUNTRY. The sign for GLOBE is shown
as a circle (standing for Earth) with a horizontal line (standing
for equator). Of course, there are many circular objects, small
and large and extra large (like a globe). In order to differentiate
between the signs representing different such objects, one has
to insert additional auxiliary markers. Thus the sign for BALL
has semicircles suggesting the standard shape of tennis ball, the
sign for BUTTON has four holes, thus typifying buttons (some of
which have only two visible holes or invisible holes). In addition
to GLOBE (with the line for equator), we have signs for ATOM and
CELL shown by inserting plus and minus signs into the circles. The
plus sign is suggestive of atoms having charge at the center, and
the minus sign symbolizes that cells have a nucleus. The sign for
KNIFE is drawn as very sharp object. Finally, the sign for TEETH,
is represented very schematically and resembling more the teeth
of a saw than human teeth, which are not so sharp. But there are
teeth that are very sharp, which have a triangular shape, like for
instance, teeth of a shark. More likely for most of us is to meet
teeth of a dog, not of a shark, which however can lead to a very
painful even if not tragic experience. Because of that, the sign for
teeth in Nobel also stands for DOG. The sign for ENVELOPE is shown
as an open letter, while the sign for SIGNAL has an appearance as
one can see on records of healthy hearts on electrocardiograms.
Signals of similar shape appear on various instruments, and they in
fact represent technically the derivative of the actual signal, which
is usually in the shape of tall narrow wave, technically referred to
as soliton (Latin and Italian "solo" = "single"), a solitary wave that
propagates, retaining its shape:

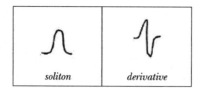

| soliton | derivative |

Derivative of a curve in fact describes the slope of a curve, which in the case of soliton, is maximal at the half height on the left of the peak and minimal (equal magnitude but negative) halfway at the right of the peak. More on this, for those who care, can be found in any calculus book.

We continue with illustrations of combinations of signs just introduced, which as one can see, lead to not so modest increase of our current vocabulary in Nobel. The words are occasionally grouped for the sake of comparisons, but at the end, in alphabetical order, we give some comments and explanations for all, over two hundred, signs shown. In order to break the monotony, occasionally we digress and touch on some interesting side details as well as on some painful memories, however, all the comments tend to be informative, adding thus an educational component to the learning of Nobel. Traveling foreign countries, just as learning foreign languages, is broadening our horizons, and Nobel is trying to share this experience.

NOON	HIGH NOON	LUNCH *noon meal*	EVENING *part of time*	SUPPER *evening meal*
APE *brain—not brain*	MASK *face—not face*	HEAT *above fire*	ASHES *below fire*	HARA-KIRI *knife in belly*
BELLY DANCE	INCENSE *smoke above*	CANDLE *flame above*	TORCH *fire above*	HOUR *part of day*
TRIANGLE	SQUARE	RHOMBUS	SPHERE	TOP

BOTTOM	**EXTREME** *top and bottom*	**SPIKE** *part of signal*	**VIEW** *above eye*	**APPEAR** *below eye*
BITE *part of apple*	**THORN** *part of hook*	**WING** *part of bird*	**ROOM** *part of house*	**FEATHER** *part of wing*
CHAPTER *part of book*	**PROLOGUE** *detail of book*	**EPILOGUE** *detail of book*	**BRANCH** *part of tree*	**TWIG** *part of branch*
LIGHT *part of lightning*	**BEAM** *parallel light*	**LASER** *parallel beam*	**MORNING** *first part of day*	**AFTERNOON** *last part of day*
DETAIL *part of part*	**SUBTOTAL** *part of total*	**FINITE** *part of infinite*	**FRAGMENT** *part of hard*	**CHIP** *part of fragment*
REGION *part of a country*	**AMPUTATION** *cut part of body*	**BIOPSY** *cut detail of a body*	**THIN** *above close to below*	**THICK** *not thin*
AIR *overlapping above*	**ATMOSPHERE** *overlapping air*	**KILL** *knife in heart*	**INJURE** *knife in body*	**SCAR** *path of injury*
BUBBLE *air under water*	**ALERT** *awake awake*	**IGNORANT** *empty brain*	**TABULA RASA** *empty empty brain*	**CELL DIVISION** **(MITOSIS)**

CANCER *uncontrolled cell division*	**LEUKEMIA** *blood cancer*	**TELESCOPE**	**MICROSCOPE**	**SOIL** *top part of ground*
MINUTE *part of hour*	**SECOND** *part of minute*	**ORGAN** *part of body*	**TISSUE** *part of organ*	**TOOTH** *part of teeth*
HEEL *part of legs*	**BRIM** *part of glass*	**STAMP** *part of letter*	**RIM** *part of wheel*	**FIGHT** *part of battle*
NOISE *not signal*	**ELECTRO-CARDIOGRAM**	**LANGUAGE** *sign between mouth*	**LOUD** *mouth above*	**SHOUT** *above loud*
WHISPER *mouth below*	**SLICE** *cut him*	**MIDNIGHT** *opposite to noon*	**TACIT** *mouth and not*	**AMONG** *between between*
METAL *overlapping heavy*	**SILVER** *heavy & crown*	**GOLD** *more than silver*	**FOOL'S GOLD (PYRITE)** *gold—not gold*	**GOLD STAN-DARD** *gold on podium*
BULLDOG *square face dog*	**MERCURY** *liquid metal*	**CINDER** *ash—not ash*	**COPPER** *electricity metal*	**LEAD** *soft metal*
MAGNET *metal & hook*	**REPRISAL** *injury against injury*	**CHAIN** *overlapping rings*	**FREE** *no chains*	**CHALLENGE** *silver ahead*

BENEFIT *silver behind*	**PLANTATION** *fields fields*	**LIFE** *heart signal*	**LIVING** *life life*	**RESIDENCE** *house of living*
INVESTIGATE	**BARE** *without cover*	**CRIME** *lot of injury*	**VANDALISM** *damage picture*	**SABOTAGE** *damage factory*
DAMAGE	**RUIN** *damaged house*	**MASSACRE** *kill kill*	**GENOCIDE** *kill kill kill*	**OVERKILL** *kill killed*
ASSASSINATION *kill authority*	**CRITICAL** *life-death*	**FIRE RETAR-DANT**	**SING** *mouth & music*	**MUFFLER** *kill noise*
BEAK *bird mouth*	**CONVERSATION** *mouth parallel*	**ARGUE** *mouth perpendicular*	**QUARREL** *mouth battle*	**SPELL** *speak alphabet*
CAT *not dog*	**BEAR** *teeth teeth*	**TIGER** *not a bear*	**MOLECULE** *touching atoms*	**BOND** *overlapping atoms*
DISCUSS *conversation & argue*	**QUANTITY** *lot of signals*	**QUALITY** *ratio signal to noise*	**SIGNATURE** *signal path*	**PARROT** *speaking bird*
CACTUS *plant with many spikes*	**LAUGH** *smile smile*	**SERIOUS** *not smile*	**SOLEMN** *not laugh*	**COMEDY** *laugh & text*

SENTENCE *part of text*	**WORD** *detail of text*	**DICTIONARY** *word against word*	**THESAURUS** *word parallel word*	**RECIPE** *text on food*
LIBRETTO *musical text*	**PRESCRIPTION** *medical text*	**AUSTRIA-HUNGARY** *dual monarchy*	**AUSTRIA** *west part*	**HUNGARY** *east part*
ANTHEM *Country & music*	**COAT OF ARMS**	**CURRENCY** *country money*	**COMPUTER** *brain—no face*	**COUGAR** *mountain teeth*
COUNTY *detail of a country*	**MONARCHY** *crown & country*	**PRINCIPALITY** *not kingdom*	**REPUBLIC** *country & king not king*	**UTOPIA** *dream country*
PIPE *part of pipe & vent*	**VENT** *part of pipe & vent*	**MAP** *picture & globe*	**INDULGE** *lot of satisfaction*	**EMPIRE** *country over country*
HILARIOUS *laugh laugh*	**INCOMPLETE** *not complete*	**DEFICIENT** *complete & not*	**FEDERATION**	**CONFEDERACY**
SIMILAR *equal but not*	**BLOW** *part of fight*	**GOLD COIN** *gold & money*	**SILVER COIN** *silver & money*	**AVERAGE** *middle between*
ATLAS *book & globe*	**AUSTRALIA** *down under*	**DISSIMILAR** *different & not*	**HARDCOVER** *book & hard*	**PAPERBACK** *book & soft*

ROMANCE *book & heart*	**ARCTIC** *part of globe*	**ANTARCTIC** *part of globe*	**PENGUIN** *Antarctic bird*	**CONTINENT** *global & local*
SUB-CONTINENT *part of continent*	**LOCAL** *not global*	**NATIONAL** *between state*	**INTERNA-TIONAL** *among states*	**MIGRATORY BIRD** *bird & globe*
TIRE *soft part of wheel*	**DIFFICULTY** *heavy heavy*	**HEAVY** *basic sign*	**LIGHT** *not heavy*	**MARRIAGE** *overlapping rings*
SINGLE *without marriage*	**DIVORCE** *cut marriage*	**BIGAMY** *parallel marriage*	**CELIBACY** *no marriage*	**BATTLEFIELD** *field & battle*
ORCHARD *fruit field*	**HARVEST** *time of crop*	**SEED** *into field*	**CROP** *out of field*	**CULTIVATE** *seed & harvest*
MEADOW *grass field*	**GARDEN** *part of field*	**PHEASANT** *bird of fields*	**SLAVERY** *equal chains*	**COHABIT** *marriage—not a marriage*
SLAVER *ship & chains*	**SLAVE TRADE** *slave & money*	**MARRIAGE FOR LOVE**	**MARRIAGE FOR MONEY**	**WORLDWIDE** *world wide*
EAST *shown on globe*	**WEST** *shown on globe*	**NORTH** *shown on globe*	**SOUTH** *shown on globe*	**EQUATOR** *emphasized on globe*

ECUADOR	TROPIC	ENCOUNTER	VIS-À-VIS	POLYMER
state of the equator	*part of equatorial region*	*come face to face*	*face against face*	*touching molecules*
DNA	PROTEIN	SAME	BULL'S EYE	
molecule of life	*molecule of living*	*equal above and below*	*center of target*	

The descriptions given for various combinations are very terse at best, and in the case of some words shown, they leave room for imagination while in some cases may even have not be warranted. Let us briefly comment on a few.

The sign for FINITE is shown as "part of infinite," which seems appropriate, though mathematicians may frown, not because it is not correct, but it is incomplete, being a truth but not the whole truth! Namely part of infinite can be finite but can also be infinite. To see and understand this, simply consider all positive integers: 1, 2, 3, . . . , an infinite collection, because there is no end in counting. Now if one considers all numbers less than hundred, which is a PART of an infinite sequence of numbers, there is FINITE number of those, but if one considers all numbers greater than hundred, which is again a PART of an infinite sequence of numbers, their number is infinite—showing thus that part of infinite can be finite and infinite. Well, Nobel is a language, it is not mathematics and may allow minor mathematical digressions, just as is the case with natural languages. For instance, it is not uncommon to hear lovers speaking of an infinite love—but how you measure infinity?

Another sign that deserves an expanded comment is the sign for AIR. Clearly, the word "air" represents a challenge for pictographic languages as it has no form, it is invisible although it is all around us and we can feel it (especially on windy winter days) if not touch it. Nobel resolves the challenge by simply combining the ABOVE signs, on the basis that air is overlapping above the ground. For simplicity, GROUND is not shown, though it is implied.

Finally, let us comment also on the signs for AUSTRIA and HUNGARY, two countries left after collapse of AUSTRIA-HUNGARY at the end of 1914-1918 WWI. Their signs reveal some of the potential in Nobel in *positioning* components of a sign when new signs are made as *parts* of existing signs. Austria-Hungary, when alive, included some dozen nationalities beyond Austrians and Hungarians: Poles, Italians, Czechs, Slovaks, Ukrainians, Ruthenians (or Rusyns), Romanians, Slovenes, Croats, Bosnians, Serbs, and Romanies (Gypsies), Austria being at (and controlling) the west of the dual monarchy, as the country was known internally, and Hungary being at (and controlling) the east of the dual monarchy. Being known as *dual monarchy* give rise to the sign of Austria-Hungary as a country with *two crowns*, which forms the basis for the sign for AUSTRIA as *western part* and HUNGARY as *eastern part* of Austria-Hungary.

The signs for England, Scotland, Wales, and Northern Ireland are similarly indicated on Union Jack (the flag of Great Britain and now United Kingdom) as parts of United Kingdom:

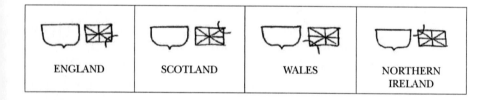

| ENGLAND | SCOTLAND | WALES | NORTHERN IRELAND |

This way of constructing signs by indicating their parts could be applied to few other countries and other objects. Thus when extended to PIPE & VENT, one arrives at signs for PIPE and sign for VENT. But there are also limitations of this kind of design of novel signs. Consider, for example, former YUGOSLAVIA, which when collapsed in 1991 gave rise to six countries (alphabetically): BOSNIA AND HERZEGOVINA, CROATIA, MACEDONIA, MONTENEGRO, SERBIA, and SLOVENIA. Even if we would like to use corners of hexagon to represent the six countries, the geography of the region is more complicated. Thus, for example, Bosnia is in the center of Croatia (and historically was part of Croatia some five hundred years ago before it fell to Turkish onslaught and became part of the Ottoman Empire). Croatia is one of few countries without center (i.e., the geographic center of the county is outside the country). So to come to a sign for Yugoslavia, a different approach has to be taken. So we decided that the sign for Yugoslavia be based on the more recent history of the country, actually on its disappearance. The country was mostly the design of the English and French after WWI, who knew little of aspirations of people not so far away. As some may recall, Yugoslavia disintegrated and, in fact, did not exist, but politicians and military in Belgrade insisted on calling the remnant part of the country (Serbia and Montenegro) Yugoslavia. This incident led to the sign for Yugoslavia (to be illustrated in the coming second part of this book, where there are signs for some sixty countries). There the sign for Yugoslavia is shown as the country that *exists and does not exist.*

There is one additional sign that we have to introduce, which will later find considerable use. We have seen the sign for WITHOUT, but what about the sign for WITH? Here it is:

WITH
basic sign

The sign can be looked at as the beginning of the sign WITHOUT, and with some imagination one can think of WITHOUT as being constructed by crossing the sign for WITH, although WITH was derived from WITHOUT, not the other way round. We will see considerable use of this sign on coming pages, even though the sign WITHOUT has a higher frequency of occurrence.

In order to proceed, we have limited the above illustrations to some two hundred words, even though we could have constructed five times more. It is difficult to exhaust possibilities for construction of additional combinations of already introduced signs. All one has to do is to browse through a larger dictionary, which would bring new words under consideration. Potential of Nobel for development, that is, for extending in the future, has been already demonstrated by the sign for WORLD PEACE, the term you will not find in dictionaries. For example, a sizable *Merriam-Webster's Collegiate Dictionary* (tenth edition, 1993) lists twenty entries involving the word *world,* including world war (defined as "a war engaged in by all or most of the principal

nations of the world") but, of course, does not list the term *world peace.*
This is not surprising, because there is no such in recent history. The
twentieth century has been marked and marred by two world wars
and hostilities that extended into cold war for the most of the time
after the wars. Hopefully the twenty-first century will bring us, if not
world peace, at least cold peace, which would be better than cold war.
The signs for COLD WAR and COLD PEACE can be easily constructed in
Nobel by combining the signs for COLD (to be introduced later), the
sign for WAR, and the sign for PEACE.

There is another word, a word of the past, the present, and
the future, which will not be found in most dictionaries of any
language, if in any, yet it is associated with a simple sign in Nobel.
We have seen the very simple sign for the word HIGH NOON, the
opposite of which gives us the sign for HIGH MIDNIGHT:

HIGH
MIDNIGHT

In a way, it is somewhat surprising that such a word has not
received acknowledgment in public and in dictionaries, in view
of it being in a way more important than HIGH NOON. The extent
to which most people have been acquainted with high noon is
when it received much attention through an outstanding Western
film, considered by some as possibly all-time the best Western,
with Gary Cooper and Grace Kelly as the lead actors (directed
by Fred Zinneman, filmed in 1952). In contrast, HIGH MIDNIGHT
every night changes the date, every year changes the year, every
century changes the century, and once in a while, changes the
millennium—aren't these important times? Yes, they are. And HIGH
MIDNIGHT can do even more, as was the case with the December 31
of 1999 when the entire world celebrated the coming twenty-first
century—a year ahead! Strictly speaking, the twenty-first century
started after December 31 of 2000, as has been noted by those with
more acute technical education. This reminds me of the true birth
date of my mother, which was around Christmas 1899, a few days

before 1900. My grandmother wished that my mother be born in the coming twentieth century and arranged with local priest to change records and set the date of her daughter for mid-January 1900,which, speaking again technically, was nineteenth century, and all the effort was unnecessary!

We will later demonstrate the power of Nobel by revisiting a single sign, that of HEART, and will on this sign illustrate the multitude of combinatorial possibilities that results from combinations of signs and arrows of Nobel. Let us comment on those 250 or so signs from the previous few pages.

AFTERNOON = *part of the time.* It would be better to define afternoon as a part of a day, but we use *part of day* in Nobel to stand for hour. In a similar way to *afternoon* are constructed signs for *morning, noon,* and *evening,* where the positioning of the overlap suggests the time of the day. The sign for *day* is shown as *overlapping time,* which is less suitable for indication of noon and evening.

AIR = *overlapping above.* It is not easy to come up with a sign for something that is invisible, like air. We took advantage that air is *above* ground, which led to the sign *overlapping above.*

ALERT = *awake awake.* To be *watchful and quick to act* (as dictionaries define *alert*), one has to be more than awake, hence emphasizing awake!

AMONG = *between between.* Emphasizing *between* suggests being surrounded, that is, being *among.*

AMPUTATION = *cutting part of the body.* Compare the signs for *surgery, amputation,* and *biopsy,* which are shown as cutting body, part of the body, and detail of the body.

ANTARCTIC = the most *southern part of the globe.*

ANTHEM = *country tune. Country* is shown as a *shield* (countries are supposed to *shield* their people and some do). Tune is symbolized by the sign of *musical note.*

APE = *brain—no brain.* Among animals apes are clearly at the top regarding their brain functions, but compared to humans, they are still some distance behind. This is summarized in the sign brain—no brain.

APPEAR = *under eye. Appear* means to become visible, and this can be represented as coming *under eye.*

ARCTIC = the most *northern part of the globe.*

ARGUE = *mouth against mouth.* Against is shown as being *perpendicular.*

ASHES = *under fire.* Ashes are *under fire* and whatever is left after fire.

ASSASSINATION = *kill authority. Knife into heart* kills. *Authority* is suggested by the sign of *crown,* symbol of kings. Most assassinations involve higher authorities, such as kings, presidents, and leading politicians.

ATMOSPHERE = *overlapping air.* Air is *overlapping above* the ground.

AUSTRALIA = *down under.* Down Under is the standard reference to Australia in England, which then I presume, becomes "Up Above" country. I have made but a single short three weeks visit to Australia and New Zealand, too short to investigate such linguistic perplexities. Be that as it may, *down under* gives Nobel opportunity for a simple sign to represent *Australia.*

AUSTRIA = *western part of Austria-Hungary.*

AUSTRIA-HUNGARY = *dual monarchy.* Hence a country with two crowns.

AUTUMN = *season of fruits.* Autumn and fall are precise synonyms, and hence there is no need to have two different signs for them. Some synonyms have close meaning but differ slightly, in which case there is room for two alternative signs.

AVERAGE = *middle between. Middle* is shown as a *line through middle* of a *circle.* This is essentially the same as the Chinese character for middle, which is a line across a square—this stands for circle, as Chinese characters tend to have angular (square) form rather than being round).

BARE = *without cover.* The sign for *cover* is shown as *overlapping below.* The sign for *below* is shown as semicircle curved down, which looks like a *cover.*

BATTLEFIELD = *field & battle.*

BEAK = *bird mouth.*

BEAM = parallel light. *Light* is shown as part of *electricity* (in fact, it should be part of lightning, which is shown in Nobel as a *lot of electricity,* but for simplicity, we use just single electricity sign here).

BEAR = *teeth teeth.* The sign of *teeth* stands also for *dog,* to remind one of fierce dogs (such as a Doberman pinscher), whose teeth can be a threat and, in comparison teeth of bear, are by far more threatening and dangerous, hence doubling the sign for teeth.

BELLY DANCE = *belly & music*. *Belly* is shown as the *lower part of the body*. *Dance* is shown as *legs* and *music*, which explains the sign for belly dance.

BENEFIT = have *silver behind*. The sign is related to the sign for ADVANTAGE, which is represented as having burden behind, and which is to be contrasted to the sign for BURDEN, which is represented as having burden ahead. "Silver behind" symbolizes what is sometimes referred to as "being born with a silver spoon in a mouth."

BIGAMY = *parallel marriage*. The practice of having *parallel marriage*, which is illegal in all countries, is different from practice of having two or more wives (as is the case with Moslems in some countries and was the practice of early Mormons), which has been legal. In the case of bigamy, neither wife knows of her competition!

BIOPSY = *detail of surgery*. *Biopsy* often precedes *surgery* and is technically and literally a detail of the procedure.

BITE = *part of apple*. Of course, one can bite other things, and we selected apple, being one of the common fruits, not because of the biblical story of Adam and Eve.

BLOW = *detail of a battle* = *part of fight*. In a battle, there is a lot of fighting, so *fight* makes *part of battle*. In a fight, there are a lot of blows, so *blow* makes *part of fight*, and becomes a *detail of a battle*.

BOND = *overlapping atoms*. *Overlap of atoms* forms chemical *bond*, and chemical bonds tend to be strong, sometimes very strong. One tends to overlook chemistry behind many kinds of bonds, including glue and magic glue, and thus it appears appropriate to base a sign for *bond* on *overlapping atoms*, although there are other kinds of bonding.

BOTTOM = *lower part of a mountain*. Many objects have top part and bottom part, but top parts and bottom parts of mountains are most visible, so *mountain* has been selected for the sign for *bottom*.

BRANCH = *part of a tree*. There are other parts of a tree, like stem, roots, treetop, twigs, and even stump, after a tree has been cut. The signs for branch, treetop, and root are similar, all being shown as parts of a tree, but positioned differently: at the side for *branch*, at the top for *treetop*, and at the bottom for *tree root*.

BRIM = *part of a wineglass. Brim* is an outer edge of any hollow object, including hat, and glass (*wineglass*) was selected as being a common and easily recognized hollow object.

BUBBLE = *air under water.* Bubbles are formed when air or another gas is under water. We selected *air* as the gas, air bubbles being the most common bubbles seen, often daily when boiling water, though other kind of bubbles need not be uncommon, such as bubbles in Coke, soda, and beer, to mention a few common drinks.

BULLDOG = *square face dog.* Breed of dogs with strong jaw used in England to fight bulls. Because of the strong jaw, their *face* appears, at least from a distance, somewhat *square.*

CACTUS = *plant* with *many spikes. Spike* is shown as top part of the sign SIGNAL, which is sharp enough to represent spike.

CANCER = *uncontrolled cell division.* Dreadful cancer is, one can say, a molecular illness, caused by continuous cell division. *Cell division* (mitosis) is a natural process, but in the case of cancer, it continues *uncontrolled,* spreading and eventually destroying enough of healthy cells to cause death.

CANDLE = *flame above. Flame* suggests the tip of the burning *candle,* and the sign *above* suggests that the flame can be carried. Similar to the sign for candle are the signs for *incense* as *smoke above* and the sign for *torch* as *fire above.*

CAT = *not dog.* The sign for cat is based on the strong association dog-cat, the two most common domestic pets. Other similar strong associations involve coffee-tea or fruit-vegetable, all of which are shown as reciprocals.

CELIBACY = *not marriage.* Celibacy is here presented as the opposite to marriage, hence use of *reciprocal.*

CELL DIVISION = *cell division.* Here we have interpreted the slash as the mathematical sign for division, such as slash used in 1/2, 2/3, etc.

CHAIN = *overlapping rings. Overlapping rings* means a "lot of rings," which makes chain. A *pair of overlapping rings* is in Nobel a sign for *marriage,* which is also viewed by some, especially some unhappy couples, as a kind of chain.

CHAPTER = *part of book.* Book, like many things has several parts, like *chapter, section, prologue,* and *epilogue.* Nobel differentiates *chapter, prologue,* and *section, epilogue* using the sign for *part* and *part of part*, at the *top left corner*, and at the *bottom right corner*, respectively. See a similar situation with, for example, the signs for parts of a tree: *branch, stem, top of tree*, and *root*.

CHALLENGE = *silver ahead*. At first glance, this combination is perplexing. However, recall the sign for *burden*, which is shown as having *difficulty ahead*. But, if the difficulty ahead is very valuable, then it presents a challenge!

CHIP = *part of a fragment* = *detail of hard* (object).

CINDER = ashes and not ashes. ASHES = *below fire*.

COAT OF ARMS = *country symbol*. Symbol is something that represents another thing to which it is related, associated, has resemblance, or is assigned by convention. In Nobel, *symbol* is shown as a *sign on podium*, which by implication suggests its publicity.

COMEDY = laugh & text. *Comedy* is *text* that should bring a *laugh*.

COMPUTER = *brain and no face*. The sign may be seen as opposite of the sign for *idiot* = *face and no brain*. Computers have a sort of brain and no face. Thus Nobel adopted the sign *brain and no face* for computers, despite that computer brain, and artificial intelligence of computers is of a different kind from brain and intelligence (or lack of it) of humans.

CONFEDERACY = *weakly overlapping countries*. Federacy and confederacy are forms of strongly and weakly interacting states, respectively, that is, states with lesser and greater self-governments. In Nobel, both are represented as *overlapping countries* (states); the difference is in the degree of overlap.

CONTINENT = *global and local*. Continent is a sizable part of the globe and is not the globe, hence, globe and not globe.

CONVERSATION = *parallel mouth*. Conversations are usually informal, pleasant exchanges of thought, views, and news, hence the use of the sign of *parallel*, which in general stands for *agreement*. In contrast, *argue* is in Nobel represented as *perpendicular mouth*, and the sign of *perpendicular* in general stands for *against*.

COPPER = *electricity metal*. *Metal* is shown as *heavy* (difficult) object. *Copper* is a very good electricity conductor metal, so we use the sign of electricity as an indicator. Silver is an even better electricity conductor, but is more expensive, and is therefore not used for making electric wires, except in special cases.

COUGAR = *mountain big cat*. The sign for *cat* is *opposite to dog*, thus *big cat* is shown as using the *teeth* sign *twice*. The plain sign *big cat* in Nobel stands for *tiger*, which is the biggest cat (particularly the endangered Siberian tiger). Some could have expected that the sign *big cat* should stand for lion, but *lion* is represented in Nobel as *king of animals*, an attribute that lion may or may not deserve, because the outcome of a fight between lion and tiger are somewhat unclear (both animals live in some proximity only in India). Be that as it may, because we have a sign for lion, let *tiger* keep the title of *the big cat.*

COUNTY = *part of region* = *detail of a country*. *Region* is shown in Nobel as *part of a country*. County is still smaller (usually administrative) unit of a country, thus can be viewed as a detail of a country. For example, Iowa is between Mississippi on the east and Missouri on the west and is about three hundred miles across and two hundred miles from the northern border with Minnesota, and the southern border of Missouri has one hundred counties, so counties cannot be large (at least in Iowa).

CRIME = *injure injured*. There are so many different crimes and we need a simple solution! To stab a knife in someone else's body is a crime, the seriousness of which can be measured by the depth of the injury and the site of the injury. But it need not be crime, it can be superficial and unintentional. So, in Nobel, *knife into body* is taken to represent *injury*, not a crime. However, *knife into injured* is definitely a *crime*, and most often a serious crime—so we solved the problem!

CRITICAL = *life or death*. *Life* is shown as *heart signal*, *death* is the *opposite*, hence use of the fraction.

CROP = *output of field.*

CRY = *shout shout*. The sign for *loud* is *above mouth*, implying *above* normal voice of *mouth*. The sign for *shout* is *loud loud*, implying *above above* normal voice of *mouth*. Hence, the sign for *cry* is *shout shout*, implying *above above above* normal voice of *mouth*.

CULTIVATE = *seed and harvest.*

CURRENCY = *country money.*

DAMAGE = *knife into suitcase*. Clearly, by pushing *knife into suitcase*, one will make *damage*, though such instances of damage must be very rare. Most damage to suitcases occur at airports, where suitcases are handled by professionals who are not professional enough. On my recent trip, I departed Des Moines, Iowa (USA), with two suitcases and traveled via Chicago, Frankfurt, and Madrid to arrive at Santiago de Compostela in Galicia, northwest part of Spain. On my arrival, I was to collect *three* suitcases! One suitcase was fully broken into two parts, and each half packed in a heavy plastic bag. Even knives could not do such damage.

DEFICIENT = *complete and not complete.* If one buys something, particularly something new, one expects it to be complete, not having missing parts. But, if there are some missing parts, then what was supposed to be *complete is not complete*; it is *deficient.*

DETAIL = *part of part.*

DICTIONARY = *word against word.* Pick up any *dictionary*, particularly dictionaries between different languages; there you will find listing of *words against words.*

DIFFICULTY = *heavy heavy*

DISCUSS = *converse and argue.* In discussions, sometimes one has to argue besides agreeing, hence the sign for *discuss* can be viewed as a superposition of conversation (*parallel mouth*) and argue (*perpendicular mouth*).

DISSIMILAR = *different and not different.* Objects which are *dissimilar* may have some parts similar while other parts are different, hence they are *different and* (in some parts) *not different.* Compare this with the sign for *similar*, which is in Nobel shown as *equal and not equal.*

DIVORCE = *cut marriage.* Simple and clear sign for complicated and unclear process!

DNA = *molecule of life.* DNA forms the molecular base of heredity—thus the essence to perpetuation of life. Its structure was reported by Francis Crick and James Watson just about fifty years ago (in 1958) and consists of double helix held together by weaker bonds (bonded by hydrogen atoms located between two oxygen atoms, the so-called hydrogen bonds).

EAST = *east direction of globe.*

EASY = *crossed difficult. Difficult* is shown as a heavy (weight).

ECUADOR = *country identified by equator.*

ELECTROCARDIOGRAM = *heart beat picture.*

EMPIRE = *country over country.* This was the case with Roman Empire, British Empire, Ottoman Empire, Russian empire and many others that have not called themselves empire, but were dominating other countries.

ENCOUNTER = *come face to face.* The sign for *come* is shown by *legs,* while *face to face* (*vis-à-vis*) is shown as *face against face. Against* is shown as *perpendicular.*

EPILOGUE = *detail at the end part of a book* (compare with PROLOGUE).

EQUATOR = *emphasized on the sign of globe.*

EVENING = *part of time* (see for more: AFTERNOON)

EXTREME = *top and bottom.* Shown as the *top and* the *bottom* of a *mountain.* Indeed, in the case of mountains, those are the extremes.

FALL = *season of fruits.*

FEAR = *teeth in body and mind.* This sign is among some that are, at first sight, in a way the most abstract—yet, as one will see, the sign does maintain close relationship with what it represents, once it is explained. *Fear* is an unpleasant and threatening emotion of *body and mind* caused by awareness of an immediate danger. It is not uncommon to experience such emotion in childhood and even in later years when approached by an unfriendly dog (*teeth*). Just as the sign for *satisfaction* is in Nobel represented by inserting *heart* into *overlapping signs of body and mind* so, in parallel, Nobel encrypts *fear* by inserting *teeth* (symbolizing threat of an unfriendly dog) in *overlapping signs of body and mind.*

FEARFUL = *with fear.*

FEARLESS = *without fear.*

FEATHER = *part of wing = detail of bird.* Birds have feathers all over their bodies, not only wings, though those of the wing tend to be the largest (of course, with exceptions, such as the tail feathers of peacocks). Wings have not been selected because of the size of feathers but because it is easy to draw bird and identify wings.

FEDERATION = *strong overlap of countries* (states). Compare to the sign for *confederation,* which is shown as a *weak overlap of countries* (states).

FIGHT = *part of a battle.*

FINITE = *part of infinite.* Again one of the half-truths, because part of infinite can also be infinite. Consider a line, it has infinite length and contains infinite number of points. But so does half a line.

FIRE RETARDANT = *kills fire.*

FRAGMENT = *part of hard* object. *Hard* is one of the basic signs, which is in a form of a *diamond* (rhombus), diamond being the hardest natural substance, being number 10 on Friedrich Mohs' (1773-1839) scale 0-10 of hardness, which lists various minerals, placing those that scratch others above on the scale. Talc (basic magnesium silicate mineral, which in compacted form appears as soap stone), for example, is of hardness number 1 (that means extremely soft).

FREE = not *chains.* "Not" is shown by *crossing.*

GARDEN = *part of field.*

GENOCIDE = *kill, kill, kill.* It is bad to kill a single person (children, sick, and old included). It is bad to legally kill (execute), not only because occasionally an innocent is mistaken for guilty (or deliberately mistaken) but because it is unnatural and antinatural. Animals (and a few plants) kill for food, not for entertainment or rage. Humans appear to be the exception as, besides "usual" killing, they introduce serial killing (unknown among animals), when a single sick mind perpetuates killings; massacre, when gangs perpetuate killings of their opponents; and genocide when politicians, generals and governments arrange killings of minorities on a large scale. This was the case with million of Armenians killed by Turkish authorities' approval in the 1900s; several million Jews exterminated by Nazis during WWII in Dachau, Auschwitz, Buchenwald, Belsen, Mauthausen, and a dozen other concentration camps throughout the Gross Deutschland of Hitler; thousands of Jews, Serbs, and Romanies (Gypsies) and other "undesirables" killed by puppet quisling Ustashe government of Croatia in Jasenovac in the 1941-1945 era of WWII. Of hundreds of thousands killed in Jasenovac camp, only records on some thirty-six thousand victims survived. They have been made available on the Internet by the Institute for Jasenovac, initiated by

a group of survivors now in New York. In the list, I found
nine persons with rather uncommon surname Randić
(there are less than around fifty people in Croatia and
an additional fifty in the whole world with that surname).
Two dozen houses of the village of Kostrena St. Barbara
on the north Adriatic coast, which has at most some one
hundred houses, are called Randići, from where all these
people moved around. The nine victims mentioned (and
thousands unmentioned) were all partisans during WWII
and were most likely captured by Germans and delivered
to Ustashe as war prisoners, but ended in the notorious
Jasenovac camp.

One would think that with the end of WWII there will
be end of this sad madness, but genocides continues. Tito is
responsible for killing some hundred thousand war prisoners
who surrendered in Bleiburg (now in Austria). Killing war
prisoners is not a novelty. Russians killed during WWII, with
approval of the entire politburo and with signatures of Stalin
and Beria, over twenty thousand Polish military officers in
Katyn around 1940, discovered by Germans in 1943. Let's
mention a few more recent genocides: the killing of five
thousand Kurds by nerve gas in 1988 by Saddam Hussein; the
massacre of large scale of Tutsi in Rwanda in 1994 by Hutu
militia; and the killing of Bosnian Moslems in July of 1995
in fictional UN safe-haven Srebrenica by Serbian General
Mladić, still at large. Genocides hopefully one day may stop,
but our memories will continue and ought to be spoken.

GOLD = *silver silver*. As is well known, sterling silver (objects made of
925 parts of silver and 75 parts of copper) are all marked with
a sign so that they could be differentiated from silver-plated
objects, which contain silver only on their surface. This
official mark of authenticity we symbolized in Nobel with the
sign of a *crown*. Similar practice is used to differentiate golden
objects from gold-plated objects, so we inserted the sign of
two crowns to signify gold. The sign of *three crowns* is reserved
to indicate *platinum*, a heavy, precious, ductile noncorrosive
metal, which is currently even more valuable than gold.

GOLD COIN = *golden money*. Sign obtained by superposition of the
signs for *money* and *gold*.

GOLD STANDARD = *gold on podium.* Standard of the basic currency of a country in terms of gold of specified quality, hence the gold quality that is public, which is suggested by placing gold on a podium.

HARVEST = *time of crop.*

HEAT = *above fire.*

HEAVEN = *above sky.* The sign of *above* (semicircle open up) when *double* means *high above* and when *triple* stands for *sky*, which is *high high* above. Heaven, which is also a synonym for sky but can stand also in place of the Deity and the blessed dead, is shown by adding another semicircle to the sign for sky.

HEAVY = *basic sign.*

HEEL = *part of leg.*

HOUR = *part of day. Day* is shown as *overlapping time.*

HARA-KIRI = *knife in belly.* Ritual suicide practiced by Japanese samurai by pushing a sword into belly and cutting (hara in Japanese) belly (kiri in Japanese)

HARDCOVER = *hard & book. Hard* is shown as *diamond,* the hardest natural substance, allotrope of carbon. The other allotropes are graphite, a lustrous soft black form of carbon used, among other things, in pencils; elusive fullerenes, apparently present but unnoticed in soot; and related to fullerenes, the nanocones and the nanotubes, both of more recent date. Fullerene C_{60}, built from sixty carbon atoms and named by Harry Kroto buckminsterfullerene to honor Buckminster Fuller, American designer of geodesic domes, in view of the molecule's similar internal structure, was reported for the first time in 1988.

HIGH ABOVE = *above above.*

HIGH NOON = *part of noon.* In common parlance, noon is the time around midday. *High noon* is the precise time of noon, hence *part of noon.*

HILARIOUS = *laugh laugh.* High spirit is indicated by excess of laugh—hence *hilarious* became *lot of laugh.*

HOUR = *part of day.* To be exact, it is 1/24 part of day.

HUNGARY = eastern *part of dual monarchy* (Austria-Hungary).

HUNGRY = *empty body.* Body here stands for stomach. The sign for "empty," *crossed zero,* is mathematical sign of set theory, the branch of mathematics dealing with properties of collections of numbers (objects).

IDIOT = *face and no brain*. Idiot is a mentally retarded person with very little mental capacity, sometimes estimated at the level of a child of three years old—but that may be misleading, because children of age three are mentally very alert. Hence, *idiot* has a *face*, but has *no brain*.

IGNORANT = *empty brain*.

INCENSE = *smoke above*. Like *candle* (*flame above*) and *torch* (*fire above*), which can be stationary, *incense* can be stationary but can also be carried around, which is suggested by the sign *above*, which is also used for signs for *carry*, *bring*, and *send* (to be introduced in part 2 of this book).

INCOMPLETE = *not complete*. *Not* is shown by using *reciprocal*. The sign for *complete* is obtained by superimposing the sign of *body* and sign of *mind*. Body and mind make a *complete* person.

INDULGE = *lot of satisfaction*. "*Lot of*" is shown by *doubling*. *Satisfaction* is shown as *complete happiness*, that is, *happy body* and *happy mind*. "Happy" is here, for simplicity, shortened by using the sign of heart.

INJURE = *knife in body*. Whether accidental or pushed deliberately, *knife in a body* causes *injury*.

INTERNATIONAL = *among countries* = *between nations*. The sign *between a country* stands for *inside a country* and thus refers to *national* issues. Issues *among countries* or *between nations* then relates to *international issues*.

INVESTIGATE = *magnifying magnifying glass*. Recall Sherlock Holmes, a character of Sir Arthur Conan Doyle's (1859-1930) stories, which are prototypes of investigations, and his use of magnifying glass.

KILL = *knife in heart*. Knife in heart is for sure to kill a person, though there are hundreds of other ways people are killed, most often driving a car!

LANGUAGE = *sign between mouths*.

LASER = *parallel parallel light*. The word is an acronym, an abbreviation constructed from the first letters of *light amplification by stimulated emission of radiation*. It was introduced in 1960 by development of device that produces coherent emission of electromagnetic radiation in ultraviolet, visible, and infrared parts of spectra of atoms and molecules. To refer to laser as extremely parallel light is almost an understatement. Light of laser was sent to the moon and was reflected back!

LAUGH = *lot of smile.*

LEAD = *soft metal.* Indeed, lead is one of most soft but rather heavy metals with a low melting point (at only 327.5 degrees Celsius, in contrast to gold, which is above 1,000 degrees Celsius and iron, above 1,500 degrees Celsius).

LEUKEMIA = *blood cancer. Blood* is shown as *heart liquid,* and *cancer* as *uncontrolled cell division.*

LIBRETTO = *musical text.* Libretto (from Italian *libro* for *book*) gives text of an opera, is the *text* that accompanies *musical* work.

LIFE = *heart beat.* Life is more than heartbeat, but recall we are in the process of construction of universal language and not elaborating on life as known to biology. Plants are, for example, alive and have no heart. Chinese used combinations of characters that represent "wet tongue" to stand for life some four thousand years ago, and again plants have no wet or dry tongue. Of course, if one's tongue is dry, one is dead, just as if one's heart stops beating. Critics may say that Nobel is oriented too much to human perceptions of the world around—and that is true, because it is intended for communication between humans.

LIGHT = *part of electricity.* The sign clearly differentiates the sign of *light* (illumination) and the sign of (not difficult), which is simply given as *crossed heavy.*

LIVING = *heart beat beat.* Doubling of the heart signal sign suggests duration, prolonged activity.

LOCAL = *not global.* "Not" is shown as *reciprocal.*

LOUD = *above mouth.* The sign suggests *above* normal voice of *mouth.*

LUNCH = *midday meal.* Midday is shown as *noon,* and meal is shown as *full plate.*

MAGNET = *metal* with a *hook. Metal* is shown as *heavy* (weight).

MAP = *picture of globe.* More correctly, map is a representation usually on paper and on flat surface of the whole, or various parts of the globe. The flag of the United Nations depicts one such two-dimensional representation of the whole globe. There are unavoidable inaccuracies in presenting larger parts of the globe as a map, which, if more accurate at the equator, tend to distort and augment the polar regions. But, when considering smaller areas of the globe, two-dimensional flat maps are quite accurate. Indeed the same appears true when looking at the earth around you if traveling short distances. So much so that some people apparently still believe (or pretend to believe) that the Earth is flat—at least this seems to be the case with some of the three thousand members of the Flat Earth Society of New York.

MARRIAGE = *overlapping rings*—basic sign.

MASSACRE = *kill, kill.* Massacre can involve half a dozen victims to several hundred victims and usually refers to killing of helpless and unresisting people, most of the time innocent victims. Massacre has been perpetuated from the biblical times as illustrated by Herod's slaughter of innocents, when, around the time of birth of Christ, Herod massacred an estimated ten thousand male children up to the age of two years in Bethlehem and its surroundings. Of more recent time, massacre appears to be a regular activity of various drug gangs, which are reviving the memories of the Saint Valentine's Day Massacre and the time of Al Capone in 1929.

MASK = *face & not a face.* Mask covers face for disguise, which can be by displaying a different face or a grotesque figure—in any case, *not the face* of the holder.

MEADOW = *grass field.*

MERCURY = *liquid metal.* It is the only metal that is liquid at room temperature. It is highly toxic, and because of that, its use, which was widespread in thermometers and barometers, has been stopped.

METAL = *overlapping heavy.* Metals are heavy, except perhaps for aluminum (and its alloys), the lightest of metals. So the sign for *metal* is shown as *overlapping heavy.*

MICROSCOPE = *lens above lens.* Lens is depicted as magnifying glass, for better recognition. Microscope is an optical instrument consisting of *overlapping lenses* that make it possible to enlarge images of small objects. The same can also be said of the telescope, which is used to enlarge distant objects. In order to distinguish, the two overlapping lenses for the sign of *microscope* are put *one above the other*, and for the sign of *telescope*, overlapping lenses are put *one next to the other*.

MIDNIGHT = opposite of noon. *Noon* is the middle *part of day* (time), while the opposite is shown by *reciprocal*.

MIGRATORY BIRD = *bird over the globe*. Migration is known among animals, fishes, birds and insects, some of which cross several thousands of miles annually. We show migratory birds as flying over the globe, which in fact they are doing, maintaining high navigational skills so that they return to the same place that they left and almost always at the same time as a year before.

MINUTE = *part of hour* = *detail of a day*. Hour is shown as part of time, thus minute, being part of hour, is also part of part of time. *Part of part* is the sign that represent word *detail*.

MOLECULE = *touching atoms*. This would be a fair description of molecules for a layman, though more accurate characterization will be to speak of *bonded atoms*, overlapping atoms, but we already use the sign of *overlapping atoms* to stand for *bond*, including chemical bond.

MONARCHY = *country & crown*. Historically, crown and scepter symbolize the authority of a sovereign, which is simplified in Nobel by using only *crown* as a symbol of *authority*.

MORNING = *part of time* (of a day). *Morning, noon, afternoon* and *evening* are all shown as *part of a time* (of a day) and are differentiated by placing the sign "*part*" approximately at the appropriate part of the watch.

MUFFLER = *kills noise*. "Killing" is suggested by *knife*. *Noise* is *opposite to music* (shown as musical note). *Opposite* is indicated by using *reciprocal*.

NATIONAL = *between a state* meaning, in fact, *within* a state.

NOISE = *opposite to music*. *Music* is represented by *musical note*. *Opposite* is indicated by using *reciprocal*.

NOON = *part of the day* (around twelve o'clock).

NORTH = *north direction of globe*.

ORCHARD = *fruit field*.

ORGAN = *part of a body*.

OVERKILL = *kill killed*. *Merriam-Webster's Collegiate Dictionary* (tenth edition) lists the following three meanings of overkill: (1) a destructive capacity greatly exceeding that required for a given target; (2) an excess of something (as a quantity or an action) beyond what is required or suitable for a particular purpose; and (3) killing in excess of what is intended or required. The sign depicting *two knives in heart* covers *the first two meanings of overkill*. The third meaning of overkill is listed below.

OVERKILL = *kill over kill*. Killing in excess of what is necessary.

PAPERBACK = *book & soft* sign. Soft (*crossed hard*) suggests soft or paperback covers of a book, just as *book & hard* suggest books with hard covers.

PARROT = *bird & mouth*, which suggest *speaking bird*.

PENGUIN = *bird of Antarctic*. Penguins are the only birds of the Antarctic, even though, due to a cold stream from Antarctic along the coast of Chile penguins also live at Galápagos Islands, which are around equator.

PHEASANT = *bird of fields*. As mentioned, a contender for the same "title" would be partridge, but pheasants are more abundant.

PIPE = *part of pipe & vent*.

PLANTATION = *lot of field*. The sign for *field* is the same as depicted in Chinese characters and it is supposed to represent rice fields. Nobel has adopted this sign also to acknowledge the early lead in construction of universal writing initiated by Chinese.

POLYMER = *touching molecules*. Long chain consisting of repeating molecules.

PRINCIPALITY = *country of prince*. Prince is not king, hence the sign for *prince* in Nobel is shown as opposite (*reciprocal*) of *king*. Principality used to be more numerous in middle ages, but few survived. One of the best known is Monaco, which will survive as long as the ruling prince has a son as follower, in which Prince Rainier III, who died in 2005, succeeded (with the help of American actor Grace Kelly, whom he married). The burden of saving the Principality of Monaco is now on his son, the current Prince Andrew II.

PROLOGUE = *detail at the beginning part of a book*.

PROTEIN = *molecule of living*. All living creatures down from viruses (that can crystallize) and bacteria (that can live indefinitely as long as food is available) to plants, animals and humans are built from proteins. Proteins are complex, lengthy folded chains of twenty basic smaller molecules, known as amino acids, as building block units. Observe the similarity and relationship between the sign for DNA, as molecule of life, which is responsible for hereditary properties of living matter, and protein as molecule of living.

QUALITY = *ratio of signal to noise*, as is quality in transmission of signals defined.

QUANTITY = *lot of signal*. If one has a *quantity* of something, then there is *lot of* something. Here the sign for "signal" is used to represent "something" or "anything."

QUARREL = *battle between mouth*, which is what verbal conflict between antagonists is.

RECIPE = *food & text*. *Recipe* is *text* that describes how to prepare *food*. Later we will see the sign for *menu* as a *list of food*.

REGION = *part of a country*. Region is usually a large *part of a country*, an area sometimes without strict boundaries characterized by some specific features and sometimes by local self-government.

REPRISAL = *injury against injury*. This sign follows the traditional "eye for an eye" mentality.

REPUBLIC = *kingdom and not*. In many countries, there is little difference between the periods when they had been a kingdom and when they became a republic, because the persons in power continued to keep all the power they could. The only formal apparent distinction between kingdom and republic is lack of dynasty, but even this is sometimes doubtful. So when any republic is under a dictator, it is better if the dictator has no blood successors! In short, some *republics* are like *kingdoms* even if they are *not kingdoms*. And even when this is not the case, many presidents are treated as kings, if not better.

RESIDENCE = *house of living*.

RHOMBUS = *geometry: diamond* shape. *Geometrical* objects in Nobel are indicated by the sign of *compass*. *Rhombus* is shown as *diamond* shaped, although they are more general geometrical objects defined by having all four sides equal, but internal angles can be very different.

RIM = outside *part of a wheel*.

ROMANCE = *love book. Romance* as a love story is shown as a *book*, with sign of *heart* that suggests love narrative.

ROOM = *part of a house.*

RUIN = *knife into house.* This sign may appear childish, because knife can do but little damage to a house. In fact, the situation is just opposite: if you "attack" a house with a knife, it is the knife that is to be ruined and not the house. Most ruins are the result of burning, destruction, or "eating" of them by weather, which cause buildings to collapse. But how to arrive at a *simple sign* to stand for ruins? Well, if we focus attention on *damage*, then recall that *damage* has been shown as *knife in suitcase*, so by analogy, "knife in house" is extended to stand for *damage to a house*, and damage to house will eventually ruin the house. One may have noticed by now that *knife* in Nobel, as well as in real life, can be a tool of destruction, and in that connotation, "knife into house" can be interpreted as "destruction of house," which is the spirit of the "childish" sign.

SABOTAGE = *knife into factory.* Perhaps another "childish" sign, but it fits the analogy with the sign for ruin.

SCAR = *path of injury.* Many *injuries*, particularly cuts, will leave their *path* on a body.

SEED = *into field.*

SENTENCE = *part of text.* Text is simply speaking a collection of sentences.

SERIOUS = *not smiling.*

SINGLE = *without marriage.* This combination differentiates single from celibacy (not marriage), which is shown as *reciprocal* to marriage.

SLICE = *thin cut.* The sign for *thin* in Nobel is shown by placing the signs *above* and *below* very close. Consider, for example, a sheet of paper, which is thin, and the *above* part of which is very close to the *below* part of it—which explains the root of the sign.

SHOUT = *loud loud.* The sign for *loud* in Nobel is *above mouth*, which suggests *above* normal voice of *mouth*. The sign for *shout* is *loud loud*, implying *above above* normal voice of *mouth*.

SIGNATURE = *path of a signal.* Signature is a trace (*or a path*) one leaves behind when writing one's own name, and *signal* is something that passes a message—what, in fact, *signature* does, passing the message of authenticity of the person who signs a document.

SILVER = *heavy & crown*. Objects made of sterling silver (925 parts of silver and 75 parts of copper) are all marked with sign a sign of authenticity so that they could be differentiated from silver-plated objects, which contain silver only on their surface. In Nobel, the sign of a *crown* inscribed on *heavy* symbolizes the official mark of authenticity of silver.

SILVER COIN = *silver and money*. By combining the sign for *money* and the sign for *silver*, we obtain a sign for *silver coin*.

SIMILAR = *equal and not*. *Similar* object are almost *equal*, but *are not*.

SING = *mouth and note*. The sign of musical *note* suggest *mouth* is *singing*.

SOIL = *top ground*. *Soil*, which is the upper level of earth, which may be dug or plowed and used for growing plants, is the *top* part of the *ground*.

SOLEMN = *not laughing*. *Solemn* may stand for dignified and ceremonial events, but it also stands for highly serious occasions—definitely occasions for *no laugh*. Compare this sign with the sign for *serious*, which is given as *not smiling*.

SOUTH = *south direction of globe*.

SPELL = *speak letters*. This exercise appears rather unique to English (and American) language. Was the lack of writing rules deliberately introduced in medieval England, to keep the privilege of literacy to few, or was it due to lack of education, widespread in medieval times—this is a matter of speculation. That even today educated people may have problems with spelling is witnessed by the fact that a former US vice president could not spell the word potato—which, in a way, need not be surprising, as vice presidents are not likely to eat them often. President Andrew Jackson (1829-1837) was known to spell the same word differently on a single page!

SPHERE = *geometry: globe*. *Geometrical* objects in Nobel are indicated by sign of *compass*. In order to distinguish sphere from circle, which is shown in Nobel as *compass* and *circle*, the sign for sphere is shown as *geometry and globe*, in view of a globe having an approximate shape of a *sphere*.

SPIKE = *part of signal.* Here we took the advantage of the *shape* of the signal sign, which has sharp extremities but which otherwise has nothing in common with spike.

SQUARE = *geometry: square. Geometrical* objects in Nobel are indicated by sign of *compass.*

STAMP = *part of a letter.* Stamps are, as a rule, placed at the upper right corner of envelopes, so is the sign *part* placed in the upper right corner of *envelope.*

SUBCONTINENT = *part of a continent.* The sign for *continent* is shown as *the globe and not globe.*

SUBTOTAL = *part of total. Total* is show as *sum of sum.*

SUPPER = *evening meal. Evening* is *part of time,* and *meal* is *full plate.*

TABULA RASA = *empty empty brain.* Tabula rasa is Latin for "blank slate" and was used by John Locke (1632-1704), an influential British philosopher, who held the view that all ideas one has come from one's experience, and *none are innate* to a person. Politically he held the view that the authority of those who govern comes solely from the consent of those governed, which is the essence of democracy. The wording of the US Constitution has been apparently strongly influenced by his views on how to govern.

TACIT = *spoken but not.* Tacit, which means implied but not spoken is shown as spoken but not spoken.

TELESCOPE = *overlapping lens.* Lenses are depicted as magnifying glass, for better recognition. Telescope is optical instrument consisting of *overlapping lenses* that make it possible to enlarge distant objects. The same can be said of microscope, which is used to enlarge images of small objects. In order to distinguish the signs for telescope and microscope, overlapping lenses for *telescope* are put *one next to the other,* while the overlapping lenses of *microscope* are put *one above the other.*

TERRITORY = *ground & country.* Etymology of the word comes from French *terra* for *land,* and *territory* represents geographical area under jurisdiction of a government. Land is in Nobel represented as *ground,* thus the origin of the sign.

THESAURUS = *word parallel word.* In contrast to *dictionaries,* which list word *against* word (usually words of different languages), in thesaurus, words of similar or *parallel* meaning are collected together.

THICK = not thin. "Not" is shown by crossing. "Thin" is shown as *above* close to *below.*

THIN = *above* close to *below.* Consider, for example, a sheet of paper, which is thin, or any other thin object. For all them, the *above* part is very close to the *below* part—which explains the sign.

THORN = *part of a hook.* Thorn is a sharp pointed part of a plant, which is shown in Nobel as a part of a hook, even though, except for hooks used in fishing, hooks need not have so sharp and split tops.

TIGER = *big cat.* Cat is in Nobel shown as opposite (*reciprocal*) to dog, hence use of *teeth. Big cat* is shown represented by *doubling* the sign of teeth.

TIRE = *soft rim. Soft* is shown as *crossed hard* (diamond), and *rim* is shown as *part of a wheel.*

TISSUE = *part of an organ* = *detail of body.* Organ is represented in Nobel as part of a body, so tissue, which is part *of an organ,* becomes part of a part of a body.

TOOTH = *part of teeth.*

TOP = top *part of mountain.*

TORCH = *fire above. Above* is shown as *semicircle open up,* like a tray or plate that one can *carry* around, thus tacitly implying that torch (*fire*) can be carried, but it can also be stationary.

TREASON = *knife into country.* This sign is an illustration of another destructive use of knife!

TRIANGLE = *geometry: triangle. Geometrical* objects in Nobel are indicated by sign of *compass.*

TROPIC = *part of equatorial part of the globe.*

TWIG = *part of a branch* = *detail of a tree. Branch* is in Nobel shown as *part of a tree,* so *twig* is *part of a part* or a *detail of a tree.*

UTOPIA = *dream country.* Named after the book *Utopia* of Sir Thomas More (1478-1535), English Renaissance humanist and statesman. He was writing about an ideal peaceful state that would be based on perfect society. Nowadays *utopia* stands for an imaginary and remote place or impractical schemes for improvement of social organization. Because More objected that the king of England be the head of the Church, he was beheaded.

VANDALISM = *knife in a picture.* Vandalism is deliberate destruction of property, and in particular works of art. This is why we selected the sign *knife into picture* to represent vandalism. In fact, in 1956 on two occasions, two deranged persons attacked Leonardo da Vinci's masterpiece, *Mona Lisa*, in the Musée du Louvre in Paris, the first throwing acid on the picture and the second throwing a stone, which "hurt" the elbow of Mona Lisa.

VENT = *part of pipe and vent.*

WEST = *west direction of globe.*

WHISPER = *below mouth.* The sign suggests *below* normal voice of mouth.

WING = *part of bird*

VIS-À-VIS = *face against face. Against* is shown as *perpendicular.*

WORD = *part of sentence* = *detail of text. Sentence* is shown in Nobel as *part of text,* and *word,* being part of sentence, becomes *part of part* or *detail of text.*

WORLDWIDE = *globe-wide.* Wide is crossed *narrow.*

W = 800

Our word count stands at about 800, to be exact 815, which included nine countries (Australia, Austria, Austria-Hungary, Ecuador, England, Hungary, Northern Ireland, Scotland, and Wales). We started with sixty basic signs, and by using their combinations, we added another 100 words. By adding overlap of signs as an operation, we arrived at 200 words. Continuing by using combinations of overlap signs, doubling, crossing, inversion, reciprocal, and fractions, we more than doubled the number of words, reaching a total of over 400 words. Adding to the initial set of sixty basic signs twenty conventional signs, of which half are standard mathematical, including plus and equal signs, known to even illiterate people, we arrived at a new total of some 550 words.

Thirty additional basic signs allowed further increase in signs of Nobel. With the help of these additional basic signs, we constructed 275 additional words (half of what we already have) climbing to just above 800 words. This is the number of words that C. K. Ogden considered sufficient to express any text written in English language in simplified "Basic English." Of course, we cannot claim such a feat, because we collected words not for their importance, but convenience. The reason for this is to outline the basic methodology and the spirit of Nobel graphical language. But we ought to point out that we are at the beginning of our climb on "Mount Nobel," and we hope that we have not lost many climbers, as the slopes that we climb do not seem to be too steep. Let me try to assure you, that even though we may have passed a visible fraction of the path, perhaps one-fourth, the rest of the journey will be of similar nature, and will not require strenuous effort on those willing to continue.

PART 2

BASIC ARROWS

Arrows

We started with 60 basic signs, added another 30 signs and 25 conventional signs, approaching thus the total of 120 signs of Nobel. There are still a number of important words that we have not yet considered. For example, five important signs that will add to the 120 are the signs for PERSON, CLOSE, SUDDEN, MALE, and FEMALE—yet to be considered. The reason why we have left these five signs for the end is that they need additional explanations because connection of these concepts with the selected signs is somewhat tenuous. But, in counting the signs of Nobel, we should not include the 25 conventional signs, which are adopted in Nobel but have been around for quite a long time. Hence, currently we are still under 100 signs.

We now proceed to introduce arrow signs as a vital component of the Nobel language. As we will see soon when the already introduced signs of Nobel are combined with arrows, they create signs for a multitude of additional words of Nobel. In Nobel, there are about sixty different arrows that can be combined with signs, but we will start with the following thirty shown below.

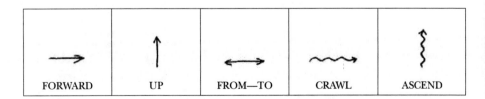

| FORWARD | UP | FROM—TO | CRAWL | ASCEND |

⇉ PUSH	→ → FOLLOW	⇌ FRICTION	↻ EXCHANGE	✕ MIX
⮌ FINE, REFINE	⋖ CHOOSE	⋖ PREFER	⤳ AVOID	⌐ GOOD
⤸ SELF	⤹ INWARD	⤾ OUTWARD	⤿ ALL	⤳ ILLEGAL
⤳ JUMPY	U IMPROVE	∫ CURE	⤚ MERGE	↑↑ USE
⤸ RETURN	↗ PRAISE	⅋ CUMBERSOME	⅋⅋ COMPLEX	⅋⅋⅋ COMPLICATED

The names of most of the arrows shown are rather transparent; a few may require a comment. A wavy arrow for CRAWL is to suggest that this is a slower form of locomotion, while double arrow for USE is suggesting a repeated activity. The folding shape for the arrow to represent REFINE is to suggest that by repeating activity again and again (as implied in folding) one refine a product. The arrow for ALL can be thought of as obtained by connecting the INWARD and the OUTWARD arrows, thus including both the *inside* and the *outside*, that is, including everything or *all*. The ILLEGAL arrow suggests literally "dealings under the table," which are illegal, of course. The SELF arrow points back suggesting *self*, just as in an oil painting of the empress of Austria with her family, Maria Theresa, the empress, was depicted with her hand pointing to herself, so as to leave no doubt who is in charge. Finally, we have three strange-looking highly involved arrows, each successive arrow showing additional loops. They certainly look *complex* and *complicated*, which explains their names. The first of the three, labeled CUMBERSOME, also deserves its name as it appears to point to the right but in a rather convoluted way.

By using the *inversion* operation, we can immediately from these thirty arrows obtain an additional dozen arrows:

BACK	DOWN	CRAWL BACK	DESCEND	PULL
MISUSE	SOAK	BAD	WORSEN	DEATH
OTHERS	BLAME			

Thus, in fact we already have, rather than thirty arrows, more than forty arrow types to be combined with other signs. Let us first examine possibilities of simple crossing of arrows, which lead to several new words. Besides the obvious or trivial NOT FOLLOW and NO FRICTION obtained by *crossing* the FOLLOW and the FRICTION signs, by crossing arrows we can obtain in addition:

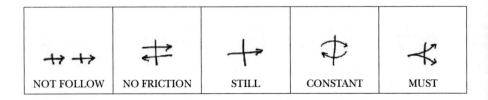

| NOT FOLLOW | NO FRICTION | STILL | CONSTANT | MUST |

OPTION	IMPARTIAL	CRUDE	NOT ALL	

Clearly, something that is not *changing* is *constant*; something that is not *refined* is *crude*; if one has no *preference*, one is *impartial*; if one has no *choice*, one *must* do it; and if one is not moving *forward*, one is *still*.

In addition to crossing as an operation, we can use *reciprocals* to convey an opposing meaning to an arrow, as shown below:

SEPARATE	NONE	ELEGANT	SIMPLE	SIMPLISTIC
NO OPTION				

Observe how we obtained simple constructions for some rather sophisticated concepts, such as *elegant*, or *simple* and *simplistic*. Opposite of *complex* is *simple*, while *simplistic*, which means overly simple, implies tendency to ignore *complications*. To *separate* is obviously the opposite action to *mix*, and opposite to *all*, in Nobel means *none*.

Combinations of Signs and Arrows

Combination of basic signs, though very useful in arriving at new words, has obvious limitations in producing a rather finite number of signs. Languages need an inherent capability to develop and expand, and even if we double the number of signs, this will not dramatically increase the vocabulary of Nobel. As we will see now, with use of arrows our capability to increase vocabulary will not just double but increase by an order of magnitude. A single sign when combined with arrows can result in a dozen, two dozen, and even more new signs. We are ready now to consider combinations of arrows and signs which will illustrate the hidden ability of Nobel to generate a large number of words, which are still easy to replicate, easy to understand, and easy to remember. We will consider one by one each of the thirty arrows and combine them with basic signs and their derivatives and will comment on occasional combination that may not be immediately identified.

FORWARD-BACK ARROW

The first pair of signs, before-after, suggests that the left side belongs to the past and the right side to the future. Thus, for example, one first asks (please) and then *thanks*, one first *arrives* and then *departs*, or one sends *invitation* before receiving *response*.

BEFORE	PLEASE	ARRIVAL	DRAFT	INCOME
AFTER	THANKS	DEPARTURE	MASTERPIECE	SPENDING
MACH	RETREAT	INVITATION		
VINEGAR	ADVANCE	RESPONSE		

Let us add, for those who may not be familiar with wine production and consumption, that before fermentation starts, we have *mach*, and if we leave unused wine in bottle, we will get vinegar (unless sulfites have been added to preserve wine from getting spoiled). Before showing combinations of various signs with FORWARD-BACK arrows, we have first grouped combinations of FORWARD-BACK with time:

NOW	NOT NOW	SOON	NOT SOON	EARLY
LATE	YESTERDAY	TODAY	TOMORROW	DAILY

TONIGHT	PREMATURE	DEADLINE	NOW AND THEN	WEEKLY
DAY BEFORE YESTERDAY	DAY AFTER· TOMORROW	RECENT		

Consider the first two signs in the last row. While in English language one needs three words to describe such days, in some languages there is a single word for such day. For example, in my native Croatian language, these words are *prekjučer* and *prekosutra*, respectively, which literally translate to "over-yesterday" and "over-tomorrow." Because Nobel is a *universal* language and should hold for all languages, it has to take notice of words in other languages besides English. Thus we have to add "the day before yesterday" and "the day after tomorrow" as additional words of Nobel even if not listed in dictionaries of English language.

In some situations, we use but a single arrow or a pair of opposing arrows, such as forward (or back) arrow, or a pair of forward arrows, but not both, as illustrated below:

ENTRANCE	EXIT	IN	OUT	VISIT
INPUT	OUTPUT	PLEAD	THANKFUL	GLASS

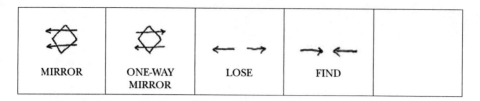

MIRROR	ONE-WAY MIRROR	LOSE	FIND	

Perhaps only the last pair of signs, LOSE-FIND, needs a comment. When something is lost, we don't know where it is; it could be in front of or behind us, left or right, here or there, so arrows showing opposite directions seem an appropriate sign for *losing* or *lost* item. By reversing the arrow directions, we convey the opposite sense—to *find*.

In the following section, we have collected few signs obtained by doubling and tripling the arrow signs.

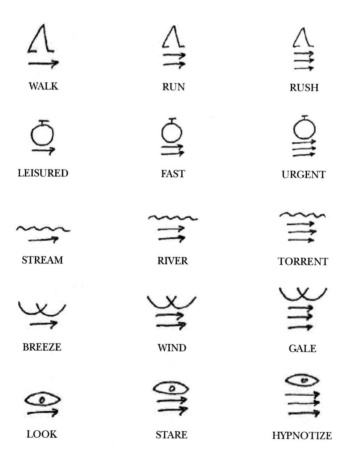

WALK RUN RUSH

LEISURED FAST URGENT

STREAM RIVER TORRENT

BREEZE WIND GALE

LOOK STARE HYPNOTIZE

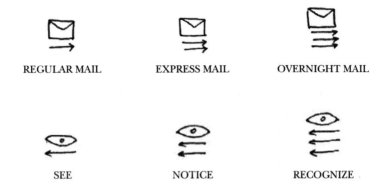

Forward direction in Nobel relates to the future and the back direction to the past. This allows one to understand the signs for excuse, when first one says *please* and then *thanks*. We continue with combinations of forward-back arrows with various signs, including doubling of signs.

BEAUTIFUL	UGLY	REGRETS	ACID	ANTACID
SOUR	FAT	SLIM	SUPERVISE	TRANSIT
BUD	TIMBER	FIREWOOD	CHASE	SEARCH
PARDON	AMNESTY	KIND	CHIVALROUS *kind over kind*	GENTLE

GENEROUS	UNKIND	MEAN	BRING	SEND
CARRY	ALWAYS _before and after_	EXCUSE _please-thanks_	SHUTTLE _arrival-departure_	NEVER _not before—not after_
APOLOGY _excuse—excuse_	TRAVEL	DIARY _daily text_		

If something is *beautiful*, it is for *picture*, hence an arrow into picture. *Ugly*, of course, is opposite, hence reciprocal. Before *flower* comes out we have *bud*; if something has to be done *before* and *not later*, then certain time we have a *deadline* to meet; while *thanks—no thanks* expresses *regrets*; and finally, *after tree* is cut, we have *timber* or *firewood*. *Masterpiece* (see p. 144) represents something very beautiful, hence it comes from beautiful, from something in a picture. *Search* is to look forward and back, while if one *supervises* one continually looks at it.

FROM-TO

If the BACK-FORWARD arrows are fused, we obtain a bidirectional arrow that stands for both back and forward or the past and the future, as illustrated below. We may refer to the horizontal bidirectional arrow as a FROM-TO arrow, and set alone, it indicates the EXTENT. By combining the sign of PART with the bidirectional arrow FROM-TO, one obtains the signs for FROM and TO.

FROM	TO	EXTENT _from-to_		

UP-DOWN ARROWS

We will list numerous combinations of signs with the UP and DOWN arrows and end with comments on a few sign interpretations that may be less apparent. For many signs, we give a hint that will help one to connect the sign with its meaning. In Nobel, the direction "up" generally signifies the "good," and the direction "down" the "bad," just as the "left" and the "right" signify the "past" and the "future."

ABILITY *overlapping potential*	ACQUIT	ANGRY *heart down*	ANTIQUE *old old*	BRAND-NEW *new new*
CALM *waves go down*	COLLABORATION *touching of work*	COMPETENT *overlapping potential*	DIARRHEA *excretion excretion*	DIGEST *in and out of body*
DISTURB *waves go up*	EBB *sea goes down*	EUPHORIA *pleasure over pleasure*	EXCRETE *out from body*	FECES *overlapping excretion*
FEED *into body*	FLOOD *water water water*	FLY *wings up*	FORCE	GUILTY
HAPPY *pleased pleased*	HAPPY HOUR	HIT *through target*	HOVER *fly and not fly*	HUMMINGBIRD *bird that hovers*
IDLE *not producing*	INACTIVE *not active*	INDIGESTION *not digestion*	INNOCENT	LAND *fly down*

MISS *down and target*	**MUSCLE** *body force*	**NEW** *up time*	**NEWS** *overlapping new*	**OLD** *down time*
PATIENT *angry and not angry*	**PAY** *put down money*	**PLAY** *not work*	**PLEASED** *heart up*	**POTENTIAL**
POURING *rain rain*	**PRECIPITATION** *rain and not rain*	**PRICE**	**RAIN**	**STRONG** *overlapping muscle*
TALENT *natural potential*	**TIDE** *sea goes up*	**UNPLEASANT** *not pleasant*	**URINE** *body water*	**VINDICATE** *guilty is found not guilty*
VINTAGE *wine age*	**WEAK** *not strong*	**WORK** *lifting ball*		

Let us start to explain the last word, WORK, which can be viewed as *lifting* a weight, which is shown as a *ball*. In physics, work means to move against force, hence by lifting we are moving against gravitational force. Before one can work, one has to have potential, which is indicated as an arrow *entering* a ball. Force itself is shown by combining potential to work and work in a single arrow. The same single arrow passing through body is to signify *body force*, which are *muscles*. On the other hand, overlapping body potential, which also means *natural potential*, is to signify *talent*. A patient person is one who may be angry but does not show it, hence a sign of *angry* and *not angry*. Similarly, if you were thought guilty but are found not guilty, you have been vindicated. Finally to *pay* means put *money down*! Most other signs hardly need explanation.

Some of the rationales already given or to be given for words to come may appear to be bordering on pictographic and ideographic content of a sign. But one should remember that we are striving to come up with a linguistic system and that languages occasionally allow one to use imagination more liberally. This can be illustrated by etymology of many words in various languages. Consider for example *muscle,* which derives its origin from *mouse,* and which in many languages is adopted. For instance, in Croatian muscles is translated (from Latin origin) as "small mouse." But how did muscle get its name in the first place? Well, one may be surprised, but Romans imagined that as one folds the arm, the moving bumps under the skin appear as though a mouse is crawling under the skin! Hence the word *muscle* for *mouse.*

To the above words we can add the following geographic names:

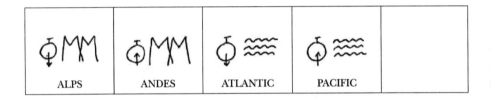

| ALPS | ANDES | ATLANTIC | PACIFIC | |

The words are based on the concept of the Old World and the New World.

CRAWL

Wavy arrow is suggesting slow motion, hence crawling (like a snake). We have collected a few signs with this arrow:

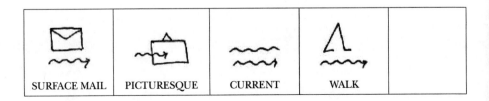

| SURFACE MAIL | PICTURESQUE | CURRENT | WALK | |

ASCEND-DESCEND

To ascend and to descend have a connotation of a gradual rather than a sudden action, thus *crawling up* becomes to *ascend* and *crawling down* to *descend*.

FRESH	STALE	EFFORT	TIRED	CAPACITY
ascend in time	*descend out time*	*ascend out of body*	*descending body*	*ascend into body*
PLEASING	DISPLEASING	IVY	AMBITION	ENDURANCE
		climbing tree	*climbing target*	*tired & not tired*
EXHAUSTED	TEDIOUS	NICE	VIGOR	
tired tired	*overlapping tired*		*ascend through body*	

PUSH-PULL

Double arrows suggest more forceful action to MOVE and MOVE BACK.

ACCUSE	HURRY	ACT/ACTIVE	MAKE	WILL
WISH	DUTY	NEED	DESERVE	MAYBE

SUSPEND	PROMOTE	ALIENATE	DELIVER *bring bring*	DISTRIBUTE *send send*
MERIT	IMPEACH	BREAK	DISCARD	DELAY *push later*
BICYCLE *legs push wheel*	MOTORBIKE *wheel pushes legs*	FLIRT *push heart*	PRODUCTION *factory output*	NECESSARY *need need*

We can combine PUSH and PULL arrows to obtain the following:

COMPRESS	EXPAND	DESIRE	TENSION	PROLONG

FOLLOW ARROWS

A sign for FOLLOW is based on combining two arrows. By simply writing one arrow after another, one obtains a sign for *follow*. Below we illustrate use of the sign on nine words. When the arrows depicting follow are crossed, one obtains the opposite: does not follow. By doubling the sign, we obtain the sign for the word CONTINUE, and its crossing gives the sign for INTERRUPT.

LEAD	FOLLOW	HUNT *hook follows*	WOO *following heart*	OBEDIENT *follows authority*
EXCESSIVE *glass after glass*	CONTINUE *follow follow*	INTERRUPT *not follow not follow*	TOIL *continual work*	

FRICTION ARROWS

By having opposing arrows, one is suggesting *friction*, just as when one is rubbing hand over hand in opposite direction. In a figurative sense, friction suggests some difficulties as is illustrated on the following sign combinations:

JEALOUS *friction in heart*	ADVENTURE *friction on travel*	BUDGET *money friction*	ILLNESS *friction in body*	CORRUPTION *friction in justice*
MUTINY *friction on ship*	INCOMPATIBLE *friction in bed*	COMPATIBLE *not incompatible*	TROUBLE *friction friction*	DISCORD *friction in house*
OIL *liquid with friction*	GREASE *soft lard*	VISCOUS *oil with friction*	SYRUP *sweet liquid*	BREATHE *breathe in-out*
TANKER *oil ship*	NAPHTHA *oil under ground*	STRIKE *factory friction*	GENERAL STRIKE *industry friction*	PAIN *pain*

TORTURE *push pain*	HEALTH *not illness*	SHAKE		

FINE

This arrow appears as folded, and its form suggests repetition, which is one of the ways to refine a product.

FINE	CRUDE *not fine*	REFINE *fine fine*	PRIMITIVE *crude crude*	HUT *coarse coarse house*
COURTEOUS *fine heart*	GALLANT *fine fine heart*	RUDE *crude heart*	VULGAR *crude crude heart*	LAWN *refined grass*
VILLA *refined house*	CABIN *coarse house*	POLISHED *refined refined*	UNPOLISHED *not refined not refined*	SOPHISTI-CATED *refined brain*
UNSOPHISTI-CATED *crude brain*				

CHOOSE

This arrow points to two directions or two possibilities to choose from:

CHOOSY *choose choose*	**NO CHOICE**	**PROMISCUOUS** *not choosy*	**MUST** *no choice*	**OFFER** *choose or not*
DECIDE *cut choice*	**APPOINT** *authority chose*	**REASON** *brain choice*	**EMOTION** *heart chooses*	**PASSION** *emotion emotion*
FATE *time chooses*	**APATHY**	**COMPULSORY** *must must*	**FORBIDDEN** *must not*	**ABSOLUTELY NO** *must not must not*
ALTERNATIVE *parallel choice*	**DESTINY** *path of fate*	**DEPRESSION** *not with emotions*	**EVOLUTION** *natural choice*	**ULTIMATUM** *must must must*
UNDECIDED *no decision*	**ABSURD** *against reason*	**REASONABLE** *parallel to reason*		

AVOID-SOAK

This arrow is bent out of the way as if it avoids some obstacle.

WATERPROOF	SHY	BOYCOTT	SHUN	OUGHT TO
avoids water	*heart that avoids*	*avoid avoid*	*avoid avoid avoid*	*not to avoid*
WORKAHOLIC	CONSIDER	IMPREGNATE	WET	ELUDE
soaked in work	*soaked in brain*	*wet wet*	*soaked in water*	*continually avoids*
IRESPONSIBLE	DIPLOMAT	POLITICIAN	LAZY	
avoids duty	*avoids battle*	*soaked in battle*	*avoids work*	

GOOD-BAD ARROWS

GOOD is pointing *up* and BAD is pointing *down*.

FINE	TERRIBLE	VIRTUE	SIN	PLENTY
overlapping good	*overlapping bad*	*good heart*	*bad heart*	*good scale*
WICKED	CHASTE	VILE	SINFUL	DEBT
sin over sin	*virtue virtue*	*overlapping bad*	*lot of sins*	*bad money*

GOOD LOOKING *good picture*	**IMPECCABLE** *virtue above virtue*	**PORNOGRAPHY** *sinful kissing*	**BAD-LOOKING** *bad picture*	**HOPE** *coming good time*
HOPELESS *coming bad time*	**OPTIMISM** *good future*	**PESSIMISM** *bad future*	**GOOD TIME**	**BAD TIME**
GOODNESS *all good*	**EVIL** *all bad*	**TEMPTATION** *to sin or not to sin*	**AWFUL** *extremely bad*	**WONDERFUL** *extremely good*
PRUDENCE *path of good over bad*				

SELF-OTHERS

SELF arrow bends back to point toward itself; OTHERS is just opposite, it bends away, pointing outward.

SELFISH	**ALTRUIST**	**HOME**	**INDOORS**	**OUTDOORS**
AUTONOMY *self-government*	**SELF-ADMIRA-TION**	**SELF-ADDRESSED**	**SELF-APPOINTED**	**SELF-CONTROL**

INWARD-OUTWARD

Inward and outward or inside and outside arrows are of similar shape, the former being bent inward and the latter outward. When used alone, inside-inside represents volume and outside-outside a surface.

INSIDE	OUTSIDE	FEEL *inside heart*	ENVY *feel jealous*	EROTIC *inside kiss*
ALCOHOL *inside wine*	ANGER *inside angry*	AFFECTION *feel to love*	CONTEMPT *not feel to love*	SKIN *outside body*
SURFACE *outward outward*	VOLUME *inward inward*	CAFFEINE *inside coffee*	TONGUE *inside mouth*	LIPS *outside mouth*

ALL

This arrow is obtained by combining the INWARD and OUTWARD arrows into a single arrow.

NONE *crossed all*	SOME *part of all*	FEW *part of some*	ONLY *crossed some*	SEVERAL *crossed few*
MOST *all but not all*	NEVERTHELESS *all parallel*	ETERNAL *all time*	IN SPITE OF *all against*	

ILLEGAL

Slight "under" bent arrow suggest dealings that are done "under" the table, which is illegal. We used this arrow also to indicate illegal leaving of a prison (ESCAPE) and have changed the direction of the sign for cases when people are illegally imprisoned (on false charges, prejudice, and such) or being framed, even though this may be the only single word that uses the redirected "illegal" arrow. We have left two blank cells adjacent to the word FRAME in case enlightened readers come up with additional illustrations.

BRIBE	CONTRABAND	BLACK MARKET	HOUSEBREAK	BLACKMAIL
CORRUPTION	ESCAPE	ARSON	TRESPASS	PIRACY
ADULTERY	RUSTLE	FRAME		

Observe the opposite direction of the illegal arrow in the last sign. When someone is framed, he or she is illegally imprisoned.

JUMPY ARROW

This arrow suggests jump or jumpy motion.

INCLUDE	EXCLUDE	MODERN	ARCHAIC	KICK
JUMP	WASH	DIALYSIS	MONEY LAUNDERING	BLOOD TRANSFUSION
MIGRATE	FUNNY	JOKE	INFECTION	INFECTIOUS
TENNIS	TABLE TENNIS	BOUNCE		

Observe the positioning of the jumpy arrow for INFECTION and INFECTIOUS, the difference when one gets infection and when one is a carrier of infection. The same pattern positioning of jumpy arrow is also in INCLUDE-EXCLUDE, MODERN-ARCHAIC, and in soon-to-be introduced signs for IN SEASON and OUT OF SEASON.

IMPROVE-WORSEN

The IMPROVE arrow can be thought as made by connecting the pair of vertical down-up friction arrows (which mean difficulty) into a single arrow suggesting improvement, going up. The opposite arrow, connecting up with down arrow, represents worsening.

HEALING	DYING	SUCCESS	FAILURE	MISCARRIAGE
INFLATION	HYPER-INFLA-TION	MISJUDGE	THERAPY	GROUP THERAPY
WRECK				

CURE-DEATH

By extending the IMPROVE-WORSEN arrows outside body we arrive at signs for CURE-DEATH arrows, which indicate the end of the processes such as HEALING and DYING, EXPIRING. All illustrations listed below use the up-down "dying" arrow, except for the last illustration representing "cured" body.

DEATH	EXTINCT	ENDANGERED	ANARCHY	DROWN
RESURRECTION	COLLAPSE	CAPSIZE	AUTOPSY	LETHAL
TOMB	CEMETERY	COMMON GRAVE	MAUSOLEUM	MORTUARY

VULTURE	BALLAST	BURIAL	CURED	

RETURN

Bending of the arrow suggests return.

REPEAT	PRACTICE	ROUTINE	BEHAVIOR	MORAL
POLITE	IMPOLITE	ETIQUETTE	HOMECOMING	BOOK RETURN
AGAIN	OFTEN	REPEATEDLY	RE-ELECT	CHANGE
RECALL				

PRAISE-BLAME

This slightly bent up or down arrow stands to suggest not only PRAISE (curved up) and BLAME (curved down) but also, when turned up, GO AWAY; and when turned down, it may represent COME HERE. In addition, curved down arrow suggests to THROW AWAY or to COPY and, if crossed, suggests original. The meaning of curved arrow is to be determined from the context.

GO AWAY	WAIT	FASHIONABLE	BLESS	RECOMMENDATION
PRAISE	CHEER	PRAY	COMPLAINT	WASTE
LOITER	COME	ABDICATE	EXTRAVAGANT	CURSE
DEMON-STRATE	LITTER	REPRODUC-TION	COPY	IMITATE
SAVE	ORIGINAL	DISMISS	SUMMON	

MISCELLANEOUS ARROWS

Here we have collected additional signs using a few arrows that may not occur as often as is the case with already-shown illustrations.

HEART TRANSPLANT	CONSTANT	MONEY EXCHANGE	MIX	BLEND
SEPARATE	MEET	RENDEZVOUS	FAVORABLE	IMPARTIAL
UNFAVORABLE	MERGE	CONFLUENCE	COMBINE	FOCUS
BUT *merge against*	HOWEVER *merge parallel*	EXERCISE	WEED	

In Nobel, EXERCISE is shown as *use of the body,* which in fact good exercise is, while WEED is shown as *grass without use,* as weed has been described in the first edition of Webster's dictionary of the English language. This optimistic view on weed has been changed since we find more bureaucratic attitude in the subsequent editions of Webster's dictionary where weed is defined as *any plant growing where it is not desired.* This revision is not only showing some hostility but is also not quite correct, because the same plants not desired at some sites, like plantations, may be desired elsewhere (e.g., national parks).

Let us end with set of signs involving the three highly involved arrows:

CUMBERSOME, COMPLEX, and COMPLICATED

CUMBERSOME	COMPLEX	COMPLICATED
ELEGANT	SIMPLE	SIMPLSTIC
AWKWARD	EMBARRASSED	FRUSTRATED

$W = 1,400$

With thirty arrows plus a dozen of their "negatives," obtained by reversing the direction of arrows, we constructed 600 additional words, totaling just above 1,400 words in Nobel. This is about quarter of the vocabulary of Nobel that this book will consider. Before we introduce additional novel signs, we will consider modification of a dozen current signs that broaden our ability to consider related objects.

Modifications of Signs of Nobel

We started with sixty basic signs, added another thirty signs, and promised another half a dozen signs that need some introduction. If we do not count the conventional signs, such as +, −, =, ?, %, #, Σ, ∞, ♪, etc., which are not the signs of Nobel but have been adopted by Nobel, we are still below one hundred signs of Nobel. However, counting different signs may be somewhat ambiguous, because several of the signs that we have already seen can be viewed as composed rather than basic signs. Consider, for example, the following signs:

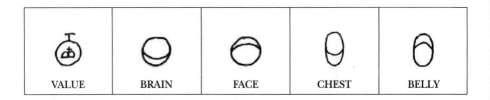

VALUE	BRAIN	FACE	CHEST	BELLY

To which we may add:

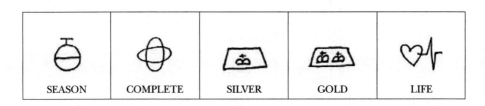

SEASON	COMPLETE	SILVER	GOLD	LIFE

all of which may appear as new signs but all of which are simple constructions based on still simpler basic signs. Thus the sign for VALUE is constructed by overlapping the signs for TIME and MONEY, and of course, time and money are valuables. Similar situation is with the sign for SEASON, which is constructed as a superposition of TIME and GLOBE, in view of seasons referring to global time.

By now we have become familiar with the basic operations with signs which include overlap of signs, doubling and tripling of signs, setting signs to touch one another, inversion of signs, and crossing of signs, and finally, constructing reciprocals and making fractions with signs in numerator and denominator places. In the following, we will introduce two additional operations on signs that are used in Nobel, though to a lesser extent. The first is referred to as *modification,* by what we consider slight changes of a sign that conveys another meaning. By modifying a sign, we can add to it an additional meaning related to that of the "master" sign. The second is referred to as *emphasis,* which consists in doubling part of a sign and in this way adds another meaning to the original sign.

MODIFICATIONS OF SIGNS

Consider the sign for HOUSE and the set of signs shown below:

| HOUSE | BUILDING | STATEHOUSE | BARN | GARAGE |
| PARTHENON | PALACE | TOWER | HIGH-RISE | FACTORY |

The last, FACTORY, which shows a profile of typical factory halls, we have seen. We represent BUILDING as a structure with *flat top,* and STATEHOUSE with a typical *cupola,* while BARN and GARAGE are shown as lacking any interior structure. The PARTHENON is a well-known Greek temple on the Acropolis at Athens. In Nobel, this classic building represents ARTS, being itself such a fine example of human artistic achievements. We represented PALACE as a hybrid of a house and building, while TOWER and HIGH-RISE are shown as narrow and tall.

We will soon introduce additional modification of few signs that justify such novelty, which is not so widely used. Besides the sign for HOUSE, there are a few additional signs that lead to a number of modifications (shown below). ARMCHAIR offers COMFORT, thus this sign represents also comfort. VIPER is shown as "mean" snake, hence the head of the snake is turned *down*, the direction of "bad" in Nobel! We represent DESK as TABLE with drawing, while PINE tree is shown as an overlapping TREE.

CHAIR	ARMCHAIR		SNAKE	VIPER
TABLE	DESK		TREE	PINE

Traditional signs also allow a few modifications as shown below:

BATTLE	ATTACK	DEFENSE	ELECTRICITY	ELECTRONIC
TRANS-MISSION	RADIATION			

DEFENSE is shown as opposite to BATTLE, while ATTACK is depicted as pointing swords *forward*. By adding an arrowhead to ELECTRICITY, we obtain a sign for ELECTRONIC, and by inverting the sign, we have a sign for TRANSMISSION. Finally, radiation is shown as bidirectional arrow by fusing the signs of electricity and transmission. With these few modifications, we can construct almost fifty additional signs:

HOSPITAL	HOSPICE	CLINIC	COURTHOUSE	OFFICE
CREDIT UNION	BANK	TREASURY	X-RAY	MICROWAVE
BLOCK	DOWNTOWN	POWER PLANT	RADIO STATION	TV STATION
ART	GAUDY	CRAFT	FORTRESS	FLYING FORTRESS
ANACONDA	COBRA	RATTLESNAKE	REPEL	RESISTANCE
CASTLE	COMPUTER	POLICE	POLICE STATE	STABLE

CHURCH	MOSQUE	SINAGOGUE	TEMPLE	CHAPEL
CATHEDRAL	ABBEY	CROSS	CHRIST	

The last sign, that of Christ, is shown as a PERSON ABOVE CROSS and although thousands, if not ten thousands, have ended their painful lives nailed on crosses. Putting man on a cross was the standard death penalty of the Roman Empire, just as was hanging in the Wild West and civilized England and Germany, pushing man on a stick in the Ottoman Empire, use of Zyklon gas in Nazi concentration camps, guillotine in France, use of electric chair and gas chambers in the USA, shooting in China (with a request to relatives to pay for the ammunition used), and so on. However, we do in Nobel show respect for gods of all religions and all time, so while we discourage use of signs for person, Christ is an exception and deserves its own sign.

We can speculate that just as in medieval times nobility craved for their heraldic signs, some may wish to take advantage of Nobel and construct signs for their family name. But this may not be as simple as some may think. Consider, for example, the case of the former president of the United States, President Bush, and current President Obama. One may construct the signs for former president Bush and current president Obama as follows:

FORMER PRESIDENT BUSH	CURRENT PRESIDENT OBAMA		PRESIDENT	PRESIDENT ELECT

The sign for former president Bush is obtained by combining the sign for a PRESIDENT and the sign for BUSH, which is shown as tree / not tree. But for those who do not speak English, this sign may signify a chief of BUSHMEN, members of a group of short-statured peoples of South Africa who are today practically extinct. Nobel, by being an international universal language, should not construct its signs on local languages (like English, despite its widespread presence). So former president Bush, unless he takes the burden on himself to advertise himself as "tree and not tree," will not be recognized by the above sign by speakers of languages other than English. In contrast, in the case of current president Obama, we can present a sign that depicts a PERSON and YES, WE CAN, which is what the current president was campaigning about. Instead of "person," we can also use the sign "president-elect" (which is depicted as "president and not president" and is shown at the right, together with the sign for president, which is in Nobel shown as "king and not king," because many presidents of many countries live and behave as kings). This sign for current president Obama is not to be misunderstood, it is in a way universal, just as Nobel language is universal, and millions and millions of people all over the world who heard of Yes, We Can will immediately correctly identified person accompanying this slogan.

Current president Obama is not the only person who can be represented by Nobel. Any person who has some *unique* accomplishment can use such accomplishment as his "signature." For example, Nikola Tesla, the genius of electricity, could be shown as the PERSON BEHIND ELECTRICITY, and BENJAMIN FRANKLIN as the PERSON BEHIND LIGHTNING. A representation of President Monroe could be based on his doctrine, a statement on US foreign policy of December 1823 that expressed opposition to the extension of European control or influence on the Western Hemisphere, which has been summarized in AMERICA TO AMERICANS; former Vice President Quayle could be PERSON of INCORRECT SPELLING, though I am sure his spelling is at least a hundred times better than mine, and people need not be ashamed if they could not spell words correctly—it is all the fault of the medieval English who could not design decent writing rules! And while the vice president has a problem with potatoes,

I am sure he would have no problem spelling chateaubriand, "a large tenderloin steak usually grilled or broiled and served with a sauce (as béarnaise)," or spelling beef Wellington, "a fillet covered with pâté de foie gras and baked in a casing of pastry" (as described in *Merriam-Webster's Collegiate Dictionary*). I myself could be a PERSON *behind* NOBEL.

There is no end to inventing individual sign-names in Nobel just as there has been no end to heraldry. So we strongly suggest that people should, at least for the time being, till Nobel indeed becomes a widespread universal graphical language, refrain from constructing their own heraldic signs in Nobel. Exceptions are always possible, and there are people who deserve more attention than others. So let us end with a story of five Jews (I have no idea where this story originates or from whom I heard it for the first time), who may deserve their own signs in Nobel:

> The first Jew said that everything is in the *brain*: the Ten Commandments, don't kill, don't steal, and so on. That was Moses.
>
> The second Jew goes a bit lower from the brain and said that everything is in your *heart*: love your neighbor. That was Jesus Christ.
>
> The third Jew goes a bit lower from the heart and said that everything is in your *stomach*: pay the workers, give them food. That was Karl Marx.
>
> The fourth Jew goes still bit lower from stomach in a body and said that everything is in *sex*. That was Sigmund Freud.
>
> The fifth Jew comes and tells, all this is relative. That was Albert Einstein.

Perhaps, if we are to make exceptions, the five Jews: Moses, Christ, Marx, Freud, and Einstein deserve special attention? Though I have to admit that I am somewhat reserved, particularly about Karl Marx, who definitely caused a problem for many. Otherwise why would someone knock his nose from his grave monument in London? Actually, I was surprised that only his nose was defaced. I would have expected someone would hit him over his head and spill his brain.

Let me end this "political" anecdote with three signs for three persons:

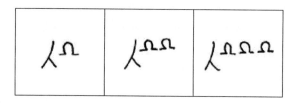

The first is characterized by a *single* horseshoe (symbol of iron), the second by *two* horseshoes (symbol of steel) and the third by *three* horseshoes (symbol of stainless steel). If these are to represent some "important" people (and just for the sake of argument, we will confine here the meaning of "important" by requesting that their names appear in larger dictionaries, such as the *Encarta World English Dictionary*).

Well, the middle case may be the easiest to solve, if one is a student of political science, or if one knows foreign languages, in this case German or Russian. English *steel* is German *Stahl* on which is based the name of Stalin (1879-1953), the general secretary of the Soviet Communist Party, the dictator of the USSR from 1922 to 1953). Russian language adopted a number of German words, and *Stahl*, which in Russian becomes *stal*, for *steel*, is the root of the name Stalin adopted (his full name is Iosif Vissarionovich Dzugashvili, originally from Georgia). The sign is thus appropriate; we are not arguing that Stalin deserves the attention. Although his reasons for selecting the name may be different, it turned out that indeed his heart was of steel, if you only recollect those whom he directly or indirectly eliminated, starting with Leon Trotsky and ending with millions dying from starvation.

The next sign some may guess, like those interested in heraldry, particularly of Americans. One would then find that the "stainless steel" of America is Dwight D. Eisenhower (1890-1969), the supreme commander of the Allied forces during WWII. Namely, the Eisenhower family crest simply consists of a diagonal band with three horseshoes. Thus we have not invented the sign for Eisenhower; it was there in books of heraldic crests. I came across it by visiting Mamie Eisenhower Public Library in Broomfield, a suburb of Denver, where she lived for a while.

Thus we have two strong political and military personalities tied to horseshoes. Who could be the third person of similar standing and has some connection with horseshoe? Well, to solve this puzzle, it helped to live in Iowa. Many outside Iowa do not know about a number of distinguished, outstanding, and/or popular figures that came from Iowa. The short list includes

James Alfred Van Allen (1914-2006) scientist, space physicist, who established the existence of radiation belt around Earth

Johnny Carson (1925-2005) TV entertainer, comedian, who was performing on TV screens for thirty years

Norman Borlaug (1914-) agronomist, Nobel Peace Prize 1970, active in developing agriculture to improve food resources against starvation

William "Buffalo Bill" Cody (1846-1917) scout, Pony Express rider, showman

Wyatt Earp (1848-1929) lawman, known for the gunfight at the OK Corral

Mamie Eisenhower (1896-1979) the First Lady 1953-1961

George H. Gallup (1901-1984) a pioneer in use of statistical methods for determining public opinion on social, economic, and political issues known

Herbert Hoover (1874-1964) US president (Presidential Library is in West Branch, one mile off Interstate 80 (from New York to San Francisco), some ten miles east of Iowa City)

Glenn Miller (1904-1944) bandleader and composer

John Wayne (1907-1944) film actor, particularly known for his Western movies

Grant Wood (1891-1942) artist, painter of a well-known painting *American Gothic*, depicting farmer, his wife, and farm fork in between

Our candidate for the third coat of arms is Herbert Hoover, president of the United States (1929-1933). He may have been very unpopular because he opposed government assistance during the Great Depression but has more than deserved our admiration for his continuing humanitarian work after presidency for some twenty years. To get more details on his work on fighting hunger all over the globe, as emissary of Presidents Roosevelt and Truman,

one should visit Herbert Hoover Presidential Library in West
Branch, Iowa. In order to see what his connection with *horseshoe* is,
one should visit the tiny house and, next to it, the smith shop of
his father next to the library. Of the three persons, Hoover is the
only one who knew firsthand how one makes horseshoes! Stalin
in his youth was attending an Orthodox Christian seminary and
Eisenhower was a college coach.

Mentioning foreign languages, you may be tempted to add
Nobel to your list, even if this is your first foreign language. Nobel
may even encourage readers to pay some attention to foreign
languages. America is mostly a single language country. We have
excluded languages of native populations, like Mohawks in the
east, Dakotas in the mid-Plains, Navajo in the southwest, and many
other Indian tribes not to be overlooked, including Mohicans
and Mohegans, which are confused in the well-known book of J.
F. Cooper, *The Last of the Mohicans*, a kind of classic of the early
1800s. More important, however, is the fact that Mohicans moved
to Wisconsin and are not extinct, and neither are Mohegans, as
the book of Cooper would imply. Ojibway is one of the Dakota
languages, with some 50 thousand speakers in north Minnesota
and neighboring Canada; Navajo speakers, some 150 thousand,
are most numerous. Their language was used in WWII as a code
language for communication in the US army. Alive are also
languages of native people of Alaska and Hawaii. This, of course,
does not mean that they are not endangered. According to some
analysts, if there are less than a million speakers of a language,
that language is on a route to become extinguished. That may be
a pessimistic position or a realistic position, but being an optimist
and knowing that experts have been more than once mistaken, I
maintain that these small languages, today in an age of computers,
will be saved and cherished and may survive. I may say that I may
have vested interest in hoping that experts are mistaken, because
my native language is a Croatian dialect that is about halfway
between Croatian and Slovenian languages, and appears not to
have changed much during the past one thousand years. It is
spoken by less than half a million people and is not well understood
in other parts of Croatia.

Being a *single*-language country, it is not surprising that many
people in the USA speak only English, although the number

of the Latino population has increased in the last dozen years visibly so that it is not uncommon to see in some western states up to Colorado, bilingual notices on buses, airports, etc. There are tiny pockets of bilingual area in the USA, like for example, Amana Colonies (seven villages in east Iowa), where people speak German, and pockets in Louisiana where French is spoken. It is not unfortunate to have a single-language country; most countries are such, but it is the mentality that one can get around with a single language that is unfortunate. So one way to break this barrier is to learn Nobel and, hopefully, after Nobel other languages. In Europe, the situation is quite different, because on average, every one hundred to two hundred miles one comes into a region of different language. So it is not surprising to meet people who speak several languages; to know three to four languages is not uncommon. I cannot boast as being person of many languages. When asked, this is the way I explain part of my foreign language experience: I am fluent in Russian. I have read A. P. Chekhov's short stories in original and also part of Solzhenitsyn's work, but I was twenty years under Stalin. I know enough German to read technical books (without dictionary), but I was four years under Hitler. I know less Italian. Enough to ask some important questions, like *dove e ostaria* (where is place to drink), because I was six months under Mussolini. Unfortunately, I know nothing French, but Napoleon was not in my time!

Speaking of foreign languages, let me end with two short anecdotes. While visiting for a year around 1975 the State University of New York at Buffalo, I met there a very friendly biophysicist, Dr. Robert Rein, who incidentally survived WWII living in Belgrade. In fact, he was all the time hiding his background, because he was Jewish, and had this been found out, that would have been his end. He would then join forty thousand Jews killed in a suburb of Belgrade by Serbian Nazi-puppet authorities. One day in Buffalo, Robert asked me to correct English of one of his manuscripts. My English, as some observant readers may have noticed for some time, is far from perfect. It is not Queen's English, it is not Oxford English, or to be loyal to my alma mater, Cambridge University, where I got my Ph.D. degree, it is not Cambridge English, but at the same time it is not pidgin English. I refer to it as approximate English. Two people speaking two different approximate English can help one another, because their approximate English need not involve the same errors, and thus they can correct one another. So I took the manuscript of Dr. Rein, made improvements that I thought were appropriate, and on returning the manuscript to him, told him that in English you don't have triple *e*, just double *e*, such as "has been" and not "has beeen." On this, Robert answered, "When you speak seven languages you have triple *e*." I am sure that "has beeen" was a typing error, and I was not serious in raising this point, but his answer is instructive to those who speak only English and expect that everyone else should write perfect English. Some of us have a good excuse for our bad English: when you speak seven languages, or understand seven languages or dialects even if not speaking, you may be pardoned for some imperfections. I may, to be honest, say that I did not count Italian (yet) in my list of seven languages, but I included Nobel!

The other anecdote relates to my first days in Cambridge, England, where I came as a graduate student. A week after my arrival, I got a letter from Dr. Walker, Cambridge resident, who indicated that he was interested in Croatian language and would like to meet me and to invite me for cup of tea. I obliged and met Dr. Walker in his apartment full of books, newspapers, and papers. He then asked if he could read a Croatian poem from a booklet so that I hear him. The poem was an epic one from the time of fights with the Turkish invading Europe, considered one of the pearls of Croatian literature. I should add that Croatian language has four accents, ascending, descending, short, and long, but these are implied and never printed, except for books for those learning language, like the booklet that Dr. Walker was reading from. At one point, Dr. Walker stopped reading and asked me a grammatical question concerning one word in that poem. Croatian grammar is quite difficult, there being seven cases (like in Latin), and I never claimed to understand it nor have a desire to waste time studying grammar more than I was forced by the school system, where you have Croatian language as a subject for eight years. Dr. Walker asked for a particular noun whether it is dative or accusative, that is, the third or the fourth case. I tried to answer testing, "to whom," "to what," and "what" used as auxiliary test for dative and accusative, and the noun could fit both cases. Then, just to give some answer, I said "dative." Dr. Walker looked at me first, and then said, "If a word ends on *a*, both dative and accusative end on *u*, but dative has short accent and accusative has long accent—and here is shown long accent" (or was it opposite? I do not recall and never tried to find out). I was amazed. Here is a person learning Croatian, and he knows such a tiny, tiny detail of grammar of Croatian language of which I have never heard in eight years of schooling, and of which many ordinary people, not language scholars, in Croatia probably never heard! Even more surprised I was when, two weeks later, I visited for the first time the Philosophical Library of Cambridge University, and on the board next to the entrance/exit, there was an announcement, "Official translator for the following 26 languages . . ." The announcement listed in two columns twenty-six languages, Croatian included, and was signed by Dr. Walker. I later learned that Dr. Walker was an Austrian living in Cambridge and working to complete a German-English dictionary that his uncle started and came to letter *K* and died. Dr. Walker was engaged to complete that dictionary. In short, there is difference between us, ordinary people, and true polyglots, people who not only speak many languages, but speak them well! Dr. Walker was an impressive polyglot, but you will not find him in the Guinness book of records. According to Berlitz, of the well-known Berlitz schools of foreign languages, the person who knew the most languages was a librarian in the Vatican Library who knew one hundred languages, which included several languages of American Indians. Perhaps after this information, Nobel will receive more attention as a "first-aid kit" in the "shrinking" planet, where more and more opportunities will arise at meeting people from different corners of the globe.

Let us continue with Nobel. Before meeting additional signs, let us point to similarities and difference between the signs for HOSPITAL, HOSPICE, MORTUARY and CLINIC. HOSPITAL is shown in Nobel as a BUILDING for the SICK, while HOSPICE is BUILDING for the DYING. In contrast, MORTUARY is BUILDING for the DEAD, and CLINIC is building for the SICK that come and go, and don't stay in like in hospitals. Earlier we have shown the signs for three vipers; Asian COBRA is shown as the KING VIPER, not because it is the most venomous, because it is not when compared with several Australian vipers, but because it is most likely the best known worldwide as poisonous snake. The second is the RATTLESNAKE of North

America, which makes noise, hence it is shown as a NOISY VIPER. The third is the common European ADDER, which can be shown as JUMPY VIPER, despite the fact that it does not jump but crawls as all other snakes do. However, in some area of Europe (e.g., Croatia), it is known as the jumpy snake because during hot summer days, it tends to rest in lower branches of brushes (to avoid heat), and when surprised, it jumps down to the ground—hence the name "jumpy."

Below we show modifications made on the sign TEXT:

TABLE	LIST	CONTENT	MARGIN	POEM

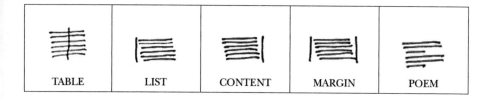

The vertical line in the sign LIST suggests column of numbers 1, 2, 3, . . . or letters a, b, c, . . . , while the vertical line in the sign CONTENT suggests the pages where different items of the list are to be found. The sign for MARGIN suggests space on both sides of the text. With the above signs, novel combinations are possible as shown below:

COMPILE *list list*	PHARMA-COPOEIA *list of drugs*	MENU *list of food*	WINE LIST *list of wines*	DESERTS *list of sweets*
SCHEDULE *time list*	ENEMY LIST *hate list*	CATALOG *alphabetic list*	INDEX *alphabetic content*	TIMETABLE *time & table*
CALENDAR *day & table*	PROSE	LITERATURE	RHYME	

We have seen the modifications of the signs for PLATE, the signs for SOUP and FOOD. SOUP was shown as plate with WATER inside, while the sign for FOOD was shown as full plate. The sign for BREAD, the basic food, can also be viewed as a modification of the sign for PLATE. Here are few additional combinations of such signs:

PLATE	SANDWICH *bread above and below*	HUNGRY *need food*	COOK *make food*	BAKERY *lot of bread*
TRAY *wide plate*				

The sign for season leads to a dozen additional signs:

SEASON *global time*	SPRING *season of flowers*	SUMMER *season of bathe*	AUTUMN FALL *season of fruits*	WINTER *season of snow*
YEAR *overlapping seasons*	MONTH *part of year*	LEAP YEAR *jumping year*	IN SEASON	OUT OF SEASON
SWALLOW *bird of spring*	SEASONAL *season in-out*			

The sign of PERSON,

PERSON

which has been adopted from Chinese characters also provides several modifications to be seen below. This sign may be known to over billion people, people in China, Korea, and Japan, so in adopting this Chinese character into Nobel we wish to indicate some appreciation for the very ancient form of universal writing. Here are few modifications of the sign for person:

STOP	GO	SURRENDER	ARMS	HEAD

They lead to a number of combinations, such as:

ENOUGH	MORE	MORE THAN ENOUGH	SUSPEND	RESUME

Finally, let us illustrate two modifications of the sign for LEGS and its use. The "crossed legs" stand for relaxation, as people do tend to relax sitting with legs crossed. I may add that after my quadruple heart bypass surgery my cardiologist advised against sitting with crossed legs, because then heart has to work harder to pump blood into legs the blood vessels of which are somewhat compressed.

RELAX	STRADDLE	VACATION *relax relax*	HOLIDAY *day to relax*	

EMPHASIS

Another way of modifying a sign is to emphasize part of the sign as illustrated below:

ARMCHAIR	DECK	SEAT	PYRAMID	CUBE
PARALLELE- PIPED	PLATFORM	HORIZONTAL	VERTICAL	SLOPE
LEANING	CONTRADICT	CONSISTENT	BLADE	BLUNT
HORIZON	ZENITH	LATITUDE	LONGITUDE	LUXURY
SOFA	WORKDAY	HOLIDAY	PEOPLE	

PYRAMID, CUBE and PARALLELEPIPED are new signs that can be viewed as obtained from TRIANGLE, SQUARE and RECTANGLE by stressing their sides. In this way, one can transform these two-dimensional geometrical objects into three-dimensional geometrical objects. PARALLELEPIPED is defined as a geometrical object, a polyhedron, consisting of six faces that are parallelograms. In simple language, a parallelepiped looks like a shoe box if all its sides are perpendicular to one another. A parallelogram is a four-sided plane figure in which opposite sides are parallel and of equal length, and if all angles are equal, it is illustrated by a sheet of paper, but in general only the pairs of opposite angles have to be equal. In a similar manner from the shape of DIAMOND (which is technically called RHOMBUS and is defined as an equilateral parallelogram having angles usually but not necessarily oblique) we would obtain a sign for three-dimensional OCTAHEDRON. But many people encounter such geometrical objects like RHOMBUS, OCTAHEDRON and PARALLELEPIPED very rarely, if ever, and therefore it would be uneconomical for Nobel to waste these relatively simple signs on such esoteric geometrical objects. We decided therefore to assign to these signs, including CUBE, another interpretation given below:

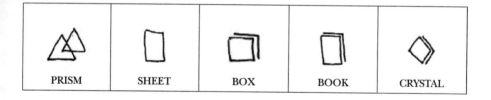

| PRISM | SHEET | BOX | BOOK | CRYSTAL |

In addition, we will interpret the sign of overlapping TRIANGLE to represent PRISM and RECTANGLE to represent SHEET, such as sheet of paper, because as we will see, we have more use for the words PRISM and SHEET than for the words TRIANGLE and RECTANGLE. Now we should add that we don't want to disappoint mathematicians by ignoring the true meaning of the signs adopted for more useful needs. From time to time, one will have a need to refer to TRIANGLE and CUBE in particular, and possibly even to RHOMBUS, OCTAHEDRON and PARALLELEPIPED. In order to allow for such possibilities, we will introduce a sign of COMPASS to represent GEOMETRICAL interpretation of the above-mentioned objects. Thus we have already seen signs:

COMPASS	TRIANGLE	SQUARE	RHOMBUS	SPHERE

The words PYRAMID, BOX, BOOK, and CRYSTAL lead to another dozen new words of Nobel. The sign for PYRAMID also stands for SOLID and STABLE in view of the great stability of such object, as testified by the Great Pyramid of Giza (Egypt), built by Egyptian King Khufu (Cheops in Greek) over 2500 years BC.

BAKE	CAGE	GIFT	ICE	ICE CREAM
ICEBERG	UNSTABLE	FAT	CRYSTALLINE	AMORPHOUS
BIBLE	KORAN	SAFE	TEXTBOOK	STUDY
HARDCOVER	PAPERBACK	RESEARCH	SCIENCE	SCIENTIST

TECHNOLOGY	PSEUDO-SCIENCE	ASTRONOMY	ASTROLOGY	ALCHEMY
CHARLATAN				

By having a sign for SCIENCE, we can continue with list of several sciences and specialties as illustrated below:

MEDICINE	PREVENTIVE MEDICINE	FORESTRY	BOTANY	ORNITHOLOGY
OCEANOGRA-PHY	HISTORY	PEDAGOGY	GERIATRICS	GEOLOGY
GEOMETRY	PODIATRY	PEDIATRICS	CARDIOLOGY	BIOLOGY
GEOGRAPHY	METEOROLOGY	NUMISMATIC	THEOLOGY	THERAPEUTICS

We could continue with adding additional sciences and specialties. One may find some of such specialties rather esoteric, or to say the least, words that are to be hardly used in daily communication. But that all is a matter of personal interests and circumstances. For example, one could consider ORNITHOLOGY, the science of birds, a rather esoteric word, which in a way it may be. The last time that I have come across it was listening to the opera *Madam Butterfly* of Puccini, when Madam Butterfly was inquiring about the season when robins nest, the time when her husband promised to return. So a word may appear esoteric, but it may occur unexpectedly. As one can see in Nobel, we are prepared for such a situation.

Let us return to the sign for ARMCHAIR, which also stands for COMFORT and by doubling and tripling give rise to signs for LUXURY and INDULGANCE. As is illustrated below ARMCHAIR give rise to additional signs:

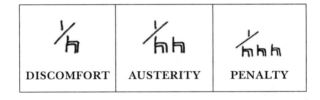

| DISCOMFORT | AUSTERITY | PENALTY |

The opposite of comfort, luxury and indulgence are: DISCOMFORT, AUSTERITY and PENALTY, which are very plausible interpretations. Having opposite signs one may be tempted to combine them just as in number of cases we arrived in this way to signs for novel words. Recall FALSE ALARM = FIRE NOT FIRE; WHETHER = CLOUD NO CLOUD; APE = BRAIN NO BRAIN, MIDDLE CLASS = RICH AND POOR, etc. However, ad hoc combination of opposites may lead to unacceptable contradictions. In the case of ARMCHAIR, combinations of opposites appear useless contradictions: COMFORT & DISCOFORT; LUXURY & AUSTERITY; INDULGENCE & PENALTY. But even these apparent contradictions occasionally may make a sense. Comfort and discomfort may be a precursor for MASOCHISM, pleasure from one's own pain, a disorder named after 19th-century Austrian writer Leopold von Sacher-Masoch. Luxury and austerity is more difficult to interpret, but surprisingly indulgence and penalty made sense, at least for Columbian Pablo Escobar (1949 – 1993), the head of notorious cocaine smuggling Medellín Cartel, who for a while lived in a special prison, "La Catedral," indulging in all the luxury that one can think of, while formally being imprisoned.

Brief Recapitulation
of a Selection of Signs

Before we continue with introduction of additional novel signs and a dozen remaining arrows, we will briefly recapitulate a selection of signs not only to reaffirm our knowledge of words that we have so far seen, but also to re-illustrate the potential of Nobel for making a multitude of combinations of signs and its inherent potential to facilitate remembering the words of Nobel. This brief summary will also better illustrate the structure of Nobel when it comes to making various combinations of signs. Among some three thousand words of Nobel that we will meet before the end of this part of the book, the sign of HEART is among the most frequently used signs. The following dozen have been the most often used signs in combinations in Nobel:

PERSON (380), HEART (280), BODY (180) LEGS (140), TEXT (140), TIME (140), WITHOUT (120), WORK (120), BRAIN (110), BOOK (120), MOUTH (100) and MONEY (100).

We have selected the sign of HEART as basic sign for which we have collected almost 150 combinations we could think of. We will follow with additional combinations, which involve a few novel signs that will be later discussed at greater length. We will end this recapitulation with a list of medical terms involving the sign of heart.

HEART	PLEASE	THANKS	EXCUSE	APOLOGY
BLESS	CURSE	VIRTUE	SIN	FEELING
EMOTION	PASSION	SHY	BOLD	PLEASED
ANGRY	SELFISH	ALTRUIST	AWKWARD	EMBARASSED
FRUSTRATED	KISS	EROTIC	LOVE	SENSITIVE
ROMANCE	CHARACTER	VACATION	BLOOD	BLEEDING
HEMORRHAGE	BLOODSHED	ADMIRE	ADORE	IN LOVE
ENTHUSIASTIC	ATTRACTIVE	BLUE BLOOD	BLOOD MONEY	CANDID

GOODBYE	WELCOME	HEART SURGERY	PARTY	BIRD OF PARADISE
MYOCARDITIS	MAKE LOVE	RAPE	LOYAL	PARADISE
FESTIVITY	HONEY	HIVE	HYPER-SENSITIVE	ALLERGY
HATE	TERRORISM	HELL	BILE	HOSTILITY
ENMITY	DISLIKE	DISLOYAL	MELANCHOLY	FRIGID
NOT FORGIVE	FORGIVE	INSENSITIVE	SWEET	BITTER
TASTE	LOVE-HATE	PLEED	THANKFULL	SOLICIT
GRATEFUL	INEXCUSABLE	REGRETS	PARDON	AMNESTY

KIND	GENTLE	UNKIND	MEAN	ECSTASY
UNPLEASANT	FUN	WANT	HAPPY	PATIENT
WOO	SYRUP	ARRHYTMIA	CORTEOUS	GALLANT
DISCORTEOUS	RUDE	MERCY	FAVORABLE	IN LOVE
UNFAVORABLE	PORNOGRAPHY	TEMPTATION	ANGER	AFFECTION
CONTEMPT	NICE	DISPLEASING	PLEASING	EXCITING
WILL	WISH	NEED	DESERVE	MAYBE
UPSETTING	MANNERS	MORAL	ETIQUETTE	ADULTERY

POLITE	IMPOLITE	IMITATE	SYMPATHY	RESENTMENT
KILL	MASSACRE	GENOCIDE	OVERKILL	SATISFIED
GRATIFICA-TION	INDULGE	ASSASIN	SUICIDE	FIRE RETARDANT
FRIEND	ADVERSARY	ENEMY	PET	JOY
INDEED	PATRIOT	LIFE	CRITICAL	RESIDENCE
LIVING	HOLY	DEATH	BROTHER-HOOD	HONEYMOON
EXECUTION	VENUS	SUGAR		

Few of the above signs need much explanation. We have already mentioned that heart that is beating, HEART indicated with SIGNAL, means LIFE, because when a heart stops beating, that is the end of life. However, not all creatures that are living have heart, like for instance, bacteria and viruses are living creatures, and so are plants, but have no heart. On those grounds, someone can object to the proposed sign for life given by "working heart." But language is not an exact science, nor we are building an encyclopedia of knowledge, but are constructing a language. There are liberties that one can take in language that are not possible in mathematics and rigorous sciences.

To the above words, we can add words that use slanted up, slanted down, and slanted bidirectional arrow:

BELIEVE	ATHEISM	AGNOSTICISM	RELIGION	TRUST
CONFIDENCE	DOUBT	PREMISE		

We have not exhausted combinations using heart but to continue we have to introduce two important signs: MALE and FEMALE.

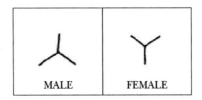

MALE	FEMALE

The signs for MALE and FEMALE have not been invented by this author, but have been mentioned in an article on benzenoid compounds by M. Gordon and W. H. T. Davison some fifty years ago in an article from theoretical chemistry in the *Journal of Chemical Physics* (volume 20, pp. 428-435, 1952) when discussing benzene, naphthalene, and related aromatic compounds. They considered a portion of a graphite (honeycomb) lattice, such as shown below,

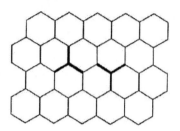

and wanted to differentiate between two carbon atoms of the lattice which have bonds in opposite directions. We adopted these two signs as they allow one more easily to construct combinations of these two signs with other signs, as will be illustrated in the next section.

There is one sign in Nobel that has been created without an apparent connection with its content. This is the sign for CLOSE, one of less than half a dozen signs of Nobel that I could claim to have "invented." This may well be the only sign in Nobel that has no connection whatsoever between its form and its meaning. As we have pointed out already several times, signs representing words in Nobel are either pictographic or ideographic. That is, they either have a direct interpretation or an indirect connection with what they represent. Thus HEART represents human organ but is indirectly related to LIKE and LOVE. The word CLOSE apparently is an exception—which, as saying goes, confirms the rule! The word ADJACENT is related to the word close and it is shown as *overlapping close.*

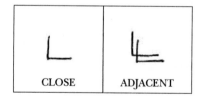

Let us add combinations we can construct using HEART and the signs MALE, FEMALE, CLOSE and ADJACENT:

DEAR	DARLING	INTIMATE	RELATIVE	CLOSE RELATIVE
BOYFRIEND	GIRLFRIEND			

These are not many, but very important words! In all so far, we have constructed almost 170 words involving the sign of HEART.

We will end with list of additional words that involve the novel signs MALE, FEMALE, CLOSE and ADJACENT. Although we have added only four signs, the number of combinations increases visibly as the following pages illustrate. To these four signs, we may add the sign for FAMILY and the sign for SEX. The sign for family is obtained by superposition of the signs of man and woman, who when overlapping make a family. The sign for SEX can be viewed as even stronger superposition of signs for MAN and WOMAN, or more generally MALE and FEMALE, as the centers of the signs coincide.

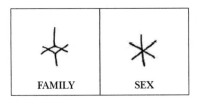

FAMILY	SEX

"Ladies first," so we will start with WOMAN or FEMALE.

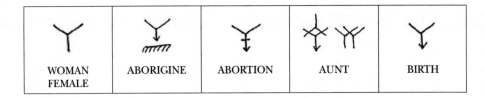

WOMAN FEMALE	ABORIGINE	ABORTION	AUNT	BIRTH

BIRTH DATE	BIRTHDAY	BIRTHRATE	BREEDING	DAUGHTER
GRAND-MOTHER	GRAND-DAUGHTER	LADY	LESBIAN	MOTHER
MOTHER'S DAY	NEWBORN	OLDER SISTER	PROSTITUTE	QUEEN
SHE	SISTER	SORORITY	STILLBORN	UNCLE
VIRGIN	YOUNGER SISTER			
MAN MALE	AUNT	BROTHER	CASTRATE	FATHER
FATHER'S DAY	FRATERNITY	GAY	GENTLEMAN	GRAND-FATHER
GRAND-SON	HE	KING	OLDER BROTHER	SON

FAMILY	ANCESTORS *parents parents*	AUNT *parents' sister*	CLAN *lot of families*	GRAND- PARENTS
PARENTS *father & mother*	TRIBE *lot lot of families*	UNCLE *parents' brother*		
SEX	MASTURBATE *sex & not sex*	MENOPAUSE *falling sex*	NEUTER *cut sex*	ORAL SEX *mouth & sex*
ORGASM *extreme sex pleasure*	ORGY *lot of sex*	PUBERTY *rising sex*	VENEREAL DISEASE *sex disease*	

Let us comment on some of the words shown on the previous pages. Let us start with BIRTH, which is shown as female output. Observe the difference between BIRTH DATE and BIRTHDAY, the former being more basic event, hence inclusion of the sign for BASE, GROUND. The sign for BREEDING is shown as overlapping birth, while ABORTION is represented by *crossing* the sign for birth. The sign for FAMILY is shown by overlap of the sign for man and woman, which is then used for construction of signs for FATHER, MOTHER, and PARENTS by adding arrowheads to the part of signs corresponding to male and female. By adding additional arrowheads, in analogy with signs for CHILD and BABY, one obtains sign for daughter and son, as those growing into mother and father (to be such one day in the future). The sign for child is also used for construction of signs for ADULT = not child and TEENAGER = child and adult simultaneously. The signs for SISTER and BROTHER are shown as overlapping females and overlapping males, where the overlapping relates to having common parents. The signs for GAY and LESBIAN are related to the sign for FAMILY, which is represented as overlap of MAN and WOMAN, except that here we have overlap of persons of the same sex. The sign for SEX can be viewed as obtained by a full overlap of the signs of male and female, and if arrowhead is added to this sign, one obtains signs for PUBERTY as "growing sex" and MENOPAUSE as "declining sex."

We will continue with listing of new words involving the sign for PERSON and the sign for PEOPLE. The sign for people is obtained from the sign for person by emphasizing it.

PERSON	ADMIRAL	ASTROLOGER	ASTRONOMER	AUTHOR
AUTO-BIOGRA-PHY	BABY	BOSS	CABINET	CAPTAIN
CHARLATAN	CHILD	CHILDREN	COAUTHOR	CROOK
DOCTOR	EUNUCH	EVERYBODY	FAMOUS	GANG
GOOD-LOOK-ING	HOST	JUNIOR	KILLED	KILLER
LEADER	MASTER	ME	MEETING	MONARCH

MUSICIAN	NOBODY	OLD	ORPHAN	PRESIDENT
PRINCE	SAILOR	SCIENTIST	SENIOR	SLAVE
SOLDIER	SOMEBODY	TEAM	TEENAGER	TODDLER
TSAR, CZAR	VISITOR	WHO		
PEOPLE	ADMINISTRA-TION	ALONE	ASSEMBLY	AUDIENCE
BUREAUCRACY	CROWD	DEMOCRATS	ELECTIONS	HUMANITY
JUDICIARY	MILITARY	NATION	ORGANIZATION	OTHERS
OVER-POPU-LATED	PLEBISCITE	POLITICIANS	POPULAR	POPULATED

PROGENY	PUBLIC	REPUBLICANS	SIGN LAN-GUAGE	THEM
THEY	UNPOPULAR	VOTE	WE	YOU

Before we continue, let us again briefly comment on a few words. The sign of PERSON is used in various combinations to enrich the vocabulary of Nobel. If the sign of person is in front of another sign it signifies a higher rank, and if it is behind it stands for lower rank. Thus person in front of a ship is captain, and person behind ship is sailor; person in front of ill (sickness) is doctor, and person behind ill (sick) is nurse. Similarly, one can have a person ahead of work to represent foreman, and a person behind work, a worker, and person in front of money is banker and person behind money is teller. Observe the distinction between signs for SCIENCE and PSEUDOSCIENCE: the first is pulling us up (all way up to the moon!), the other is pulling us down, as illustrated with signs for ASTRONOMY (positive) and ASTROLOGY (negative), the popularity of the latter only reflects on one side the widespread ignorance of science and its impact on the life and the living of today and on the other side illusion based on wishful thinking of many who are desperate to evade difficulties and realities of hard life.

Among the signs constructed using PEOPLE, one can find among others the signs for NATION, ORGANIZATION, ADMINISTRATION, BUREAUCRACY, SIGN LANGUAGE and HUMANITY. All these signs are shown as "people around," inserting the appropriate sign that characterizes country, goal, government, desk, sign, and the globe, respectively. One should distinguish between the sign for MEETING, shown as people around a TABLE, and the sign for BUREAUCRACY, shown as people around DESK. Let us draw attention of readers to signs: SIGN LANGUAGE and HUMANITY, both of which have some relevance to Nobel. By adding a crown over sign language, we obtain the sign for Nobel, which one may interpret as the "official" sign language—at least it is official for this book!

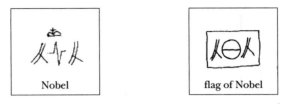

Nobel   flag of Nobel

On the other hand, the sign for humanity, "people around the globe" is taken as a sign for a flag of Nobel, which is light blue, just as is the flag of the United Nations, but instead of a flat diagram of the earth, it has instead the sign of humanity. Hopefully, one day this flag will be seen flying over countries of different languages. We end this section with signs for THIS, THAT, THEESE, and THOSE. The novel sign which is reflection of the sign CLOSE is interpreted to stand for ASIDE.

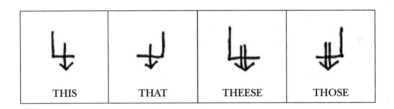

THIS   THAT   THEESE   THOSE

W = 1,700

Since the last count of words, by introducing modifications and emphasis on a dozen signs and adding signs for *male, female, family, sex, person (people),* and *close,* we added another 275 signs getting close to 1,700.

Brief Comparison
of Blissymbolic and Nobel

As mentioned, Blissymbolic, a universal language designed by Bliss after WWII, demonstrated clearly that fully functional written sign language is possible. We are not going to discuss here specific features of Blissymbolic but will only compare at random twenty-five selected words of Blissymbolic with their counterparts in Nobel to illustrate visual differences between the two sign languages. We leave to readers to judge on the similarities and the differences not only between the two sets of signs but also between the signs and their interpretation.

OPPOSITE MEANING	RAIN	SIMILAR	TEENAGER	UP
SAD	SNOW	THANKS	WANT	YES
OR	READ	TELEPHONE	UPSET	WOMAN

□	⊐	—	□◉)⅔	Λ̂
PAPER	ROOM	SKY	TELEVISION	WALK
⊥	△⚲△	○	□	♀̆
PERSON	SCHOOL	SUN	THING	YOUNG

By a close look at the above signs and seeing what they represent, one can discern some common features between Blissymbolic and Nobel, besides the obvious identities for signs of *heart, legs, up* arrow, and *down* arrow. For example, the sign for eye in Blissymbolic appears to be a small circle with a dot that appeared in the words *read* and *television*. In Nobel, the sign for eye is shown by a more "realistic" pictograph. One can see some logic in the signs for *rain* and *snow*, but if one is not told in advance what these two signs represent, it would be very difficult to guess. This is not the case with Nobel, because about half of the signs of Nobel shown for the same twenty-five words can be correctly guessed even by those who see them for the first time!

We will not continue with the discussion of the Blissymbolic and Nobel but should mention that both languages have their own internal logic or system, and twenty-five words are clearly too few to reveal the structure of Blissymbolic. Although it may be interesting and even instructive to make a close comparison between the two languages, I have to admit that I have been too busy with Nobel to have time for studying other sign languages, except for learning some five hundred kanji (Chinese characters), half of which I am afraid I have already forgotten.

∨/	⊊⊋	⁼/₌	⅄/ʎ	↑
OPPOSITE MEANING	RAIN	SIMILAR	TEENAGER	UP

SAD	SNOW	THANKS	WANT	YES
OR	READ	TELEPHONE	UPSET	WOMAN
PAPER	ROOM	SKY	TELEVISION	WALK
PERSON	SCHOOL	SUN	THING	YOUNG

Among the twenty-five Nobel words shown above, there is one new arrow, a short bidirectional arrow for OR. The two semicircles, horizontal for ABOVE and vertical for PART we have already seen. Let us here add few additional signs using ABOVE:

HIGH ABOVE *above above*	SKY *above above above*	COVER *overlapping below*	MOON	STAR
BREEZE *air moving*	WIND *air running*	GALE *air rushing*	DELIVER *bring bring*	DISTRIBUTE *send send*

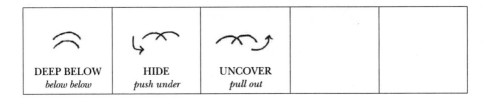

DEEP BELOW	HIDE	UNCOVER		
below below	*push under*	*pull out*		

By combining two signs of PART so that they overlap, we obtain a sign for COMMON, as something that has overlapping parts. By doubling and tripling the sign of common, we obtain signs for ORDINARY as something very common and TRIVIAL as something very ordinary. The *reciprocals* (opposites) of common, ordinary and trivial are interpreted as SPECIAL, RARE, and UNIQUE.

COMMON	ORDINARY	TRIVIAL
SPECIAL	RARE	UNIQUE

As we see, both Blissymbolic and Nobel use a circle for SUN, but in Nobel we added the sign ABOVE and BELOW, hence CIRCLE ABOVE AND BELOW = SUN, which helps to specify the generic sign of circle, which can be so many different things. Similarly we can add sign ABOVE and BELOW to MOON (CRESCENT) and STAR in order to differentiate them from other possible interpretations of the same signs, DECORATION and sign for MOSLEM. After all, sun, moon, and star are circling the sky and appear above and below the earth.

There is one more sign in Nobel that we have not met before and which we did not introduce—because it does not need an introduction. This is the sign for SAD, which is similar to the popular sign of SMILE, but with inverted lips. This sign and a set of signs in between the SMILE and SAD can sometimes be seen in a doctor's office as indicating the scale of pain. If SMILE and SAD are

combined by superposition, one obtains a face that is not easy to
interpret: Is it a little smile with a lot of sadness or a lot of smile and
a little sadness? We took that this sign represents AMBIGUOUS.

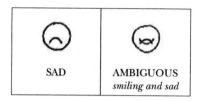

| SAD | AMBIGUOUS *smiling and sad* |

We will end this stage of Nobel by listing about twenty-five signs
based on the sign combinations for BRAIN. As already mentioned,
the number of combinations possible with this sign is much
bigger, over one hundred, but the selected two dozen occur more
frequently and in particular suffice to illustrate the power of use
of arrows in Nobel.

THINK	THINKING	KNOW	UNDERSTAND	MEANING
IDEA *growing thought*	INTUITION	INVENTION	INTERPRET	CLEVER
DULL	WISE	STUPID	BOTHER	TENSE
MISUNDER-STAND	REMEMBER	MEMORY	FORGET	RECOLLECT *think back*

| CONSIDER | OBSESSED | STUPID ERROR | FOCUS | ADVISE |

We have by now accumulated a large vocabulary and could start writing not only sentences but also even a short text, despite the fact that we are still missing many important words. Consider, for example the following sentence:

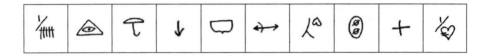

Here is its transcription in English:

| LET | GOD | PRO-TECT | THIS | COUN-TRY | FROM | ENEMY | STARVA-TION | AND | FALSE-HOOD |

We have chosen this sentence not only because of its everlasting content but also because it is one of the oldest messages that came down to us from the period of some four thousand years ago. The above message was found on one of Babylonian clay tablet written in cuneiform, wedge-shaped script found on ancient Sumerian, Assyrian, Babylonian, and Persian inscriptions. The only new sign found in the above message is an alternative sign for THIS, which is pretty obvious.

Countries of the World

Before we continue with remaining signs of Nobel, let us return to the sign for COUNTRY, which we will use now to construct signs for a number of countries of the world. In constructing such signs, one has to take into account that proposed sign should be based on some characteristic of the country, and even this need not be unique to the country considered but at least ought to be one of the dominant characteristics and generally be associated with the country it represents. Of course, when it comes to the names of different countries and different people, one can in Nobel, just as in any other language, use their names. While names of people are rather unique (despite the name of William Shakespeare being written in a dozen different ways through history, and he is not the only one with numerous variations of a name), this is not the case with the names of countries, which may have rather different names in their native language and in English, as shown below for a selection of countries:

ALBANIA	SHQIPËRISË
CROATIA	HRVATSKA
FINLAND	SUOMI
GERMANY	DEUTSCHLAND
HUNGARY	MAGYAR
GREECE	ELLÁS
JAPAN	NIPPON
MONTENEGRO	CRNA GORA
POLAND	POLSKA
SWEDEN	SVERIGE

By being a universal language, Nobel should not give preference to the English language, hence it is desirable to solve this problem by offering a sign alternative for each country. But there are additional reasons for having sign-names for various countries, if possible. Of course we could use countries' names either in English or native language and let readers educate themselves in case they are not sure of which country one speaks. But, in addition to the name of the country, there are words that relate to specific subjects of various countries and thus we need a sign for a country to simply represent such words. Consider, for example,

mikado—emperor of Japan
samurai—soldier of Japan
haiku—poetry of Japan
sudoku—number puzzle popularized by Japan (though originally invented in the USA)
sumo—traditional wrestling of Japan

Without having a sign for Japan, representation of such words would be, to say the least, somewhat awkward.

Before listing signs for selected countries, we will list several signs using the sign for COUNTRY, which we have not seen so far:

COUNTRY	ABROAD	ALIEN	COMPATRIOT	DOMESTIC
EMIGRANT	EXPORT	EXTRADITED	FATHERLAND	HOMELAND
ILLEGAL IMMIGRANT	IMMIGRANT	IMPORT	MIGRATE	MOTHERLAND

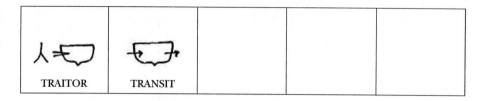

人=🝑	🝑			
TRAITOR	TRANSIT			

We are now listing fifty countries, which include extinct Austria-Hungary, the Soviet Union, and Yugoslavia, and several historic countries or regions, like Scotland, Wales, Northern Ireland, Holland, Siberia, Transylvania, and Tibet. Scotland is the only country for which two signs have been given, one as a part of the United Kingdom, and the other by using the flag of Saint Andrew, the diagonal cross. Similar sign for England, by using cross, the flag of Saint George, is not suitable, because several countries have flag with similar cross (Sweden, Norway, Finland). Of course, each of the flags is of different color, but unfortunately, Nobel is color-blind! In fact, we should have said that fortunately Nobel is color-blind, because communication in colors would be unpractical to say the least.

Argentina *silver (argentum)*	Austria *part of Austria-Hungary*	Austria-Hungary *dual monarchy*	Barbados *trident (on flag)*
Bermuda *danger triangle*	China *people over people*	Colombia *mountain coffee*	Croatia *beautiful sea*
Cuba *cigar*	Egypt *pyramids*	England *part of United Kingdom*	France *country of wine*
Greece *Parthenon*	Holland *part of Netherlands*	Hungary *part of Austria-Hungary*	Iceland *land of ice*

India *wheel of Asoka*	**Ireland** *trefoil*	**Israel** *star of David*	**Japan** *rising sun*
Korea *yin yang*	**Lebanon** *tree (on flag)*	**Liberia** *free (liberty)*	**Macedonia** *cutting knot*
Mexico *sombrero*	**Mongolia** *horses*	**Morocco** *pentagram (on flag)*	**Nepal** *flag shape*
Netherlands *under sea*	**North Korea**	**Papua** *birds of paradise*	**Poland** *fields*
Portugal *bullfight*	**Scotland** *part of United Kingdom*	**Siberia** *very cold*	**Slovenia** *Lipizzaner*
South Korea	**Soviet Union** *hammer & sickle*	**Spain** *bullfight*	**Sweden** *three crowns*
Switzerland *arrow and apple*	**Tibet** *roof of the world*	**Transylvania** *forest*	**Turkey** *Moslem but using Latin alphabet*
United Kingdom *Union Jack*	**United States** *overlapping states*	**Wales** *part of United Kingdom*	**Yugoslavia** *extinct and not extinct*

Having a sign for United States, we can continue by listing several of the states of the USA. We have listed only sixteen out of fifty, for which signs are not difficult to construct, because of some of the unique features of the states. In the case of Florida and Pennsylvania, we took advantage of etymology. Florida is from *flower* in Spanish, and Latin for forest is *sylvania*, the same word that is in the name of Transylvania, northwestern part of today's Romania, but for a short period in medieval time, Transylvania was an independent state. For Hawaii, we took volcano as a symbol, even though this is not the only state with a volcano, but Hawaiian volcanoes are widely known, visited by many, and continue to increase the size of the state! Similarly, Iowa is not the only corn-producing state, but it produces most of the corn within the USA. I was tempted to include Michigan and assign to this state a wheel, which would symbolize auto industry, as a symbol, but in current uncertainties on the survival of auto industry in the USA, such characterization would be characterization of the past, not the future, hence it would be premature.

Constructing names for states, just as is the case with various countries of the world involves numerous challenges and is best left to the people of those countries to consider, who know more about their country than outsiders. A colleague of mine, a Mexican, has seen the sign for Mexico; she was not pleased, telling me that it would be better to use *eagle and snake*, which are symbols of Mexico and part of Mexican flag. To her, *sombrero* is suggesting lazy sleeping person. Surely people sleeping in daytime need shade wherever they can find it, and sombrero (which in Spanish means *shade*) is the last opportunity—but so do people who work in sunny hours, they also need the sombrero. To most people outside Mexico (and possibly inside Mexico), sombrero is not only a beautiful piece of clothing but a representative national icon.

I have traveled forty-nine out of fifty US states and all provinces of Canada bordering the USA except Yukon. In the USA, I have missed Oregon, but I am still waiting if someone is willing to invite me for a visit. I must add that all my trips were professional, attending scientific conferences or giving invited lectures. So one may expect that I should have come up with signs for forty-nine states! But, in my defense, I may say that the task is too big for a single person. I have half a dozen signs for USA states and another dozen signs for various states of the world that I do not feel comfortable to release. Let me give you one illustration that will show dilemmas. Consider the sunny state of Arizona, which has become, next to Florida, quite popular for senior citizens and other retirees. Well, the sign can be based on etymology, which would represent Arizona as a *desert* state. It is not the only state having desert, California next to it is also known for its deserts, but Arizona is clearly ahead in this respect. If *sombreros*, which are beautiful hats, to some may be objectionable, then *desert* as a symbol of a state is not going to please many. On the other hand, Arizona has a unique wonder of the world, the Grand Canyon, and if one can come up with *simple* sign for the Grand Canyon—the problem would be solved! Well, there is a sign for *valley*, there is a sign for *great*, but there is no simple sign for *canyon*, which dictionaries describe as "deep valley with steep sides," or "deep narrow valley with steep sides and often with a stream flowing through it." Those are descriptions of canyon, which I found in *Merriam-Webster's Notebook Dictionary* and *Merriam-Webster's Collegiate Dictionary*, respectively. However, those are descriptions of canyons, and we deal with the Grand Canyon, which, of course, is not an entry of dictionaries.

We can solve the issue of the Grand Canyon from the language point of view by modifying one of the above definitions of canyon into a definition of the Grand Canyon: "The Grand Canyon is a deep narrow valley with steep sides and with a river flowing through it and numerous deep narrow side valleys." It took twenty words! Try to compose a sign for that. This would be half the length of the longest word in the Ojibway language, where the longest word takes three lines of text. Can we come up with something more reasonable?

Yes, we can! This would be politically correct, as we ought to search for simplicity. So here is my proposition:

Grand Canyon is one mile deep.

If Denver is known as the Mile High City, because it is one mile above the sea level, why not the Grand Canyon be known as "one mile deep" canyon (1.6 km), even though it is slightly deeper? However, the same can be said about Denver, because some parts of the city, if not most of the metropolitan area, are somewhat higher.

So we solved the problem for Arizona as "one mile deep state," which can be condensed in a simple sign in Nobel, but we still have to wait for the word to be spread!

Alaska *cold cold*	California *wine country*	Colorado *overlapping mountains*	Florida *flower*
Hawaii *volcano state*	Iowa *"tall corn" state*	Louisiana *fleur-de-lis*	Massachusetts *tea party*
Mississippi *bayou country*	Montana *mountain*	Nevada *tossing a coin*	New Mexico *sombrero*
Pennsylvania *forest*	Texas *longhorn cattle*	Wisconsin *dairy state*	Wyoming *geyser*

Pending:

Arizona
one mile deep

As readers have noticed, we have incorporated a dozen novel signs without introducing them properly, which we will do shortly. However, before we consider new signs, let us make a general comment concerning selection of names for countries. First, we would like to emphasize that the names shown should be considered *provisional*, that is, to be used as names proposed until better alternatives are suggested, hopefully from people of the countries themselves. The next to observe is that many countries are still missing from the list, including many of the states of the USA. For instance, we have no sign for Italy, or to be more correct, I should have said that we have no sign for Italy yet. The same is true of very visible countries of Europe like Germany and Russia, many South American countries, most countries of Africa, Arab countries, Southeast Asia, and the continent of Australia.

As mentioned, the criterion for selecting a sign for a country should be that it signifies some dominant feature of the country, for which that country is *widely known, well known, known, or should be known.* Then such a specific characteristic on which the sign is to be based has to satisfy the requirements of Nobel, the sign should be *easily recognized, easily reproduced and easily interpreted.* Thus, most countries not represented here are not excluded because there is nothing unique and characteristic about them but either because there are too many features to choose from or because a preferred characteristic has not yet been identified, and more energy and time should be dedicated to this task. It would have helped if, when younger, I was traveling more—but when I was younger, I lived in a country where you could only travel in your dreams.

Let us consider, for example, a design of a sign for the great country of Italy. Indeed this is a great country that incorporates rich heritage from the Etruscans, followed by Romans, followed by the glorious Renaissance up to the modern times. But what shall we choose to represent Italy? We could have characterized Italy by wineglass, instead of France, because Italy is the largest producer of wine, but how many people know this particular fact? France is much better known for wines than Italy, so we have to find something else that can represent Italy. The first thing that comes to mind is singing. Italy can be proud of its outstanding opera singers from the time of Enrico Caruso, Benjamino Gigli, and Mario Lanza to probably the greatest of them all, the very recently passed-away Luciano Pavarotti. To this list of the great performers, one should add opera composers, people like Gioachino Rossini (*The Barber of Seville, William Tell*), Giuseppe Verdi (*Aïda, La Traviata, Troubadour,*

Otello) and Giacomo Puccini (*Tosca, Turandot, La Bohème, Madam Butterfly*), to mention those best known outside Italy. But how to summarize and transcribe this musical talent of Italy, the opera composers and the opera singers, into a straightforward simple graphical sign?

Italy is also the country of other giants of our civilization, people like Michelangelo, who painted the Sistine Chapel, and the genius Leonardo da Vinci, of *Mona Lisa* and hundreds of inventions, including parachute, submarine, differential for changing gears, etc. To this we could add that Italy is the cradle of science in modern sense, science based on observations and experiments initiated by Galileo Galilei (1564-1642) and defended by Giordano Bruno (1548-1600), known for *e pur si muove* (but it is moving), the statement often incorrectly attributed to Galileo. Giordano Bruno maintained at that time the "heretic" thought that the earth is not in the center of the universe and was burned alive for not yielding to the medieval Inquisition. Giordano Bruno was more a philosopher of science than a scientist, and interestingly his name has been mentioned when speaking of universal languages. He has been considered as a pioneer semanticist. In contrast, Galileo Galilei was a scientist. For example, Galileo constructed a telescope and was first to observe the rings around Saturn, but even more important were his experiments with pendulums and the falling objects, for which he took advantage of the Leaning Tower of Pisa. Hence, *the Leaning Tower of Pisa*, which is known to millions and is a landmark of Italy, could be a base for a satisfactory sign in Nobel for Italy. An alternative sign could be the sign for EXPERIMENT, which is an inclined board with rolling ball, which Galileo Galilei constructed to measure acceleration due to earth gravity. Finally, a trivial fact that Italy looks like a leg of a person can be used as a description of the country. So, not to leave Italy out, we propose three signs for Italy and let Italians choose, or propose an even better solution.

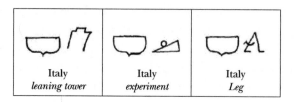

Italy	Italy	Italy
leaning tower	*experiment*	*Leg*

Let us now consider Germany, another country of Europe of great past contributions to architecture, the arts, industry, music, philosophy, science, particularly in chemistry, medicine, and physics. The country of Germany was the origin of aspirin, one of the first common analgesics (painkillers), which has been used for a long time and is today often used also as blood thinner. Germany has been one of the dominant counties in science and technology from earlier days, stretching to the time of modern physics, which includes the relativity of Albert Einstein and the quantum theory of Max Planck, which has been crowned with the development of quantum mechanics of Werner Heisenberg, who was first to formulate the exact laws that govern the inner structure of atoms and molecules. The number of outstanding Germans worth mentioning in various human activities is too long to even consider to list. For example, if one only focuses attention on music, the shortest list should include Johann Sebastian Bach, Ludwig van Beethoven, Felix Mendelssohn, and Richard Wagner. However, one could consider as the country of outstanding music also Austria, which though smaller, can claim similar fame and the same title, with Wolfgang Amadeus Mozart, Franz Joseph Haydn, Richard Strauss and Gustav Mahler. The situation is here somewhat different from the case of Italy, which had no visible rival in the field of classical theater and singing. So, regretfully, we have to give up on the classical music being a unique "signature" of Germany.

We may have better luck by considering scientists, in which Germany excelled and made impressive impact. Among mathematicians we have Gottfried Leibniz, Karl Friedrich Gauss, Felix Klein, David Hilbert, the list that can only be matched by Swiss elite of mathematical giants, brothers Johann and Jacob (Jacques) Bernoulli and Daniel Bernoulli (son of Johann Bernoulli), and Leonhard Euler. Among physicists of modern times, we have at the top: Max Planck, Arnold Sommerfeld, Johannes Stark, Albert Einstein, and Werner Heisenberg. Among chemists, we find Adolf von Baeyer, Emil Fisher, Hermann von Helmholtz, Wilhelm Ostwald, Gustav R. Kirchhoff, Robert Bunsen, to mention but very few. We could continue with biology and other sciences. The problem is to *narrow down* the list and come if possible to a single person and use him or his results to represent the science of Germany and then

Germany, rather than *continue to add* names, even knowing that additional names deserve everyone's attention.

One way to cut down names is to eliminate a few, but on what grounds? Among scientists, we could for instance delete Ostwald on being Russian-German, that is, only half German. On the same quasi principle, we should cross out Einstein being part German, part Jewish, and part American. Felix Klein would then also have to go, being German and Jewish. But this approach appears racist in a way, something to be avoided at all costs, so we will not eliminate Ostwald, Einstein, and Klein. The only person that we will eliminate is 100 percent German J. Stark, a well-known Nazi racist, who, among other things, excluded Einstein's theory of relativity from "German physics." True, Stark discovered the Stark effect, an important experimental finding that causes degenerate atomic energy levels to split in nonhomogenous electric field. Degeneracy here means that several energy states of atoms are identical in normal atoms and only when such atoms are exposed to certain external experimental conditions, one can see that the energy levels are composed of several sublevels. So we cannot deny the scientific contributions of Stark though we may all be utterly disgusted with his political engagements during the rule of Nazi Germany and World War II. Actually, some scientists have been so displeased with Stark that they have suggested that the Stark effect be renamed. Others, who may have been equally disgusted with Stark's political agenda, did not like to mix politics with science and had no choice but to tolerate the status quo, though they equally abhorred Stark's nonscientific activities. We are in position to get rid of Stark, eliminate him as an "outlier" for all the times, as nonrepresentative of Germany, even if one could design some suitable sign for his effect.

This incident, the discussion about renaming the Stark effect, appears to have brought some uneasiness among scientists who, before the question was raised, appeared to be in harmony. The question was raised on one of the Sanibel Conferences in the mid-1970s, the scientific conferences at the border areas of theoretical physics, theoretical chemistry, and theoretical biology, organized annually by Professor Per Olov Löwdin at Sanibel Island, Florida. For some time, it seemed to me that one could possibly restore the harmony by a *compromise* solution to this issue that appears to have no room for compromise, of which I have been thinking for a while. Since the Stark effect has to do with *degeneracy*, why not call it the degenerate Stark effect? The addition of the adjective "degenerate" introduces deliberately some ambiguity as it is not immediately clear whether the effect is degenerate or Stark is degenerate. This is like famous Latin translation of one of oracle at Delphi *ibis redibis nunquam peribis in bello* (You will go you will come back never you will die in war) the meaning of which depends on where one inserts comma:

> *You will go you will come back, never will you die in war*
> *You will go you will come back never, you will die in war.*

So you can interpret the label "degenerate Stark effect" as "degenerate Stark" effect, that is, an effect discovered by a degenerate person called Johannes Stark (1874-1957), if you will!

Now back to Germany. After agonizing hours, I narrowed on two people, one on the list and one not on the list given above: Gutenberg, who invented printing, and Leibniz, who, together with Newton invented calculus but was first to publish his work (which Newton, knowing of its power, selfishly kept for himself and did not publish till Leibniz). Leibniz was also an inventor of his own universal language. I selected *printing* to represent Germany but let German people consider and suggest something else.

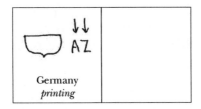

Germany
printing

The same, of course, holds for people of other countries, who may come up with better signs for their own countries—but signs ought to be simple, representative for such countries, and sufficiently widely known. We could enlarge the list of countries and states. For example, Chile is the country of "white gold," sodium nitrate $NaNO_3$, which brought the economic prosperity of Chile after 1800 when it mining started for over one hundred years. Hence, "white gold" could symbolize Chile (though after

1940 its production has been considerably curtailed). Similarly, "white horse," Lipizzaner, (associated with Spanish Riding School of Vienna, Austria), could offer a sign for Slovenia, the country where breeding of these white horses originated. Finally Ethiopia could be the "country of runners", because on all recent marathon races the top few runners came from Ethiopia.

The last country not to be ignored here is Russia. Again a big country, not only physically (involving eleven time zones) but also scientifically and culturally. In particular, we could list writers as apparent contributors to our present-day cultural development, people like Aleksandr Pushkin, Ivan Turgenev, Fyodor Dostoyevsky, Leo Tolstoy, Anton Chekhov, Maksim Gorky, Aleksandr Solzhenitsyn, and Boris Pasternak, to mention a few. I have deliberately omitted in the above list the old "classic" Gogol and more recently Dudintsev, because they are Ukrainian, not Russian. It is very acceptable to consider classic literature as a basis for a sign for Russia, just as we have considered classic music in the case of Italy. This does not deny other countries to have great literature or great musicians, but Russia has definitely a recognizable elite. The problem is how to translate this asset of Russia into a Nobel sign. There is a sign for literature in Nobel, but we need a sign for Russia as "the country of literature," and that is not so easy to compose with three basic signs, two of which will be used to cover "literature." So we have to look for some other characteristic of Russia. The most obvious feature of Russia is her enormous size! So one possibility is to use LARGE LARGE LARGE as a sign. Another possibility is to use a simple drawing of Sputnik, the first artificial Earth satellite of the Russians (technically more correct, the Soviet Union).

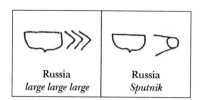

Russia	Russia
large large large	*Sputnik*

NEW SIGNS

Before introducing new signs, let us mention that FIELD, the sign used for Poland, the land of fields, is the same as in Chinese characters. Hence, besides the sign for PERSON, this is the only other sign that Nobel shares with kanji of Japan and characters of China. The following are new signs that have appeared, combined with the COUNTRY sign to make signs for the names for two dozen countries listed before:

DANGER	BEAN	CIGAR	EXPERIMENT	KNOT
TOSS	THERMOMETER	FREEZE	COLD	CORN
LONGHORN	HORSESHOE	HORSE	YIN YANG	

Horseshoe is the sign that we have seen before when speaking of Herbert Hoover, Joseph Stalin, and Dwight Eisenhower. To these signs, we should also add the sign for trefoil, which identifies IRELAND, which obviously has limited use for construction of novel signs. Another sign, which equally finds limited use in combinations, is the sign of ACORN. For each of them we found so far just a single additional combination and will be grateful if readers can enrich Nobel by their own constructions. Be that as it may, and even if no other additions are to be found, most readers will agree that "Saint Patrick's Day" and "oak tree" are very important per se and need to be absorbed in Nobel. One need neither be Irish, nor Christian, nor even religious, to observe various manifestations of celebrations of Saint Patrick's Day, which, besides green cookies, also includes green-colored beer—something I would not believe to be true had I not seen it myself. I have not tried it, because I am not a dedicated beer drinker—my preference is wine. I may add that I have not yet come across green-colored wine to be seen on Saint Patrick's Day, but "green wine" exists in name (given to young wine in Portugal).

Oak, being rather hard wood, of course, has been of considerable significance in the history of humanity. Its name in various variations appears in different countries and different places and is sometimes hidden to recent population, as is for instance in the name of the medieval city of Dubrovnik (*dub* being the medieval name for oak in Croatian, a name which has not been used for quite long time). Oak is still used for fine-quality furniture including fine-quality coffins for dead and fine quality barrels for wine for alive, so we should absorb it in Nobel.

TREFOIL	SAINT PAT-RICK'S DAY	ACORN	OAK	

Several other novel signs of Nobel are pretty obvious: CIGAR, CORN, perhaps HORSESHOE, and THERMOMETER, and finally LONGHORN, cattle of Texas, which is shown as a simplified head of an animal having long horns. Several of the signs that were used to describe some countries are traditional, like the UNION JACK, the STAR OF DAVID, and the YIN YANG, thus they need no comment. Other signs we will briefly comment on, even though they have been already introduced, just in case that reader does not immediately recall them, to save the reader searching over the previous pages:

HEAVY is shown as *bulky weight*
BEAN is shown as *coffee bean,*
EXPERIMENT, the board with a rolling ball, we already discussed as possible sign to identify Italy
KNOT is depicted as the simplest *trefoil knot.* In Nobel, *knot,* besides its literal interpretation, also represents UNIVERSE. The justification and reason for this lies in mathematics, since as mathematicians can argue knots can only exist in three-dimensional space, just as universe exists in

three-dimensional space. One can draw a knot, as we did on a sheet of a paper, which represents two-dimensional space, but the curve intersects itself and only represents knot but is not a knot—because a knot does not intersect itself. Hence, knots cannot exist in two-dimensional space. Well, this argument may have been somewhat intuitive, but mathematical arguments also exist that knots cannot exist in four-dimensional space. Because one cannot visualize four-dimensional space, it is best to trust mathematicians and accept as true that knots exist only in three-dimensional space. Those more curious should consult mathematical texts on the subject, and before we leave the subject, let us only comment on one aspect that may be confusing to some: If one can make a knot (using rope) in three-dimensional space, and three-dimensional space is part of four-dimensional space just as two-dimensional space (a plane) is part of three-dimensional space, how can knots not exist in four-dimensional space? Well, mathematicians will repeat that knots do not exist in four-dimensional space but knotted surface exist—and knot made with rope is illustration of knotted surface and not of knotted curve. It is time to get out of this knotted subject.

TOSS is a novel arrow with self-evident shape, and it is also used to signify the idea of EXIST. Observe that it is related in shape to the arrow named EXTINCT.

GLOBE is shown as ball (circle) with *equator*.

COLD is indicated by down-bent arrow on thermometer.

Now we can briefly comment on names of several countries:

ARGENTINA sign is based on the sign for SILVER, which is metal (HEAVY) on which is imprinted the sign of a crown as all proper silverware are also imprinted (but silver-plated items are not, which is done so that one cannot be swindled in buying silver-plated items and paying for them as if they are solid silver).

AUSTRIA is shown as western *part* of AUSTRIA-HUNGARY.

AUSTRIA-HUNGARY was known as dual monarchy, hence it is represented by two crowns.

BERMUDA is based on folklore of the Bermuda Triangle, a dangerous part of the Atlantic bounded by connecting Bermuda, Melbourne (Florida), and Puerto Rico—a region associated with numerous accidents, disappearance and sinking of ships and planes.

COLOMBIA is represented by signs of the mountain and coffee, that is, *mountain coffee*, as their coffee is often advertised as such.

CROATIA, as many who visited the country know, has beautiful coastline, hence the country of *beautiful sea.*

CUBA is renowned for its high quality *cigars.*

FRANCE is correctly perceived as the country of good wines and high-quality *wine.*

GREECE is identified by PARTHENON, an architecture classic of all times, the sign of which has been used in Nobel to stand for ARTS.

HOLLAND is shown as *part* of the NETHERLANDS.

HUNGARY is shown as eastern *part* of AUSTRIA-HUNGARY.

ICELAND is country of ICE (solid water).

INDIA is indicated by the wheel of an early ruler, Asoka (wheel appears on the Indian national flag).

IRELAND is indicated by CLOVER LEAF.

ISRAEL is indicated by the STAR OF DAVID.

JAPAN is shown as the country of *rising sun.*

KOREA is indicated by yin yang.

LEBANON is indicated by tree (which is on its national flag).

LIBERIA is based on sign for *free* (crossed chains), based on its name as being the first black people's free country in Africa.

MACEDONIA is symbolized by *cutting a knot* as told by the legend on Alexander the Great, the ancient emperor of Macedonia.

MOROCCO is identified by pentagram (STAR), which appears on its flag.

MALTA (not shown) could be identified by characteristic cross known as Maltese cross, an emblem of medieval Knights of Malta (that has resemblance with cross used by the order of medieval Templar).

MEXICO is symbolized by *sombrero*, a shade hat.

MONACO (not shown) is the principality known for its casinos, gambling, hence *tossing a coin* for luck could represent Monaco.

MONGOLIA has been known through history for its horses, which made it possible for Mongols to travel fast and long distances and which brought Genghis Khan (1162-1227) to Europe (and took Mongols back to Asia).

NETHERLANDS is shown as a country "under the sea" in view of their successful exploitation of land that was under sea and is below sea level.

NEPAL has a unique flag shape among all nations.

NORTH KOREA is shown by superposition of the direction "north" with yin yang.

PANAMA could be shown as the country that connects (overlaps) *two oceans*—by having a Panama Canal that allows passage of ships between the two oceans.

PAPUA is the country of *birds of paradise.*

POLAND derived its name from the word *fields* hence is identified by the sign for field.

PORTUGAL, just as SPAIN, are countries indicated by bullfight, which is shown as a BATTLE with ANIMAL. But because in Portugal at the end of a fight, a bull is not killed but spared, we inverted the sign for battle, which then means "defend," so in Portugal in bullfight at the end, a bull is defended (not killed).

SIBERIA is known for its freezing winter temperature, the coldest reported at below minus 70 degrees Celsius or minus 96 degrees Fahrenheit, hence it is appropriate to characterize the country as *very cold.*

SLOVENIA, the home of Lipizzaner white horses (bred in small village Lipizza).

SOUTH KOREA is shown by superposition of the direction "south" with yin yang.

SOVIET UNION is identified by the communist symbol of hammer and sickle (which were to symbolize peasants and workers).

SPAIN just as PORTUGAL are indicated by bullfight, shown as BATTLE with ANIMAL, but because in Spain at the end of a fight, a bull is killed, we left the *battle* sign.

SWEDEN continues to use the symbol of *three crowns* so we will also keep it.

SWITZERLAND is known for the story of William Tell and his son and an apple put by Austrian ruler on a head of a boy demanding that father with arrow hits the apple. William Tell had two arrows and made a hit. When asked why he had two arrows, William Tell told the (Austrian) ruler, "If I miss, the second arrow is for you."

TIBET is known as a roof of the world, hence we use signs of *globe* and *roof.*

TRANSYLVANIA (like Pennsylvania) owes its name to the word for forest (based on Latin) hence we show besides the shield *two trees* (wood or forest).

UNITED STATES is shown as full overlap of states (countries) as continuation of the signs for FEDERATION and CONFEDERACY, which show lesser and lesser overlap of countries involved.

YUGOSLAVIA is shown as extinct and not extinct, in view of the fact that when it collapsed, Serbia kept the name YUGOSLAVIA (that means South Slavs), which it was not. In fact, YUGOSLAVIA, from its very beginning when created by the French and English after WWI, never incorporated Bulgarians, the largest South Slav nation.

With the above explanations, readers should easily understand the sign assigned for the names of the shown US states. So we will go straight to listing words involving fifteen novel signs that we needed to broaden the list of the countries listed above. We start with the sign for HEAVY, which has also been interpreted as DIFFICULT, and will continue with other words listed before in the order in which they appeared for the first time. We are not giving much explanation but just a few hints that may help one to relate given sign to similar signs introduced earlier.

HEAVY/DIFFICULT

We have already seen use of the sign HEAVY or DIFFICULT in combinations of many words, like

ADVANTAGE = difficulties behind
BALLAST = dead weight
BURDEN = difficulties ahead
CHALLENGE = silver ahead
EASY = crossed difficult
MAGNET = metal with hook
PRIVILEGE = silver behind
RUST = metal with friction

Now we can add a number of metals:

COPPER = electricity metal
GOLD = silver silver (double crown)
LEAD = soft metal
MERCURY = liquid metal
SILVER = metal with crown (seal)

We continue with few additional signs for metals:

PLATINUM *more than gold*	IRON *metal of horseshoe*	STEEL *iron iron*	STAINLESS STEEL *steel steel*	CHROMIUM *shiny metal*
ALUMINUM *light metal*	URANIUM *radiation metal*			

Observe some parallelism of the signs for silver, gold, and platinum and the signs for iron, steel, and stainless steel. In both cases, addition of the indicator sign (crown and horseshoe, respectively) means a jump in the quality (and price).

DANGER

This sign has an appearance in shape of the sign SS that was a symbol of notorious Nazi storm troopers who were more than dangerous, but the similarity is accidental and is mentioned only as a mnemonic device. We will later explain the origin of this sign, which is one of less than half a dozen signs that were "invented" for Nobel. We have already seen two such signs, the sign for CLOSE and the sign for WITH. Here we will show illustrations of words involving the DANGER sign in combinations with other signs. Later, after we introduce the final set of signs, we will show additional instances of signs using not only the DANGER sign, but also closely related signs for SUDDEN and VIOLENCE.

DANGER	RESCUE	COURAGE	BLIZZARD	COWARD
sudden sudden	not danger	walk against danger	dangerous snow	not courageous
CONVULSION	VICIOUS			
danger inside body	dangerously aggressive			

BEAN/COFFEE

"Bean" is shown as the coffee bean and also is the sign that represents COFFEE, considered the most common bean.

BEAN	COFFEE	TEA	BEVERAGE	BEAD
basic sign	bean	not coffee	coffee and tea	hard bean
CAFFEINE	TEAPOT	COFFEE SHOP	TEA SHOP	NECKLACE
inside coffee	flask & tea	lot of coffee	lot of tee	lot of beads

CIGAR

The sign for CIGAR is based on the sign for CIGARETTE (which is more common among smokers) by doubling the horizontal part of the sign. One of the signs shown below stands for NO SMOKING. If we would simply cross the sign of cigarette to obtain the sign for NO SMOKING, such a sign need not be easily recognized (see the central sign below). For a better recognition, we decided therefore to cross the sign of cigarette with the BAD ARROW sign (see the next sign) so that this combination represents NO SMOKING. Thus the novel sign sends two messages: *don't smoke here* and *smoking is bad for you!* The last sign, overlapping cigarettes, is the sign that indicates "the space for smokers," which informs smokers that they are welcome to indulge in smoking in such places.

CIGAR *basic sign*	CIGARETTE *basic sign*	NO SMOKING	NO SMOKING *cigarette is bad*	SMOKING AREA

EXPERIMENT

The sign for experiments is based on Galileo Galilei's experiments with rolling balls. Galileo investigated free fall and came to the right solution that the length of the path traveled is proportional to the square of the time, but in order to make as precise measurement as possible, he constructed a board at a slope in order to slow the rolling balls, besides introducing very small units for length and time so that results are expressed by large numbers, at the time when only integer numbers existed.

EXPERIMENT *basic sign*	LABORATORY *lot of experiments*	GUINEA PIG *experimental animal*		

CHAIN

CHAIN is not a basic sign but obtained by overlap of rings. We have already seen a number of signs involving chain, so instead, here we will present few additional signs involving overlapping rings that stand for marriage. Two overlapping rings indicate MARRIAGE, which, in figurative sense one can view as a sign that indicates that person has lost some of the liberties associated with youth and, in other words, has become "chained." Below we show combinations of signs derived from the signs for MARRIAGE:

BRIDE	BRIDEGROOM	CONCUBINE	HAREM	HUSBAND
woman before marriage	*man before marriage*	*wife not a wife*	*overlapping wives*	*man after marriage*

SPOUSE	WIDOW	WIDOWER	WIFE	
marriage & person	*woman with dead marriage*	*man with dead marriage*	*woman after marriage*	

KNOT/UNIVERSE

As already explained the basic sign of a (trefoil) knot represents also UNIVERSE

KNOT	KNITTING	PRETZEL		
basic sign	*overlapping knots*	*knotted bread*		

TOSS

Basic arrow suggesting something was thrown up represents "tossing."

TOSS *basic arrow*	GAMBLE *toss a coin*	CASINO *gamble gamble*	COMPULSIVE GAMBLER *must gamble*	CERTAIN *tossing apple*
BETTING *gamble against gamble*	BINGO *toss & lot of money*	UNCERTAIN *opposite to certain*	EXIST *toss and time*	

The sign for CERTAIN is based on an anecdote about Newton and a falling apple from a tree. According to this story, Newton was sitting under an apple tree, when an apple fell down on the ground. He then wondered why the moon did not fall on the earth, which led him to develop his theory of gravity.

HORSESHOE

Horseshow has a simple shape, resembling Greek letter omega, and is a useful sign not only to identify horse, but also iron, of which it is made, and then steel, which can be viewed as better-quality iron, and even stainless steel, of still better quality by doubling and tripling the sign, respectively—all in analogy with signs for silver, gold, and platinum. If one is superstitious (and most people unfortunately tend to be to a greater or lesser degree), one can adopt the sign of horseshoe for "good luck," which is shown as "finding a horseshoe."

Ω	⇇ Ω	∫Ω	∀Ω	／∀Ω
HORSESHOE *basic sign*	**MAGNET**	**ELECTRO-MAGNET**	**HORSE**	**DONKEY** *not horse*
∀Ω／∀Ω	→Ω←	←Ω→		
MULE *horse & donkey*	**GOOD LUCK** *find horseshoe*	**BAD LUCK** *lose horseshoe*		

Let us comment on MULE. It is a hybrid between horse and donkey—but the appearance and characteristics of offspring are visibly different if donkey male fertilized mare or stallion fertilizes female donkey. English language apparently does not make a distinction, even though it tends to prefer the offspring arriving from donkey-father horse-mother. At least this appears the conclusion, based on several dictionaries, like the two Merriam-Webster's dictionaries already mentioned, which describe mule as "offspring of the male ass and female horse" and "a hybrid between a horse and donkey; especially the offspring of a male donkey and a mare." But in many other languages, there are different words for each case. For instance, in Croatian, one speaks of *mula* and *mazga* respectively, *mula* being *mule*. Hence, Nobel, being an international language, needs to consider the two distinct hybrids as two separate words. The situation here is not as complicated as was the case of Grand Canyon, because we have signs for *horse, donkey, father,* and *mother* and, if necessary, for *stallion* and *mare,* and they are not involved. But, following the spirit of Occam's razor, which stresses preference for simplicity among alternatives, we should seek simpler signs if possible. Here are the two signs that we propose as better representations for the horse and donkey offspring:

∀Ω／∀Ω	∀Ω／∀Ω ⅄／⅄	∀Ω／∀Ω ⅄／⅄
MULE	*horse father* *donkey mother*	*donkey father* *horse mother*

Interestingly, in both cases, the offspring in appearance is more like the mother than the father, hence mule (of English dictionaries) looks more like a horse than like a donkey.

THERMOMETER

WARM, COLD, HOT, FREEZING, etc. are indicated on thermometer by up or down bent arrows.

THERMOMETER *basic sign*	WARM	COLD	HOT	FREEZING
COZY *warm & comfort*	LUKEWARM *warm & not*	FRESH *cold & not*	REFRIGERATOR *cold box*	FREEZER *freezing box*

CORN AND CANE

The two signs are similar but nevertheless suggesting two different industrial plants by offering slightly different profiles.

CORN *basic sign*	CANE *basic sign*	CORNFIELD *corn & field*	CORN EAR *corn fruit*	CORNMEAL *corn & meal*

CATTLE

Texas cattle with visibly long horns are represented by adding horn to schematized head of an animal. The sign for ANIMAL is taken to be inverted letter A, because historically the shape of letter

A comes from simplified shape of bull (cow) used already over two thousand years BC in Middle East. For this historic reason, while we use the inverted letter A as a general term for animals, we will use it also more specifically to stand for cattle. If we wish, we can have a special sign for Texas longhorn cattle, by doubling the sign of LONGHORN. There are such cattle, but it may be advisable not to be near them, unless you are on a horse.

LONGHORN *basic sign*	COW *milk animal*	CATTLE *lot of animals*	STAMPEDE *cattle rush*	RUSTLE *illegal cattle*
CATTLEMAN	COWBOY	LONGHORN CATTLE *lot of longhorns*		

Animals

By having a general sign for animals, which, as mentioned, will be also used for the most common, most useful, and in some civilizations, the most cherished animal—cow, we can proceed to catalogue signs for number of animals. In order to be fairly complete, we need a few indicator signs, which are shown below. They are in fact the signs for the LEG OF HEN and LEG OF DUCK, referred to as *indicator* signs, which will be of help to identify not only these two birds, but also closely related TURKEY and GOOSE. Just as other signs in Nobel, the indicator signs can also be doubled and even tripled, which of course does not mean that birds have different number of legs. The increase in number of an indicator sign merely indicates an increase in the size of the animal between related animals (birds), one with the single sign being the smallest and one with three signs being the largest. This is analogous to already used teeth as indicator of DOG and BEAR, which can be extended with triple teeth to stand for mythical DRAGON, heaving the largest teeth of them all.

| TEETH | HEN LEG | DUCK LEG | | |
| *basic sign* | *basic sign* | *basic sign* | | |

One can view the signs for DUCK LEG as a modification of the sign for HEN LEG.

Similarly, the sign for FIELD can be used to identify several animals. There are many birds and animal in fields and if we can single one that is most *common*, we can use the sign of field as indicator and, in this way, increase the list of signs for animals. Thus following this recipe, we arrive at the sign for RABBIT as the RODENT of FIELDS, and the sign for PHEASANT as the HEN of FIELDS, to be shortly introduced. Here we took PHEASANT as the most *common* even if not most numerous bird of fields. One is more likely to see a CROW, which we represented as BLACK BIRD, in fields than a pheasant, but crows are also city dwellers, which pheasants are not, so we give preference to pheasant as the "field" bird.

With the help of the above signs and numerous other signs of Nobel that will be used in combination with the sign for animal, bird, fish, insect, and arachnid, we will arrive at a sizable list of signs representing various animals, that is, about three hundred. At the end, we will make a few comments trying to justify particular signs; however, we would like to encourage readers to seek justification for the signs and see if they agree with our arguments, at least for those animals with which they are familiar.

We have deliberately included several perhaps less known and more exotic animals just to illustrate the possibilities of Nobel. Thus you may come across a name of an animal that you are not familiar with, such as goanna, a large Australian monitor lizard. I have to admit that not being a student of zoology and spending only one day in Sydney and one day in Brisbane, and a week on Heron Island, at the south end of the Great Barrier Reef I did not know that such giant lizards even existed in Australia. Heron Island is less than a mile long and several hundred feet wide; the island is too small for visitors, and there is no room there for large lizards. I may add, however, that from the sign for goanna in Nobel, readers who have not been in Australia and have not heard of the goanna will from the sign immediately see that this is lizard from Australia—which illustrates the educational component of Nobel. Interestingly, Heron Island is full geckos (or geckoes), small nocturnal lizards that easily walk over vertical wall of buildings. Even more interestingly, all geckos on Heron Island are female geckos (there are no males on the island and they are obviously not in demand). Female geckos can reproduce without male intervention, and because of this, the offsprings are genetically identical to their mothers, and thus the colony of Heron Island geckos is genetically rather uniform.

ANIMAL *basic sign*	ALPACA	AMPHIBIAN	ANTELOPE	BEAVER
BISON	BOAR	BRONCO	BUFFALO	BULL
CALF	CAMEL	CARIBOU	CATTLE	CHAMELEON
CHAMOIS	COW	DEER	DONKEY	DUNG BEETLE
ELEPHANT	FOAL	FOX	FOXHOUND	GECKO
GILA MONSTER	GIRAFFE	GOANNA	GOAT	HEDGEHOG
HYPOPOTAMUS	HORSE	IGUANA	IMPALA	JACKASS

JERBOA	KANGAROO	KOALA	KOMODO DRAGON	LAMB
LION	LIZARD	LLAMA	LONGHORN	MAMMAL
MAVERICK	MEERKAT	MONGOOSE	MOOSE	MOUNTAIN GOAT
MOUNTAIN LION	MOUNTAIN SHEEP	MULE	MULE *donkey/mare*	MULE *stallion/donkey*
MUSK	NEWT	OX	PIG	PLANKTON
REINDEER	REPTILE	RHINOCEROS	SALAMANDER	SEA HORSE
SEA URCHIN	SHEEP	SHEEPDOG	SHETLAND PONY	SKUNK
SLUG	SNAIL	TASMANIAN DEVIL	TOED	TOPI

TORTOISE	TURTLE	TWO-HUMPED CAMEL	UNICORN	WALLABY
WARTHOG	WATER BUFFALO	WILDEBEEST	WOMBAT	YAK
ZEBRA				

As one sees, we have arrived at over eighty animal signs, though a few signs are not animals but relate to animals.

Before commenting on the signs for animals using ANIMAL sign (the inverted letter A), let us comment on several of the less common animals' signs, which will further illustrate the direct educational note of Nobel, which often names of animals lack.

GOANNA = *Australian largest lizard.* Australia is shown as *down under*—inverted sign for a country (shield). Lizard is *animal close to the ground.*

GILA MONSTER = *lizard with poison.* Lizards, which include the gecko, iguana, chameleon, and horned toad, are not venomous, except for the Gila monster of the southwestern United States and Mexico. Hence, lizard with poison is a rather unique characterization for the Gila monster.

IMPALA = *high jumping antelope.* Impalas are elegant antelopes that are well known for their high jumps.

JERBOA = *jumping rodent of deserts.* Jerboa is small nocturnal rodent of arid areas of Africa and Asia; it has strong rear legs adapted for jumping as a way of locomotion.

KOALA = *tree marsupial.* Koalas are familiar friendly-looking creatures of trees, but did you know that they are marsupials, like several other animals of Australia and the opossum, the only non-Australian marsupial of North, Central, and South America?

KOMODO DRAGON = *the largest lizard.* Komodo dragon is the largest lizard, up to ten feet (three meters), living on the island of Komodo, of Indonesia.

MEERKAT = *standing mongoose.* Meerkat of South Africa is a mongoose (short-legged carnivorous mammal, native to India and known for capability to kill poisonous snakes). Meerkats, who live in colonies, are known to stand erect near their burrow, hence standing mongoose.

PLANKTON = tiny *sea creatures.* Tiny is shown as small, small, small and creature as animal and not animal. Planktons, which can be animals and plants, float near the surface of sea and lakes, and are the major food for fish and some aquatic animals.

TASMANIAN DEVIL = *carnivorous marsupial.* Marsupials are plant eaters, except for the Tasmanian devil. Hence, the sign, *meat eating* marsupial. Marsupials (kangaroo, wombat, opossum, and koala) are *animals with bag* (a pouch).

TOPI = *the fastest antelope.* African topi antelope has been considered as the fastest antelope. *Fast* = takes *little time, faster* = takes *less time, fastest* = takes *the least time,* hence, *little little little time.*

WOMBAT = *Australian burrowing marsupial.* Australia = down under; burrowing = hole under ground; marsupial is animal with pouch (bag).

YAK = *Tibetan cattle.* You may have seen yaks in zoological gardens, but now you know that they come from Tibet.

We continue with brief explanations of names of other animal signs shown above:

ALPACA = LONG HAIR LLAMA. Llama is shown as CATTLE OF MOUNTAIN RANGE.

AMPHIBIAN = ANIMAL between WATER and LAND

ANTELOPE = ANIMAL with characteristic *horns*

BEAVER = MAMMAL WITH HOUSE UNDER WATER. Beavers are building their lodge under water, with only tops appearing above water.

BISON = FOREST BUFFALO. In contrast to American buffalo, which live on prairies, European buffalo lived in forest (and those surviving live mostly in zoo).

BOAR = WILD PIG

BRONCO = WILD HORSE

BULL = EMPHASIZED ANIMAL. Bull has always held a central place among domestic animals.

BUFFALO = ANIMAL with characteristic *horns*

CALF = CHILD COW. Child is shown as a GROWING PERSON.

CAMEL = ANIMAL WITH MOUNTAIN. Mountain refers here to the hump of camel.

CARIBOU = WILD REINDEER. Wild is shown as opposite of "domestic," which is shown as a ROOF, hence inverted roof. Reindeer is DOMESTICATED DEER OF POLAR AREA.

CATTLE = LOT OF ANIMALS, as they tend to group together

CHAMELEON = TREE LIZARD that CHANGE COLOR

CHAMOIS = MOUNTAIN GOAT ANTELOPE

COW = ANIMAL giving MILK

DEER = ANIMAL with characteristic *horns*

DONKEY = NOT HORSE

DUNG BEETLE = INSECT PUSHING COW EXCRETION

ELEPHANT = LARGEST ANIMAL

FOAL = CHILD HORSE. Child is shown as a GROWING PERSON.

FOX = *double* FACE ANIMAL

FOXHOUND = DOG PUSHING FOX, that is, dog chasing fox, and thus pushing her to run

GIRAFFE = ANIMAL WITH *long* NECK

GOAT = ANIMAL with characteristic horns

HEDGEHOG = ANIMAL WITH LOT OF SPIKES. Spike is shown as TOP OF SIGNAL.

HIPPOPOTAMUS = WATER HORSE. Sign is based on etymology of the word; *hippo* is Greek for horse and potamus is Greek for *river*, thus hippopotamus is *river horse*, but it is to be found in lakes as well, thus water horse appears appropriate.

HORSE = ANIMAL with HORSESHOE

IGUANA = TREE LIZARD

JACKASS = MALE DONKEY. Donkey (ass) is shown as NOT HORSE.

KANGAROO = JUMPY ANIMAL

LAMB = "CHILD" SHEEP

LION = KING ANIMAL

LIZARD = REPTILE WITH LONG TAIL. Lizards have long tails, which can break and grow again.

LLAMA = MOUNTAIN RANGE (Andes) ANIMAL (CATTLE)

LONGHORN = characterized by its LONG HORNS

MAMMAL = ANIMAL with BREAST

MAVERICK = ANIMAL WITHOUT DECORATION. "Without decoration" here symbolizes *unbranded animal,* such as calf separated from its mother and herd. It becomes property of anyone who finds it and is first to brand it.

MONGOOSE = ANIMAL ATTACKING VIPERS

MOOSE = ANIMAL identified by its *flat horns*

MOUNTAIN GOAT = MOUNTAIN GOAT

MOUNTAIN LION = MOUNTAIN LION

MOUNTAIN SHEEP = MOUNTAIN SHEEP

MULE = HORSE AND DONKEY, being a combination, a hybrid

MULE = hybrid of donkey (father) and horse (mother)

MULE = hybrid of donkey (mother) and horse (father)

MUSK = DEER WITHOUT HORN

NEWT = AMPHIBIAN that looks AS SMALL LIZARD (REPTILE)

PIG = MUD ANIMAL. Mud is shown as WATER ABOVE GROUND

PONY = SMALL HORSE. Pony is a HORSE of SMALL size. FOAL can be of small size and, when very young, can be smaller than pony, but sign for foal is CHILD HORSE.

REINDEER = DOMESTICATED ARCTIC DEER

REPTILE = ANIMAL CLOSE to LAND (GROUND)

RHINOCEROS = ANIMAL WITH HORN ABOVE NOSE. Horns is shown as PART OF LONGHORN.

SALAMANDER = AMPHIBIAN that looks AS LIZARD (REPTILE)

SEA HORSE = SEA HORSE

SEA URCHIN = SEA HEDGEHOG

SHEEP = ANIMAL with characteristic *horns*

SHEEPDOG = DOG PUSHING SHEEP

SHETLAND PONY = SCOTTISH PONY. Shetland Islands are part of Scotland, hence Shetland pony became in Nobel Scottish pony. Some 150 islands about 200 kilometers (130 miles) north of Scotland have been fairly isolated, and it is known in biology that many species on isolated islands tend to shrink in size and thus consume less food. There are exceptions, of course, like Galápagos tortoise or Komodo dragon, which apparently do not lack food! SHETLAND ISLANDS deserve to have a sign of their own and we can consider the sign: COUNTRY & SCOTTISH PONY.

SKUNK = ANIMAL OF HATE SMELL

SLUG = JELLY ANIMAL WITHOUT COVER. Jelly = OVERLAPPING SOFT
SNAIL = JELLY ANIMAL WITH COVER
TORTOISE = LAND REPTILE WITH COVER. Land is shown as LOT OF
    GROUND.
TURTLE = SEA REPTILE WITH COVER. Sea is shown as LOT OF WATER.
TWO-HUMPED CAMEL (Bactrian camel) = ANIMAL WITH MOUNTAIN
    RANGE, in view of the dromedary camel, or simply camel,
    shown as ANIMAL WITH MOUNTAIN
UNICORN = HORSE WITH A HORN. Mythical creature, horse with a
    single horn.
WALLABY = SMALL KANGAROO NOT SMALL KANGAROO. Wallaby, a
    marsupial of Australia and New Guinea, resembles a small
    kangaroo but is not a small kangaroo, but a wallaby.
WARTHOG = WILD PIG WITH TUSK. Tusk is shown as OUTSIDE TOOTH.
WATER BUFFALO = WATER & BUFFALO
WILDEBEEST = is shown as UGLY ANTELOPE, being an antelope, the
    appearance of which lacks elegance.
YAK = TIBETAN CATTLE. Tibet is shown as COUNTRY THE ROOF OF
    THE WORLD. World is shown as GLOBE.
ZEBRA = ANIMAL WITH STRIPES. Stripes is a new basic sign.

We will continue to consider names of animals but using
alternative signs as indicators. In particular, we will use the
following:

TEETH	BREAST	FACE	BRAIN	LEGS
HAND	BIRD	FISH	SNAKE	INSECT and ARACHNID

We added the sign for *hand*, which we need to arrive at a sign
for *claw*. We will later explain at some length the sign for hand,

which is not necessarily obvious. We need the claw sign for a whole family of sea and water crustaceans.

With these additional signs as indicators, one can construct signs for another 125 animals, totaling well over 200 animals. We start with the sign for BRAIN. First, we listed apes and then monkeys, but comments on signs are listed alphabetically.

BRAIN	APE	GORILLA	CHIMPANZEE	ORANGUTAN
GIBBON	MONKEY	BABOON	GOLDEN LION TAMARIN	MANDRILL
PIGMY MARMOSET	LEMUR			

APE = BRAIN/NO BRAIN, in comparison with other animal apes have BRAIN, in comparison with humans, they have NO BRAIN.

BABOON = MONKEY WITH DOG FACE

CHIMPANZEE = INTERMEDIATE size APE

GIBBON = SMALL TREE APE

GOLDEN LION TAMARIN = GOLDEN MONKEY

GORILLA = LARGE size APE

LEMUR = BELOW MONKEY, that is, from the theory of evolution point of view, lemurs are less related to primates.

MANDRILL = LARGEST MONKEY

MONKEY = BELOW APES, that is, from the theory of evolution point of view, monkeys are less related to humans.

ORANGUTAN = FOREST APE

PIGMY MARMOSET = SMALLEST MONKEY

Apes are shown as having brain and not having brain, which, as already mentioned, is to suggest that they are rather clever, but not as clever as humans. Gorilla is indicated as large ape, being the biggest. Chimpanzee is indicated as intermediate (in size), and orangutan is shown as forest ape, while gibbon is shown as small tree ape. Gibbons are sometimes confused as being monkeys, but they are in fact apes. Monkeys are represented as "below apes." The sign for baboon takes advantage of its face because it looks like a dog, hence it is shown as *monkey with dog face*. Mandrill is the *largest monkey* (having length of one meter), and pigmy marmoset is the *smallest monkey*, having length of some fifteen centimeters without tail (which can be fifteen to twenty centimeters long). Lemurs are shown as being "below monkeys."

We follow with signs for forty-five animals, the signs of which are based on the sign for *teeth* (dog). Including in this group are a dozen breeds of dogs among several hundred known breeds. We have selected those that can be well characterized and recognized from their characterizations. The signs for these dozen dogs are explained at the end of the list of signs for animals involving the sign for *teeth* (dog). However, one will notice that some well-known breeds of dogs have not been included, or I may say, not included yet. Take, for example, Afghan hound, which leads the list of over two hundred breeds of dog that one can find on the Internet. To have a sign for this tall dog with silky coat, originally developed in Afghanistan as hunting dog or sheepdog, we would need a sign for Afghanistan, which we do not have currently. Or consider Great Dane, a very large dog with long legs and square face. The first thought would be to describe it as Danish dog (for which one would need a sign for Denmark, which again for the time being we do not have), however, it is not a Danish dog, but a breed of German dogs. This shows that one needs to know something about the objects to be considered! However, would we have a sign for Denmark, we could still well characterize Great Dane as Danish / not Danish dog.

After outlining a base for selecting particular signs for particular dogs, we continue with comments on signs of all animals shown, whether their signs are obvious or maybe not obvious, including brief comments for some animals that may be less familiar to some readers. In particular, this includes extinct archaeopteryx from Jurassic time, which may have been the only bird with teeth. If we can have signs for extinct species, one may argue that we may also construct signs for species yet to be discovered—such as recently discovered in Laos ROCK RAT!

TEETH	ALLIGATOR	ARCHAEO-PTERYX	BARRACUDA	BEAGLE
BEAR	BULLDOG	BULLDOG	CAPYBARA	CAT
CHEETAH	CHINCHILA	COYOTE	CROCODILE	DACHSHUND
DALMATIAN	DENTEX	DOG	FIELD MOUSE	FOXHOUND
GREAT WHITE SHARK	HARE	HOUND	HUSKY	HYENA
IRISH SETTER	IRISH WOLF-HOUND	JACKAL	JAGUAR	KANGAROO RAT
LEMMING	LEOPARD	LHASA APSO	LYNX	MOUSE

MUSKRAT	OCELOT	PANDA	PIRANHA	POLAR BEAR
POLICE DOG	PORCUPINE	RABBIT	RAT	ROCK RAT
RODENT	SAINT BERNARD	SCOTTISH TERRIER	SETTER	SHARK
SNOW LEOPARD	SPANIEL	SQUIRREL	TERRIER	TIGER
WOLF	WOLF PACK			

BEAGLE = EXPERIMENTAL DOG. Beagle has been initially known as a dog hunting rabbits, a description that would suffice to construct a sign for beagle, but it is also one of the most common dogs used for medical experiments (such as investigating drugs for high blood pressure that still strikes many and often fatally). We decided for this latter description for two reasons: first, a simpler sign for beagle is constructed in this way, and the second, and more important, to remind people that medical research, though trying to avoid animals wherever possible, still needs to test promising drugs on animals before they are given to people. Let us not overlook that there has been a drug, thalidomide, which was designed to decrease pain and discomfort of pregnant women, which was not tested on animals, or not tested enough. Its use in Europe and Africa in late 1950s and early 1960s was catastrophic, resulting in ten thousand children born with severe defects, missing arms and legs or both. The drug was not approved for use in the USA with comments that the drug needed more study—which saved many from hidden potential danger. Not long after, however, an Israeli doctor found that thalidomide helps severe complications of leprosy, which has led to revived interest in this drug, which virtually eliminated need for leprosy hospitals.

BULLDOG = SQUARE HEAD DOG

BULLDOG = BULL & DOG

DACHSHUND = SHORT LEGS LONG BODY

DALMATIAN = SPOTTED DOG

DOG = TEETH

FOXHOUND = FOX HOUNTNG DOG

HOUND = HUNTING DOG

HUSKY = SNOW DOG. Huskies are dogs pulling sledges in Alaska and have also been known as ESKIMO DOG, but the label Eskimo for Inuit people of Alaska is viewed as offensive and in 1977 at a conference in Barrow, Alaska, it was determined to officially replace the term Eskimo with the term Inuit, which means in their language "the real people."

IRISH SETTER = IRISH SITTING DOG. Irish is indicated by TREFOIL, symbol of Ireland. Setters are trained to sit next to game.

IRISH WOLFHOUND = TALLEST DOG. Irish wolfhound is the tallest breed of dogs in the world. Ireland is symbolized by TREFOIL, plant having leaf with three lobes.

LHASA APSO = TIBETAN SMALL DOG

SAINT BERNARD DOG = AVALANCHE DOG. This dog has been helping to find and save people after an avalanche.

SCOTTISH TERRIER = SCOTTISH DOG ABOVE BURROW (see TERRIER for more information). Scotland is indicated as a part of Union Jack (flag of United Kingdom).

SETTER = SITTING DOG. The dog has been trained to sit when it finds bird game.

SPANIEL = HAIRY DOG WITH HANGING EARS. Spaniel is not the only dog with "hanging ears," BEAGLE is another, but we already have a sign for beagle as "experimental dog." In order to avoid possible confusion, we added the attribute "hairy" for spaniel, being covered by a long, wavy, silky coat in contrast to beagle, which is a smooth-haired dog. Hairy is shown as *overlapping hair.*

SQUIRREL = TREE RODENT

TERRIER = DOG ABOVE BURROW. Terriers were initially bred to hunt small animals living in underground burrows, hence the sign of a *dog above burrow.* Burrow is shown as a *hole under the ground.* Hole is shown as *part of a loop.* The name *terrier* comes from Latin *terra* for earth, because it pursues animals into their burrows.

We have shown two alternative signs for bulldog, one as a "square face dog" and another as bull-dog, where its name originates from a dog to belonging to a breed developed in England for contest with bull. One may say that the first sign is more descriptive and the second is more historic, but both are equally good, though my own preference is for the descriptive sign. We continue with explanations of the other signs using TEETH as an indicator:

ALLIGATOR = TEETH of WATER

ARCHAEOPTERYX = EXTINCT BIRD WITH JAW. Extinct is shown as of DEAD TIME; jaw is shown as MOUTH WITH TEETH.

BARRACUDA = TEETH of SEA

BEAR = TEETH TEETH (bigger teeth than dog)

CAT = NOT a DOG

CAPYBARA = This rodent of South America is shown as VERY LARGE RODENT; in fact, it is the largest rodent, with height of some four feet (over one meter).

CHEETAH = The fastest land animal is shown as THE FASTEST BIG CAT.

CHINCHILLA = This rodent is well known (and bred) for its very fine hair, hence the sign FINE FINE HAIR RODENT

COYOTE = PRAIRIE TEETH (DOG)

CROCODILE = TEETH TEETH of WATER

DENTEX = TOOTH FISH. The root of the name *dent* comes from Latin *tooth,* and appears in words like dentist, denture, and dental floss.

FIELD MOUSE = FIELD & MOUSE signs. Mouse is shown as rodent of a house.

GREAT WHITE SHARK = TEETH TEETH TEETH OF SEA. This is the shark that has been attacking and eating humans.

HARE = FAST FIELD RODENT. Fast is shown as taking LITTLE TIME.

HYENA = LAUGHING "DOG". Laugh is shown as LOT OF SMILE.

JACKAL = WILD DOG. Jackal looks like wild dog.

JAGUAR = NEW BIG CAT WITH SPOTS. Jaguar and leopard are both of similar size and similar appearance, both are "big cats with spots." In order to differentiate between them, we introduced label "new" for jaguar, which lives in North America, Central America, and northern parts of South America, that is, on the *new* continent. In contrast, LEOPARD, the other "big cat with spots" lives in Africa, which is part of "old continent," is shown as "old big cat with spots."

KANGAROO RAT = JUMPING RODENT

LEMMING = SUBARCTIC RODENT. This small rodent with thick furry body and feet lives in subarctic regions. Subarctic is shown as CLOSE TO ARCTIC.

LEOPARD = OLD world BIG CAT WITH SPOTS. See more under JAGUAR, which is shown as NEW world BIG CAT WITH SPOTS.

LYNX = FOREST WILD CAT. This short-tailed wildcat lives in northern coniferous forests, hence *forest wild cat.*

MOUSE = HOUSE RODENT

MUSKRAT = LARGE AMPHIBIAN RODENT. Amphibian is shown as being *between water and land.*

OCELOT = SMALL WILD CAT WITH SPOTS. Etymology of name ocelot translated (via French roots) relates to jaguar (hence "cat with spots").

PANDA = BEAR / NOT BEAR, because although giant panda looks like bear it is not a bear.

PIRANHA = RIVER TEETH

POLAR BEAR = ARCTIC BEAR

POLICE DOG = POLICE & DOG signs combined

PORCUPINE = RODENT WITH MANY SPIKES

PRAIRIE DOG = PRAIRIE RODENT, which in fact it is.

RABBIT = FIELD RODENT

RAT = BUILDING (CITY) RODENT

ROCK RAT = the full name being Laotian ROCK RAT, thought to be extinct for eleven million years, but found in 2008 in Laos.

RODENT = GROW TEETH

SHARK = TEETH TEETH of SEA

SHEEPDOG = DOG PUSHING SHEEP

SNOW LEOPARD = SNOW & TIGER (BIG CAT) signs. Snow leopard inhabits higher altitudes of the Himalayas.

SQUIRREL = TREE RODENT

TIGER = CAT CAT (big cat)

WOLF = "DOG" (TEETH) of WOOD

WOLF PACK = LOT OF WOLVES. Wolf is shown as teeth of wood. "Lot of" is indicated by doubling.

We continue now with animals using the sign "breast," which signifies mammals, as an indicator.

BREAST	ANTEATER	ARMADILLO	BAT	BLUE WHALE
CALF	COW	DOLPHIN	FLYING FOX	MOLE
NARWHAL	OTTER	SEAL	SEA LION	VAMPIRE BAT
WHALE				

ANTEATER = MAMMAL EATING ANTS. Ant is shown as "working insect" as ants seem to be busy working, carrying food to their dwelling base.

ARMADILLO = COVERED MAMMAL. Armadillo is one of rare mammals having plated cover.

BAT = FLYING MAMMAL

BLUE WHALE = THE LARGEST WHALE, in fact, the largest animal of the world—hence not to be found in zoological gardens and aquariums, though I was fortunate to see the tops of these ocean giants and spray of misty sea as they exhaled, from a boat of the Los Angeles Aquarium, as blue whales migrated from Baja California to the Bering Sea in arctic region.

CALF = "CHILD" COW. Child is shown as *growing person.*

COW = MILK ANIMAL

DOLPHIN = MAMMAL OF SEA. The same characterization "mammal of sea" has been used also for SEAL. The distinction is that for dolphin the *breast* sign is drawn *under* the sea sign, because dolphins are living under sea, while *breast* sign for seal is drawn *above* the sea, because seals are most of the time above sea. The same convention applies to signs for WHALE and SEA LION, respectively.

FLYING FOX = VERY LARGE BAT. These large fruit eating bats of Australasia span five feet.

MOLE = MAMMAL UNDER GROUND. Most underground small animals are rodents; a mole is, however, not a rodent, thus the sign "mammal under ground." Rodents are also mammals, but we have already a sign for rodents as animals with "growing teeth."

NARWHAL = SMALL WHALE LARGE TUSK. This small arctic whale (twenty feet or six meters, which is small for whales) has a single ivory tusk.

OTTER = WATER MAMMAL with WEBBED FEET.

SEAL = is shown as SEA MAMMAL. The same is true of DOLPHIN. To distinguish them, dolphin is shown as mammal below sea and seal as mammal above sea.

SEA LION = is shown as OCEAN MAMMAL. The same is true of WHALE. To distinguish them, whale is shown as mammal below sea and sea lion as mammal above sea.

VAMPIRE BAT = FLYING MAMMAL that SUCKS BLOOD. Sucking is shown as MOUTH PULL.

BIRD	ALBATROSS	AUK	BALD EAGLE	BLACKBIRD
CARDINAL	CONDOR	CUCKOO	DODO	DOVE
DUCK	EAGLE	EMPEROR PENGUIN	EMU	FLAMINGO
GOOSE	GULL	HEN	JAY	MALLARD
MANDARIN DUCK	MARABOU	NIGHTINGALE	OSTRICH	OWL
PARROT	PARTRIDGE	PEACOCK	PELICAN	PENGUIN
PHEASANT	PIGEON	PUFFIN	ROADRUNNER	SECRETARY BIRD
SPOONBILL	STORK	SWALLOW	SWAN	TOUCAN

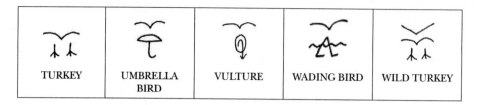

| TURKEY | UMBRELLA BIRD | VULTURE | WADING BIRD | WILD TURKEY |

Here are brief hints for the signs shown.

ALBATROSS = is shown as OCEAN BIRD in comparison with its common relative SEA BIRD (gull).

AUK = ARCTIC BIRD. There is another arctic bird, PUFFIN, which we distinguish from auk by adding in the description that puffin has a characteristic *triangular beak*.

BALD EAGLE = WHITE HEAD EAGLE. EAGLE is shown as BIRD OF MOUNTAIN.

BLACKBIRD = BLACK BIRD. *White* and *black* are shown in Nobel as triangles (to be explained later when considering colors); white is blank triangle and black is marked triangle.

CARDINAL = RED BIRD. The color red will be later introduced. It is the first color of the spectrum, which the sign is supposed to suggest. Red color can alternatively be presented as "the color of blood," but the red color of cardinal is bright red color similar to the robe of cardinals, high-ranking Roman Catholic clergy, next in rank to the Pope, who elect the pope as one of themselves.

CONDOR = BIRD OF MOUNTAIN RANGE

CUCKOO = BIRD EXPORTING EGG, in view of it laying eggs in nests of other birds.

DODO = EXTINCT TURKEY; in fact is an extinct bird of Mauritius in the Indian Ocean, which is of pigeon family, but of the size of a turkey. Turkey is shown as big hen, hence use of two hen legs as indicator.

DOVE = bird of PEACE. Peace is opposite (reciprocal) of WAR. War is lot of BATTLE.

DUCK = BIRD identified by its webbed foot

EAGLE = BIRD OF MOUNTAIN

EMPEROR PENGUIN = CZAR PENGUIN, the largest penguin. Czar is shown as KING KING. King is PERSON with CROWN.

EMU = AUSTRALIA & "OSTRICH" (BIRD with big LEGS). Australia is shown as DOWN UNDER (inverted sign for COUNTRY).

FLAMINGO = BIRD and FLAME, in view of their red or pink coloration

GULL = SEA BIRD, the most common sea bird, though seen also on inland lakes

GOOSE = bigger than DUCK, hence DUCK DUCK

HEN = BIRD, identified by its leg

JAY = NOISY BIRD. Noise is opposite (reciprocal) to *music* (musical note).

MALLARD = WILD DUCK

MANDARIN DUCK = CHINA DUCK. China is shown as PEOPLE OVER PEOPLE COUNTRY in view of having more than a billion inhabitants.

MARABOU = WALKING BIRD WITH MOUTH POUCH (BAG)

NIGHTINGALE = SINGING NIGHT BIRD

OSTRICH = BIRD and LEGS

OWL = NIGHT BIRD, owl is one of most common night birds.

PARROT = SPEAKING BIRD

PARTRIDGE = FIELD BIRD MEDIUM size. Medium is shown as BIG AND SMALL.

PEACOCK = BIRD WITH UMBRELLA TAIL. Tail is shown as BODY END.

PELICAN = SEA BIRD WITH MOUTH POUCH (BAG)

PENGUIN = ANTARCTIC BIRD

PUFFIN = ARCTIC BIRD WITH TRIANGULAR BEAK. Triangle is object of GEOMETRY (hence the sign of COMPASS). Beak is BIRD MOUTH.

ROADRUNNER = FAST RUNNING BIRD. Fast is shown as "takes LITTLE TIME."

SECRETARY BIRD = WALKING BIRD EATING SNAKE

SPOONBILL = WADING BIRD WITH BEAK AS SPOON

STORK = CHIMNEY BIRD, in view of it making its nest on chimneys

SWALLOW = SPRING BIRD, heralds of spring

SWAN = bigger than goose, hence big big goose

TOUCAN = SMALL BIRD LARGE BEAK

TURKEY = bigger than HEN, hence HEN HEN

UMBRELLA BIRD = UMBRELLA & BIRD signs. Bird of Central and South America having large crest resembling umbrella.

VULTURE = BIRD over DEAD BODY

WADING BIRD = SHALLOW WATER BIRD

WILD TURKEY = WILD TURKEY. Wild is INVERTED ROOF

FISH	ANGLERFISH	CUTTLEFISH	DENTEX	FLATFISH
FLOUNDER	FLYING FISH	GLASSFISH	GOLDFISH	LAMPREY
LUNGFISH	MUDSKIPPER	RAY	SALMON	SAWFISH
SCORPION FISH	SKATE	SQUID	STINGRAY	STURGEON
SUNFISH	SWORDFISH	TROUT		

ANGLERFISH = FISH that FISHES. This large marine fish uses its long dorsal fin extending over its mouth to attract small fish as prey.

CUTTLEFISH = SEA BOTTOM MOLLUSK. MOLLUSKS, which include clams, snails, slugs, squid, and octopus, being mostly marine animals, are shown as FISH AND NOT FISH. In particular, the name of cuttlefish is confusing because cuttle*fish* is not a *fish*.

DENTEX = TOOTH FISH. The root of the name *dent* comes from Latin *tooth*, and appears in words like dentist, denture, and dental floss.

FLATFISH = HORIZONTAL FISH. Most flatfish lie horizontally at sea bottom.

FLOUNDER = SHALLOW SEA FLAT FISH. Shallow is shown as LEGS IN WATER. Flat is indicated by sign HORIZONTAL, as flounder and other flat fish lie horizontally at sea bottom.

FLYING FISH = FLYING FISH. Flying is shown as WING UP.

GLASSFISH = GLASS FISH. This transparent fish is shown as glass, which is HARD and TRANSPARENT.

GOLDFISH = GOLD & FISH. Gold is heavy with CROWN SEALS.

LAMPREY = FISH SUCKING BLOOD. Lamprey is fish without teeth that attaches itself to another fish and sucks its blood as a parasite.

LUNGFISH = FISH that BREATHE. *Breathe* is suggested by LUNGS, which is INSIDE CHEST.

MUDSKIPPER = FISH WITH LEGS. Mudskipper is Asian or African tropical fish that can get out of water to feed and maneuver on land, climbing tree roots, using its fins.

RAY = CARTILAGE & FLAT FISH. Rays like sharks have no bones but *cartilage*, which is shown as SOFT BONE. Flat is shown as HORIZONTAL, because flat fish tend to extend *horizontally*.

SALMON = MIGRATORY FISH *between* RIVER AND OCEAN. Migratory fish that returns from OCEAN to freshwater RIVERS to spawn. Migratory nature of fish could be indicated by FROM-TO ARROW.

SAWFISH = FISH WITH OUTSIDE TEETH. This ray-fish of tropical seas has prolonged snout with visible OUTSIDE TEETH, giving appearance of a saw.

SCORPION FISH = FISH WITH POISON STING. Poison is opposite (reciprocal) of medication, hence *crossed* R sign; sting is shown as PART OF HOOK.

SKATE = BOTTOM SEA RAY. RAY is shown as CARTILAGE & FLAT FISH; *cartilage* is shown as SOFT BONE.

SQUID = OCEAN MOLLUSK. Mollusks are shown as FISH NO FISH.

STINGRAY = RAY WITH POISONOUS flexible TAIL. This is the fish that killed in 2006 not yet forty-year-old Steve Irwin, worldwide known as "the crocodile hunter." He was Australia's wildlife expert and conservationist and was killed during underwater filming in Australia's Great Barrier Reef.

STURGEON = RIVER BOTTOM FISH known for CAVIAR. Caviar is shown as UNDERWATER EGGS.

SUNFISH = SUN & FISH. Sun is shown by a circle and signs ABOVE and BELOW, as it appears on sky above and below globe.

SWORDFISH = FISH with SWORD
TROUT = RIVER FISH WITH SPOTS

We continue now with animals using the sign of SNAKE:

SNAKE	ANACONDA	COBRA	GLASS SNAKE	KING COBRA
MILK SNAKE	PYTHON	RATTLESNAKE	SERPENT	SNAKEFISH
WATER SNAKE				

ANACONDA = EMPEROR SNAKE (because of its size). It can grow to thirty feet (nine meters), compared to PYTHON, for which we reserved the sign, KING SNAKE, in view of it growing "only" to 20 feet (six meters).

COBRA = KING VIPER, even though there are more poisonous snakes than cobra, cobra is responsible for most of the human loss.

GLASS SNAKE = SNAKE AND NOT SNAKE. Glass snake is not a snake; it is in fact a limbless lizard that can grow up to four feet (well over one meter). Most glass snakes appear as snakes to all but experts who know them. Hence, the appearance can be quite misleading. There are important differences between snakes and lizards, even those without legs that appear just as snake: (1) Lizards have eyelids, they can close eyes; snakes do not have eyelids; (2) Lizards can break off their tail (sometimes in several pieces) if caught by predators by tail and can later grow new tail. It is this property, known as *autotomy* (from Greek *auto* = self; *tome* = *cutting off*) which can explains their name as glass snake, as they can break as glass in several pieces.

KING COBRA = EMPEROR VIPER; it is enormous, and it can grow 18 feet (about 5.5 meters) in size.

MILK SNAKE = MILK & SNAKE signs. According to storytelling, this snake of the USA and Mexico sucks milk from sleeping cows, a story not believed by many to be true. Otherwise, this snake is considered the most beautiful snake, at least to those not afraid of snakes.

PYTHON = KING SNAKE. King is PERSON WITH CROWN, hence, SNAKE WITH CROWN.

RATTLESNAKE = NOISY VIPER. This large venomous snake that lives in North and South America has a horny tail end that when vibrating makes noise.

SERPENT = SNAKE (synonym)

SNAKEFISH = OCEAN SNAKE FISH.

WATER SNAKE = VIPER AND NOT VIPER. This snake can bite, and its bite causes putrefaction, that is, making the area of the bite decay, but the snake is not venomous.

LEGS	ARTHROPOD	CENTIPEDE	CRAB	CRUSTACEAN
FIDDLER CRAB	HERMIT CRAB	LOBSTER	MILLIPEDE	OCTOPUS
SHRIMP				

ARTHROPOD = ANIMALS WITH COVER and MANY LEGS. This group of animals includes insects, arachnids, centipedes, and crustaceans living in seas and oceans.

CENTIPEDE = 100 LEGS but in fact most have not even half of that, while few have few hundred

CRAB = CRUSTACEAN WITH CLAW. CLAW = HAND with HOOK

CRAYFISH = WATER CRUSTACEAN WITH LARGE CLAW

CRUSTACEAN = SEA (or freshwater) ARTHROPOD, includes lobsters, crabs, shrimp, crayfish, and barnacles

FIDDLER CRAB = SMALL CRUSTACEAN LARGE CLAW. Most animals are from outside symmetrical, but male fiddler crabs have one claw enlarged. In the time of courtship, they wave the claw, like violinists—hence the name!

HERMIT CRAB = CRUSTACEAN and IN-OUT OF HOUSE. Hermit crabs have not their own shell and take empty sea snail house as theirs, to change it for bigger one as they grow.

LOBSTER = LARGE CRUSTACEAN WITH CLAW

MILLIPEDE = 1,000 LEGS (from Latin *mille* for thousand). Thousand is an exaggeration; the creature has typically between 36 and 400 legs, two legs for each of its segments.

OCTOPUS = SEA animals with SUCKING TENTACLES. Tentacles are shown as LEGS NOT LEGS. In English, one speaks of "arms of octopus," but in practice, they are also used as legs. Sucking is shown as PULLING MOUTH.

SHRIMP = SMALL MARINE CRUSTACEAN

We follow now with signs involving the sign of insect:

INSECT	ADMIRAL	BEE	BEETLE	BUG
BUTTERFLY	CATERPILLAR	CICADA	DUNG BEETLE	FLEA
GRASSHOPPER	HOUSEFLY	LOUSE	MANTIS	MONARCH

MOSQUITO	MOTH	PRAYING MANTIS	PUPA	SILKWORM
SILVERFISH	TERMITE	TSETSE FLY		

ADMIRAL = BEAUTIFUL BUTTERFLY. Beautiful is shown as FOR PICTURE, because most people most of the time take pictures of *beautiful* things around.

BEE = HONEY INSECT

BEETLE = COVERED INSECT

BUG = BED INSECT

BUTTERFLY = BEAUTIFUL INSECT. Most insects to most people are not beautiful but irritating, ugly, and even disgusting, but butterflies are an exception.

CATERPILLAR = BEFORE BUTTERFLY. Caterpillar is larva of butterfly (or moth), hence the sign "before."

CICADA = NOISY PINE INSECT

DUNG BEETLE = BEETLE PUSHING DUNG; beetle = *covered insect*; dung = *cow excretion*

FLEA = JUMPING INSECT

HOUSEFLY = HOUSE INSECT

LOUSE = HAIR INSECT

MANTIS = INSECT EATING INSECT. This is one of few insects that feed on insects.

MONARCH BUTTERFLY = KING BUTTERFLY

MOSQUITO = ATTACK INSECT, known for its attacks on people and animals to suck their blood. By infecting people with malaria, the mosquito is responsible for most deaths caused to people by all animals.

MOTH = BUTTERFLY NOT BUTTERFLY. It looks like a butterfly but it is not, it is a moth.

PRAYING MANTIS = INSECT PRAYING. Praying is shown as PRAISING GOD. This insect that preys on insects, including its own male after the act of copulation, of course is not praying to God but keeps long forelegs in a position as if praying.

PUPA = INSECT BETWEEN; insect between immature (caterpillar) and becoming mature

SILKWORM = BEFORE SILK INSECT. *Before insect* indicates CATERPILLAR, here caterpillar of silk moth.

SILVERFISH = SILVER INSECT. This insect is not a fish, but a small slivery insect that feeds on starch of books and wallpaper and food.

TERMITE = INSECT EATING WOOD

TSETSE FLY = INSECT of SLEEPING SICKNESS

We continue now with arachnids, mostly spiders:

ARACHNID	BLACK WIDOW	SCORPION	SPIDER	TARANTULA
WOLF SPIDER				

BLACK WIDOW = SPIDER WIDOW. Very poisonous spider of tropical regions of America and Asia. It is black, which explains half of its name. The other half one could have thought that comes from it being so poisonous that it makes many women widows. But this is not the origin of its name. It is called widow because of habit of eating its male and thus making herself widow.

SCORPION = ARACHNID WITH POISONOUS HOOK (which symbolizes venomous sting)

SPIDER = ARACHNID and FABRIC (that represents its web)

TARANTULA = LARGE HAIRY SPIDER. Hairy is shown as overlapping hair.

WOLF SPIDER = SPIDER WITHOUT NET. This spider is hunting its prey, rather then using net as other spiders do, hence, *spider without net*

Finally, we will end with several animal signs based by combining miscellaneous signs:

MISCEL-LANEOUS	AMOEBA	JELLYFISH	MUSSEL	OYSTER
	⊖♪✄	◇◇◇✗	△◇	‡◇
PEARL OYSTER	PORTUGUESE MAN-OF-WAR	STARFISH		
♯◇◈	½R ½R ◇◇◇✗	☆		

AMOEBA = CELL WITHOUT SHAPE. The sign for SHAPE is similar to the sign for SIZE, that is, EXTENDING IN ALL DIRECTIONS. They differ in relative orientation.

JELLYFISH = SOFT SOFT FISH NO FISH

MUSSEL = BLACK SEASHELL. Seashell is HARD UNDER SEA. Hard is DIAMOND, the hardest natural substance.

OYSTER = CRUDE SEASHELL.

PEARL OYSTER = CRUDE SEASHELL WITH PEARL

PORTUGUESE MAN-OF-WAR = POISONOUS POISONOUS JELLYFISH

STARFISH = STAR & SEA

W = 2,000

We have by now reached over two thousand words, which is just about the size of vocabulary of common people for everyday communications. It is true though that we are missing some common words and have seen a number of uncommon words, but consider the wealth of your vocabulary in Nobel—all accumulated in days or at most a few weeks, not a few months, and not toiling over them.

In addition to signs for animals shown, we can add a few related signs than involve animals one way or another, words such as:

ANTLER	BRISTLE	CLONE	COWHIDE	DUNG
FANG	FEED	HOOF	HORN	HYBRID
INVERTEBRATE	JAW	LAMB	LARD	LIZARD
MANGROVE	MARSUPIAL	MEAT	MOLLUSK	MOTHER MILK
MUTTON	PEST	PREDATOR	PREY	REPTILE
RIDE	RODENT	SLEEPING SICKNESS	SPINE	VEAL
VENISON	VERTEBRATE	WADING	WILD ANIMAL	

As just mentioned, with all this information on animals, we accumulated over two thousand words. We should add that we have not exhausted the list of animals; many others could be added. Just using as a root the word COW, we could easily add COWBIRD, COWFISH, and COW PONY (a bird, a fish, and an animal). Cowbird, a North American blackbird that lays its eggs in the nests of other birds, like cuckoo, and cowfish, various small fish with hornlike projections over the eyes, may not be so widely known as cow is. Cow pony is a more familiar domestic animal, strong and agile saddle horse trained for work with cattle, such as herding cattle. Speaking of PONY a small horse, a question can be raised: how would one differentiate, in Nobel, small horse from grown-up pony, when both are small? It does not take much time to come to the solution illustrated below:

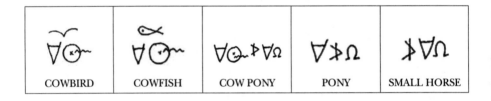

| COWBIRD | COWFISH | COW PONY | PONY | SMALL HORSE |

SMALL HORSE is a horse that is small, hence, the sign for small horse is combination of the signs SMALL and HORSE, animal identified by HORSESHOE. Pony is not a horse, it is a pony, an animal closely related to horse, the size of which is small so it looks like small horse. Hence, the sign for pony is again to be a combination of the signs SMALL and HORSE, but this time we arranged the indicator signs so that PONY is ANIMAL indicated by SMALL HORSESHOE. There is no room for confusion here, because as a rule small horses do not bear horseshoes, and even if they would, the sign for small horse and pony remain different. Finally, the sign "baby horse," which also signifies for small horse, stands for FOAL, that is one-year-old or younger horse offspring.

We may make a parallel of pygmy, small person of Equatorial Africa (about 1.5 meters in height, which is well under five feet) and DWARF, a person of unusually small stature, against SMALL PERSON. Well, small person is CHILD, and we have already shown the sign for child as GROWING PERSON. Thus the sign SMALL PERSON should be used to represent PYGMY and DWARF, not a CHILD. If one wish to further differentiate pygmy and dwarf, that is possible, as shown below:

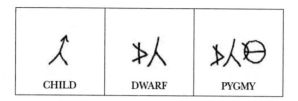

Thus DWARF is simply SMALL PERSON, while PYGMY is SMALL PERSON from TROPIC.

Let us end this zoological section with comments on two signs: GOLD and EMPEROR, both used for construction of names of animals. Here are few additional signs using GOLD:

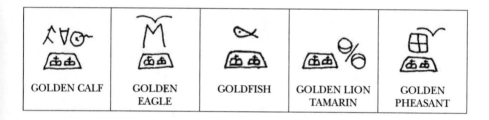

GOLDEN CALF characterizes a biblical event; a monument to golden calf was made by Aaron and worshiped by Israelites and became a symbol of false and misguided worship, such as worship of money, which appears dominant in our time as well.

There is truly and officially only a single EMPEROR in the animal kingdom and that is emperor penguin, the largest of penguins. There are though several KINGS in the animal kingdom: kingbird, a large American songbird of flycatcher family that feeds on insects caught flying; King Charles spaniel, a small spaniel; king cobra, the largest viper growing to 18 feet (5.5 meters) in length; king crab, a very large edible crab of the north Pacific and Japan; kingfish, large edible fish living in the warm coastal waters of the Atlantic Ocean; kingfisher, bird of short tail feeding on fish and insects; king mackerel, a mackerel living in warm waters of the Atlantic Ocean;

king penguin, a large penguin living on islands close to the Antarctic; king salmon or chinook salmon found in rivers of North America and north Asia, considered among the best for salmons (Chinooks are Native Americans of western Washington state); and king snake, a nonpoisonous snake of North America, a constrictor snake like the python but of smaller size, from 2 to 6 feet, preying on small animals and snakes. In all cases, the title "king" implies larger size and some dominant position. In Nobel, we continue with this tradition, and have used the title "emperor" and related title of "king" to indicate the most prominent animals of a kind as summarized below:

EMPEROR PENGUIN	ANACONDA	KING COBRA	BONOBO	
KING PENGUIN	PYTHON	COBRA	LION	

As one can see, we promoted *king cobra* into *emperor* cobra, while we are still missing *emperor animal*, having only lion as a king of animals, which is its popular title. There is a folk saying in Croatia: *Um caruje, snaga klade valja*, which says that the brain is the "emperor that rules" and body "strength is pushing logs," or more freely translated, "brain reins, strength pushes work." If we use this as the basis for animal titles, and if lion is already "king of animals," having the body strength, then the candidate for "emperor of animals" would be bonobo, also known as pigmy chimpanzee, species related to both chimpanzee and humans. It was first discovered as a species in 1928 based on examination of skull, though believed before to belong to a small chimpanzee, but in fact bonobo is a separate ape species similar but different from chimpanzee. They live south of the Congo River in the Democratic Republic of Congo; they are endangered species. They are frugivorous, that is, their main diet is fruits, though they also eat insects and small animals. They are the most similar animals to human and thus deserve the title EMPEROR ANIMAL.

Let us at the end mention that although we have listed over two hundred animals, there are still some relatively common animals that have not been mentioned. They include for example, badger, cockroach, cormorant, crane, platypus, ermine, macaque, mackerel, mink, magpie, poodle, prawn, quail, raccoon, raven, rhesus, tapir, tuna, and weasel. It is not that I have not given thought to these animals, or that they cannot be described in Nobel. They can, as can also a number of other objects and concepts not considered, but the description may require several signs, that is, at the moment, there is no obvious single three-sign combination that offered satisfactory answer. One may recall the Basic English of C. K. Ogden, who has demonstrated that by limiting vocabulary of English to eight hundred words one can in fact describe everything in simple Basic English. I looked in his dictionary of Basic English to see how he would describe *cabbage*. Well, the description took three lines in the dictionary, but it was possible. It is not simple to describe cabbage even in common English, not restricting vocabulary to eight hundred words. This is how the *Encarta World English Dictionary* describes cabbage:

> *Cabbage (leafy vegetable): a plant with a short stem and roundish head of closely layered green, white, or red leaves that is eaten as a vegetable.* [To this description is added a figure of cabbage to help you to recognize the vegetable under description.]

So it is understandable that with less than two hundred elements of Nobel, signs and arrows combined, we will face similar challenges and cannot expect to have every object and every concept reduced to combinations of very few signs. We have seen more than 80 percent of basic signs and 80 percent of arrows. The remaining signs and arrows, although accounting for less than 20 percent of basic material, will more than double our vocabulary. However, now is a time for pause, recapitulation of what we have learned to make sure that we have assimilated most of the material so far presented. Rather than repeating what has been said, we will present shortly a quiz based on several key signs so that readers can test their knowledge of Nobel.

We should also add that having few additional signs we could further increased the list of animals. In fact we have "smuggled" very few new signs (e.g. STRIPES, SPOTS) or new combinations of signs (e.g. JELLY = overlapping soft) that have not been previously introduced. Probably some readers may have even not noticed them as new signs and new combinations.

How many more signs are still there? How many arrows we have not yet seen? Well, we have approximately seen about 80 percent of signs and arrows, so there is no much more yet to be learned. By combining new and old signs and new and old arrows, we will more than double the number of words of Nobel and will arrive at some five thousand words at least. In this first part of introduction to Nobel, we included most of the words that we could construct so to give a message of the potential of Nobel to build up considerable vocabulary. Thus we have come across some words, as ORNITHOLOGY, which was mentioned before, that can hardly be viewed as words of daily use. In fact, some such words, just as some scientific disciplines may have very limited audience and very limited use. According to American physicist Richard Feynman (1918-1988), one of the outstanding scientists and Nobel laureate (1965), such discipline is philosophy of science, for which he said,

> *Philosophy of science is about as useful to scientists as ornithology is to birds.*

Attributed to Richard Feynman and quoted by Steven Weinberg, Nobel laureate 1979, from the University of Texas (as cited in the *New York Times*, December 18, 2007, in an article, "Laws of Nature, Source Unknown" by Dennis Overbye). We mentioned this just to illustrate that some "useless" words may suddenly appear in quite unexpected context and show that they may not be so useless after all.

We are ready to quote the above statement of Richard Feynman in Nobel, with which we want to illustrate potential of Nobel even at this rather "high level" of communications, except in order to do that we need a sign for PHILOSOPHY, which we have not yet considered. We have listed on p. 186 signs for twenty sciences and could augment such list easily by another twenty sciences, but PHILOSOPHY presents considerable challenge, due to its own complexity and lack of simple definition. One would think that after consulting half a dozen dictionaries, searching for explanation of the word PHILOSOPHY one would find an answer, but instead such search appears to lead to more questions. Let examine how various dictionaries explain PHILOSOPHY. We will start with some elementary dictionaries and will end with more advanced and sophisticated dictionaries.

According to *Macmillan Essential Dictionary for Learners of English* (Oxford, England, 2003) philosophy *is the study of theories about the meaning of things such as life, knowledge and beliefs.* While explaining the philosophy the above is of little help for construction of a sign in Nobel for philosophy. *Webster's Easy English Dictionary* (New York: Random House, 2001) explains philosophy as follows: *the study of what it means to be alive, what knowledge is, and how people should live.* This is informative but again not useful in contemplating a sign for PHILOSOPHY in Nobel. *Basic Dictionary* with the auxiliary title, "Pre-intermediate level, over 10,000 meanings clearly explained" (London: Bloomsbury Publishing, 2004), comes with a rather short definition for philosophy as the *study of the meaning of human existence.* This may be less informative, but allows construction of a sign:

PHILOSOPHY

This sign is fine, acceptable, but it is somewhat lengthy. Can we come across a simple alternative?

In trying to search for a possible simpler solution for the sign for PHILOSOPHY, I consulted few additional more advanced dictionaries. *The Funk & Wagnalls Standard Desk Dictionary* (New York: Harper & Row Publishers, 1984) lists five different meanings for the word philosophy, the first of which is relevant for us here:

philosophy-1. *The inquiry into the most comprehensive principles of reality in general, or of some sector of it, as human knowledge and human values.*

I let readers judge for themselves, but without those already listed "simple" descriptions of philosophy, one may have more difficulties to understand what philosophy is from such "advanced" approaches. Not being satisfied I looked in the *Encarta World English Dictionary* (New York: St. Martin's Press, 1999), which came with the following:

> philosophy-1. *Examination of basic concepts—the branch of knowledge or academic study devoted to the systematic examination of basic concepts such as truth, existence, reality, causality and freedom.*

Well, we are learning more and more about philosophy, which as we see includes beside before mentioned truth, existence, reality and causality also freedom. I am reminded of a scientific conference that I attended in 2004, which was held on the island of Brijuni, former summer residence of Marshal Tito, Yugoslav dictator, which was entitled Space, Time and Life. Well, what else is there? So this conference could be about everything. Is philosophy about everything? In order to find more finally I consulted the huge *New Lexicon Webster Dictionary of the English Language* (Encyclopedic Edition) published by Lexicon Publications in 1987, according to which

> philosophy-1. *The love of pursuit of wisdom, i.e., the search for basic principles. Traditionally, Western philosophy comprises of five branches of study: metaphysics, ethics, aesthetic, epistemology and logic.*

As already mentioned, we are looking for short definitions, and indeed definition of philosophy as *the love of pursuit of wisdom* is short. So let us follow the lead. Looking for clarification of wisdom, in the same dictionary we find:

> wisdom—*the quality of being wise—intelligence drawing on experience and governed by prudence.*

Let us continue and look for clarification of prudence:

> prudence—*foresight leading a person to avoid error and danger.*

That sounds understandable but let us check for foresight:

> *foresight—prophetic capacity, prevision.*

And finally,

> *prophetic—foretelling, containing prediction.*

Coming upon foretelling reduces philosophy to crystal gazing, which I am sure all philosophers will find offensive, just as astronomers would find it offensive to be connected to astrology.

In desperation, I recalled two well-known philosophical statements:

> *Cogito, ergo sum*—by René Descartes (1596-1650), "Father of Modern Philosophy." Translation from Latin, *I am thinking, therefore I exist.*

> *To be or not to be—that is the question*—by William Shakespeare (1564-1616) from *Hamlet.*

I think that these two statements better characterize philosophy than the various authors and committees that are behind the definitions that we quoted from half a dozen dictionaries. So we can summarize PHILOSOPHY as SCIENCE (not a theory, not a study, not love, and not a pursuit) of EXIST / NOT EXIST, which is the essence of the question raised by the prince of Denmark in *Hamlet.* This leads to a simple sign for philosophy in Nobel:

PHILOSOPHY

Hence, philosophy = *meaning of to exist or not exist* (or *to be and not to be*). Now we are ready for the Richard Feynman quote: "*Philosophy of science is about as useful to scientists as ornithology is to birds.*"

PHILOSOPHY	OF	SCIENCE	IS	ABOUT
AS	USEFUL	TO	SCIENTISTS	AS
ORNITHOLOGY	IS	TO	BIRDS	

Additional Set of Signs and Arrows

Before we end this section and start with the quiz, we will enlist an additional set of signs and arrows and will follow with a few illustrations. The signs to be shown are not difficult to recognize; most of them are self-evident. What makes this group of signs among the last to be introduced is that most of them are not used frequently. Some of the signs we have seen already, e.g., the sign of FORK with the sign for BARBADOS, and finally the sign for POWDER (SPOTS) with the sign for DALMATIAN, the sign for FABRIC with the sign for SPIDER, that some may have not recognized as new signs. Of the signs shown, perhaps the signs for SPACE and SPORT will be more used.

ARTIFICIAL	AX AXE	BAG	BALLOON	BEARD
BOTTLE	CHERRY	COMPETITION	COOPERATION	DISTANCE
EAR	FABRIC	FLEXIBLE	FORK	HANG

LEAF	LOOP	MOUSTACHE	NOSE	PIPE
POWDER	ROPE	SILK	SPACE	SPORT
SPOTS	THREAD			

To this, we may add new arrows:

INDIRECT	PASS	ERUPTION	SPREAD	DO

And finally a set of three convoluted bidirectional arrows:

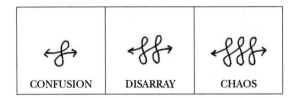

CONFUSION	DISARRAY	CHAOS

Let us comment on the few signs introduced. The sign for DISTANCE is shown as a part of a line, and LEAF is drawn as a simple as possible. There are hundred different shapes for leaves; the one selected is among those more easily to be recognized. Almost every plant has different kind of leaf. *Webster's Easy English Dictionary* (Random House) describes leaf as "one of the flat green parts that grow on a tree or other plants." But leaves need not be flat and not all are green; *Macmillan Essential Dictionary* is more accurate when describing leaf as "a flat, thin, usually green part of a tree or a plant that grows on a branch or a stem." But again, many leaves are not flat (think of cabbage!), and some are not thin, like those of several desert plants, including agaves, native to hot dry areas of North and South America. The sap of the spiny-edged thick leaves of agaves is used to make tequila and other alcoholic drinks. One need not be knowledgeable in botany to know that leaves are of so different size and shape and we need just a single sign—which clearly cannot be representative. So we selected the shape of spade, a figure on playing cards, with which many will be familiar, particularly those spending times in Las Vegas and other casinos all over the USA and the world. Another candidate would be maple leaf, which is also depicted on Canadian flag, but we have to disappoint Canadians, in view of their maple leaf being too detailed and not easy to reproduce in communications. So, in Nobel, Canada remains symbolized by a leaf, but for practical and not symbolic reasons, this is going to be a leaf familiar to gamblers and as seen on playing cards, and not a maple leaf that may be more familiar to churchgoing people!

The signs for AX (AXE) and BALLOON are easy to recognize. LOOP is shown as folded line. The sign for SPORT, the three overlapping rings, is based on the flag symbolizing the Olympic Games, which are represented by five overlapping rings. Ancient Olympic Games held during the sixth and fifth century BC were part of popular competitions in ancient Greece. Modern Olympic Games, revived in 1896, continue every four years to bring the best athletes from all over the world to test their skills along the Olympic motto, *citius altius fortius*—faster, higher, stronger (in Latin). This motto, the symbol of five interlocking rings, and another motto, "The most important thing is not to win but to take part!" were all due to Frenchman Baron Pierre de Coubertin, the founder of the modern Olympic Games. We can view our sign for SPORT, three overlapping rings, as part of activities that culminate in winning the gold medal in Olympic Games. Three overlapping rings and five overlapping rings may be placed in parallel with three-star general and five-star general, the five-star general being at the top. Good athletes are just as good generals, but only those getting Olympic gold medal may be viewed as top generals. Incidentally, the United States of America had in the past only five five-star generals, the three best known were George C. Marshall (1880-1959), well known for the Marshall Plan that has helped recovery after WWII in the war-ruined Europe; Douglas MacArthur (1880-1964) known for his "I shall return" statement when ordered (by the Pentagon) to abandon the Philippines at the time of Japan invasion; and Dwight D. Eisenhower (1890-1969) the supreme commander of the Allied forces in Europe in WWII, with responsibility for planning and supervising the successful invasion of France in June 1944, and later, from 1953 to 1961, thirty-fourth president of the United States. In connection with Marshall Plan, I may add what is not so widely known, that the initiative for the project came from President Truman, who was aware that the project can get through Congress only if it be called Marshall Plan (George Marshal was Secretary of State) and not Truman Plan.

The sign for COMPETITION and COOPERATION are related and differ only in their orientation, just as has been the case with the signs for battle and defense. The swords oriented *up* are ready for confrontation, and when oriented *down*, suggest peace, thus *peaceful competition = cooperation*. The sign for SPACE represents the coordinate *system*, mathematical invention of René Descartes (1596-1650), French philosopher and mathematician. Mathematicians refer to two-dimensional coordinate system as two-dimensional space and, analogously, three-dimensional coordinate system as three-dimensional space. Being mathematicians, they do not stop there, but continue to speak of four-dimensional space, which of course is not possible to visualize, and so on.

The sign ARTIFICIAL looks, at first sight, artificial and devoid of simple explanation. But this is not the case. The sign is related to its opposite, which is NATURAL. The sign for NATURAL, as explained earlier, symbolizes overlapping PARALLEL BODIES, which are natural positioning of bodies mating. So, opposite of parallel bodies would be PERPENDICULAR BODIES, but the sign of perpendicular bodies was already used to represent COMPLETE, an overlap of BODY and MIND. So, by rotating the two ovals by forty-five degrees, we still have perpendicular ovals but obtained a novel sign—which we took to stand for ARTIFICIAL.

The sign for ROPE, which also stands for HANG, is taken as a picture of a hanging rope. When we wish to differentiate between the two, then we add to the sign HANG the sign WITH, so rope becomes HANG WITH, which is one (brutal) use of rope. The sign for THREAD and SILK are closely related, the latter having in addition the sign FINE.

SPOTS and POWDER are similar, except for orientation. The sign for FLEXIBLE is flexible, the sign for PIPE is obvious, as are also the diverging arrows representing ERUPTION and SPREAD. Finally consider the sign for ALPHABET, the word that stands for the names of the first two letters of the Greek alphabet, alpha, the first, and beta, the second. In Nobel we use letters AZ.

We follow with illustration of number of combinations using the final set of signs and arrows, which includes also the last arrow, the DO arrow which is based on sign WITH. In fact, by doubling the sign for WITH we obtain sign for HAVE, which is an important auxiliary verb, and by adding arrowheads we created sign for DO, another very important auxiliary verb.

LONG *part of distance*	SHORT *part of distance*	SPEED *distance over time*	ACCELER-ATION *speed over time*	FAST
SLOW	EVENT *space & time*	DISASTER *bad event*	FOLIAGE *overlapping leaves*	SALAD *leaf on plate*
INSINUATE *speak indirectly*	BOTTLENECK *part of bottle*	HOLE *part of loop*	PUNCTURE *knife in balloon*	MATCH *sport competition*
CONTEST *official competition*	RIVAL	BRICK *artificial stone*	AFFECTATION *artificial behavior*	AIR CONDITIONER *artificial climate*

ARTIFICIAL INTELLIGENCE *artificial brain*	FOUNTAIN *artificial water eruption*	ARTIFICIAL LANGUAGE	ARTIFICIAL RESPIRATION	ARTIFICIAL TURF
ARTIFICIAL INSEMINATING *art. pregnancy*	ARTIFICIAL SWEETENER *art. sugar*	ARTIFICIAL SELECTION	CLEAN *without spots*	DALMATIAN *dog with spots*
SUGAR *sweet powder*	SALT *white powder*	PEPPER *black powder*	FACE POWDER	SAND *sea & powder*
SACCHARIN *artificial sugar*	CLUSTER	ACROBAT	BLIMP *overlapping balloon*	GEYSER *hot water eruption*
NEPTUNE *god of sea*	VOLCANO	ROPE *hang with*	CURTAIN *hang hang*	IRON CURTAIN
ACROSS	CREDIT CARD *plastic money*	INFLEXIBLE	AROMA *nose likes*	CIRCUS *lot of acrobats*
SPILL *water spread*	FLOOD *lot of spill*	FLOOD *lot of flood*		

Quiz

We constructed the quiz by selecting the following seven signs: ANIMAL, BODY, BOOK, BRAIN, COUNTRY, HEART, and TIME. For each sign, we display twenty-four words in which that particular sign is part of. Under each set of signs, we have listed alphabetically words that the signs represent. This will help readers to identify the correct answer. Some signs will be readily identified; others may take a little more time. Readers should take advantage of the opportunity to cross out words that they have recognized, thus leaving few alternatives to consider. At the end of the quiz, we give the correct answers in the form of a key that reveals the position of the correct answer. Thus, for example, in the first place on each quiz is the word, which is in the position 20 in the alphabetical list, the word in the next place is in the position 17 in the alphabetical list, etc. (see the last page of the quiz).

If you score on the first reading of this book, 22-24 you have outstanding knowledge of Nobel, while 20-22 is still excellent. The score 18-20 is still very satisfactory, "very good" in the usual high school characterization of grades. However, if you fail to correctly identify half of the signs, perhaps you may consider going back and reading again some of the pages that you may have read too fast. However, even that need not be necessary, because as we add new signs, we will combine them with the existing signs, and all this will help further readers to become more familiar with old and new signs.

We follow with a set of quizzes covering the following signs:

1. Animals
2. Body
3. Book
4. Brain
5. Countries
6. Heart
7. Time

The quiz is followed by a key for checking the correct answers. The key is the same for all seven quizzes and indicates the place of words ordered alphabetically at the bottom of each page by the number from 1 to 24, number 1 corresponding to the first word and 24 to the last word.

W = 2,300

We just went over 2,300 words, about eight words per page. But we could even round this to 2,500 words, because we could not list every possible word. Consider, for example, FRAME = *outside picture;* SNOWFALL = *snow & cloud;* MIDDLE EAST = *middle and east;* HAZE = *fog and not fog;* and so on.

Quiz # 1   Animals

AMPHIBIAN   KANGAROO   MOUNTAIN LION   RABBIT
ANTELOPE   LAMB   MUSK   REINDEER
BOAR   LION   PIG   SHEEP
DEER   LLAMA   PEST   SHEEPDOG
GOAT   MONGOOSE   PREDATOR   WATER BUFFALO
HORSE   MOUNTAIN GOAT   PREY   WHALE

Quiz # 2   Body

BATH	CRIME	EXCRETE	PREGNANT
BATHE	DEATH	FEVER	SKELETON
BONE	DIARRHEA	HEALTH	STARVE
CAESARIAN	DIGEST	HUNGRY	SURGERY
CHEST	DYING	INFLAMMATION	TIRED
CONSTIPATION	EXERCISE	INJURY	URINE

Quiz # 3   Book

ASTROLOGY	BOTANY	HISTORY	PSEUDOSCIENCE
ASTRONOMY	CHAPTER	KORAN	SCIENCE
AUTHOR	COAUTHOR	LOGBOOK	SCIENCE FICTION
AUTOBIOGRAPHY	DIARY	MEMOIR	TECHNOLOGY
BIBLE	FORESTRY	PAPERBACK	TEXTBOOK
BIOLOGY	HARD COPY	PHARMACOPOEIA	THEOLOGY

Quiz # 4   Brain

APE	IDEA	MEMORY	REMEMBER
BOTHER	INTERPRET	MISUNDERSTAND	STUPID
CLEVER	INTUITION	NERVOUS	THINK
CONSIDER	INVENT	OBSESSION	THINKING
DULL	KNOW	REASON	UNDERSTAND
FORGET	MEANING	RECOLLECT	WISE

Quiz # 5   Countries

AUSTRIA	FRANCE	LIBERIA	POLAND
BERMUDA	GREECE	MEXICO	PORTUGAL
CHINA	HOLLAND	MONACO	SPAIN
COLOMBIA	IRELAND	MOROCCO	SWEDEN
CROATIA	ICELAND	PANAMA	TIBET
CUBA	JAPAN	PAPUA	UNITED STATES

Quiz # 6 Heart

AFFECTION	CHARACTER	LOYAL	SHY
AWKWARD	CURSE	NEED	SIN
ATTRACTIVE	HONEY	PARTY	TEMPTATION
AXIOM	IN LOVE	PATIENT	TERROR
BLEEDING	KISS	REGRETS	TRUE
BILE	LOVE	RAPE	WELCOME

Quiz # 7   Time

AFTER	DAY	LATE	NOON
AGAIN	DEADLINE	MORNING	NOW
ALWAYS	EARLY	NEVER	OFTEN
ANTIQUE	FOOD TIME	NEW	OLD
BEFORE	FRESH	NEWS	STALE
BRAND-NEW	IMMEDIATELY	NIGHT	TRADITION

20	17	8	11
9	12	21	18
16	19	10	7
1	4	13	22
24	15	6	3
5	2	23	14

1_____   7_____   13_____   19_____
2_____   8_____   14_____   20_____
3_____   9_____   15_____   21_____
4_____   10_____   16_____   22_____
5_____   11_____   17_____   23_____
6_____   12_____   18_____   24_____

Unusual Test

Before closing this second part of the introduction to Nobel, we will offer a test on Nobel, but a somewhat unusual test. In contrast to the quiz, where we have listed answers to facilitate readers in identifying individual signs, now we will not only present signs without list of answers but also present signs most of which have not yet been explained. Readers will have to ponder and think of the nearest possible answer for each sign. If one correctly identifies one in five this is an outstanding achievement, even one in ten correct answers would be very laudable, because you arrived at the answer on your own reasoning and you have not been shown any of the signs given ever. Imagine someone gives you a list of 356 foreign words of a language that you have never heard before. For instance, words like

JAIGWA   DIBAKONIGEWIN   TIBIKABAMINAGWAD   DONDANAMA   BEMOSSESSING

or words like

NOA   TIKA   RIKORIKO   REKEREKE   HAVA

You, just like me, most likely have not only no idea what these words mean, but most of us even have no idea what language they came from, unless you are an inhabitant of northern Minnesota or New Zealand. The five words given are from the language spoken by Ojibway, Native Americans living in northern Minnesota, and from Maori language of New Zealand spoken by native New Zealanders. However, if I list the same five words in Nobel, as shown below, although you have not seen some of them before, you may get some idea what these five words mean:

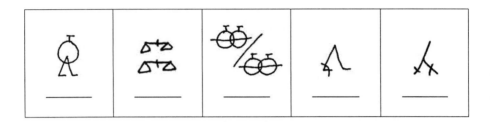

We left blank spaces for you to fill in what you may think that these words represent. We suggest that you use pencil rather than ink just in case that you may have to correct your answer. We will now present 365 words of Nobel for you to try to find what their proper interpretation is, one for each day of a year. Take your time! At the end of the test, you will find not only correct answers but also some explanations to justify the answers. As we mentioned one correct answer in five, one in each row, should be considered outstanding in view of you not having seen these sign combinations before. Some words with similar meaning may cause problems, so don't be disappointed if your guess is close but not quite the same as suggested by the indicated answers.

Words 1-35

1	2	3	4	5
6	7	8	9	10
11	12	13	14	15
16	17	18	19	20
21	22	23	24	25
26	27	28	29	30
31	32	33	34	35

Words 36-70

Words 71-105

71_____	72_____	73_____	74_____	75_____
76_____	77_____	78_____	79_____	80_____
81_____	82_____	83_____	84_____	85_____
86_____	87_____	88_____	89_____	90_____
91_____	92_____	93_____	94_____	95_____
96_____	97_____	98_____	99_____	100_____
101_____	102_____	103_____	104_____	105_____

Words 106-140

106_____	107_____	108_____	109_____	110_____
111_____	112_____	113_____	114_____	115_____
116_____	117_____	118_____	119_____	120_____
121_____	122_____	123_____	124_____	125_____
126_____	127_____	128_____	129_____	130_____
131_____	132_____	133_____	134_____	135_____
136_____	137_____	138_____	139_____	140_____

Words 141-175

141_____	142_____	143_____	144_____	145_____
146_____	147_____	148_____	149_____	150_____
151_____	152_____	153_____	154_____	155_____
156_____	157_____	158_____	159_____	160_____
161_____	162_____	163_____	164_____	165_____
166_____	167_____	168_____	169_____	170_____
171_____	172_____	173_____	174_____	175_____

Words 176-210

176_____	177_____	178_____	179_____	180_____
181_____	182_____	183_____	184_____	185_____
186_____	187_____	188_____	189_____	190_____
191_____	192_____	193_____	194_____	195_____
196_____	197_____	198_____	199_____	200_____
201_____	202_____	203_____	204_____	205_____
206_____	207_____	208_____	209_____	210_____

Words 211-240

211_____	212_____	213_____	214_____	215_____
216_____	217_____	218_____	219_____	220_____
221_____	222_____	223_____	224_____	225_____
226_____	227_____	228_____	229_____	230_____
231_____	232_____	233_____	234_____	235_____
236_____	237_____	238_____	239_____	240_____

Words 241-260

241_____	242_____	243_____	244_____	245_____
246_____	247_____	248_____	249_____	250_____
251_____	252_____	253_____	254_____	255_____
256_____	257_____	258_____	259_____	260_____
261_____	262_____	263_____	264_____	265_____
266_____	267_____	268_____	269_____	270_____

Words 271-300

271_____	272_____	273_____	274_____	275_____
276_____	277_____	278_____	279_____	280_____
281_____	282_____	283_____	284_____	285_____
286_____	287_____	288_____	289_____	290_____
291_____	292_____	293_____	294_____	295_____
296_____	297_____	298_____	299_____	300_____

Words 301-335

Words 336-365

336_____	337_____	338_____	339_____	340_____
341_____	342_____	343_____	344_____	345_____
346_____	347_____	348_____	349_____	350_____
351_____	352_____	353_____	354_____	355_____
356_____	357_____	358_____	359_____	360_____
361_____	362_____	363_____	364_____	365_____

Answers

1   BRANCH—*part* of a *tree*

2   RATION—*food* per *person*

3   PARALYZED—*person* with both *legs crossed*

4   SAMURAI—*Japan's soldier* (of previous times)

5   CIVILIAN—*not* a *soldier*

6   SQUIRREL—*tree rodent* (*rodent* = *growing teeth*)

7   PLACEBO—*not* a medication *pill*

8   BIOGRAPHY—*person's life path*

9   WARD—*part of a prison*

10   WARD—*part of a hospital*

11   SPONTANEOUS ABORTION—*birth failure*

12   ICEBOAT—*ice* and *ship* (*ice* = *solid water*)

13   WILD ROSE—*wild* and *rose* (*beautiful flower*)

14   ENCORE—*again on podium*

15   ENCYCLOPEDIA—*book of all* things

16   OPINION—brain view, hence *brain* above

17   NUMB—*without feeling* (*feeling* = *inside heart*)

18   AIRMAIL—*bird and letter*

19   MURDER—to *kill a person* (*kill* = *knife in heart*)

20   PLATONIC—*love in clouds*

21   MUMMY—*preserved dead body* (*preserved* = *protected protected*)

22   ODIOUS—*people hate*

23   LIQUEUR—*sweet brandy*

24   PESOS—*Mexican currency*

25   MIRACLE—*walking on water*

26   FIRST TEETH—*basic teeth*

27   PIGLET—*"child"* pig

28   MARE—*female horse*

29 POUND—*British currency (money)*
30 MIDDLE EAST—*middle east*
31 STERN—end *part of a ship*
32 BOW—front *part of a ship*
33 FRAME—*outside picture*
34 TEXAS—lone *star state* (hence a single star!)
35 TOMBSTONE—*stone over a grave* (*stone = hard on the ground*)
36 SNOWFALL—*cloud and snow*
37 SNOWMAN—*snow person*
38 SQUAT—*sit and not sit* (*sit = not stand, stand = not walk*)
39 SCAR—*path of injury*
40 STALLION—*male horse*
41 STEPFATHER—*father* that is *not father*
42 STEPMOTHER—*mother* that is *not mother*
43 SNOW FENCE—*snow and fence*
44 TASK—*part of work*
45 HAZE—*fog and not fog*
46 CUSTOMER—*coming again*
47 LEAP SECOND—*jumping second*
48 ANXIETY—*friction entering brain*
49 LEGAL—*parallel to law*
50 NAVY—*sea military*
51 CHALLENGE—*brain battle*
52 GUINEA—*country of experimental animal* (*guinea pig*)
53 CAMPAIGN—*battle follows battle*
54 TEAR—*cut without scissors*
55 CENT—*hundredth of a dollar* (*dollar = USA currency*)
56 READY—*now* or *not now*
57 ROB—*illegal attack*
58 LAG—*follow and not follow*
59 HELLO—have a *good day*
60 EXPERIENCE—having *work behind*
61 NOVICE—having *work ahead*
62 PROFIT (GAIN)—*revenue over cost* (*revenue = money coming in*)
63 LOSS—*cost over revenue* (*cost = money going out*)
64 DIPLOMACY—*avoiding war*
65 TAXI—*wheel* (car) *against money*
66 NORTH AMERICA—*new world* (globe) *north*
67 SOUTH AMERICA—*new world* (globe) *south*

68	FIRST—*before others*
69	LAST—*after others*
70	FOREVER—*infinite time*
71	EXPLAIN—let it *jump out of brain*
72	SUCCEEDING—*ascending goal*
73	FAILING—*descending goal*
74	LOGIC—*reason behind reason*
75	EARNEST—*without smile*
76	EMBARK—*jump on ship*
77	DISEMBARK—*jump from ship*
78	OBVIOUS—*all see*
79	SUBTLE—*not obvious* (*obvious = all see*)
80	BELLIGERENT—*soaked in war*
81	EASILY—*without effort*
82	ECHO—*sound return* (*sound = music and noise*)
83	ANIMATE—*push life* (*life = heart with signal*)
84	ANATHEMA—*curse curse*
85	SKEPTIC—*question if true*
86	NAÏVE—*does not question if true or lie*
87	ACHILLES' HEEL—*heel on a podium*
88	SCANDAL—*sin on a podium,* that is, a public sin
89	BROWSE—*jump through book*
90	ERRAND—*jumping task*
91	BAIL—*money for release from prison*
92	LIGHTHOUSE—*light* and *tower*
93	IGLOO—*snow house*
94	BURGLAR—*person illegally entering house*
95	FLAMMABLE—*catches fire, hence, hook and flame*
96	HOBO—*person jumping* from place to place
97	SCOUNDREL—*person with overlapping sins*
98	HEATHEN—(person) *without God*
99	HOMELESS—(person) *without home*
100	EFFICIENT—*without waste*
101	UNITED NATIONS—*countries around globe*
102	OFFICE HOURS—*desk and time*
103	TIME CONFLICT—*time against time*
104	FOLK—*common people* (*common = overlapping parts*)
105	REFUGEE—*person without country*
106	CHEF—*king of food*

107 INFANTRY—*foot soldiers*
108 OBSCENE—*heart in mud* (*mud = water over ground*)
109 IMPOUND—*official hook,* that is, keep legally
110 ILLUSION—to believe that *fact is not fact*
111 E-MAIL—*electronic letter* (*electronic = electric electric*)
112 EVADE—*avoid* being *followed*
113 CIVIL WAR—*country in middle of war*
114 BLUR—*awkward to eye* (*awkward = involved arrow*)
115 FATA MORGANA (MIRAGE)—*blurred blurred vision*
116 HALLUCINATE—*blurred blurred blurred vision* (and see what is not)
117 STUDENT—*person entering a book*
118 EMIGRATE—*leave the country*
119 ENCEPHALITIS—*brain inflammation* (hence *brain* and *flame*)
120 DOLLAR—*USA currency* (*currency = country's money*)
121 CELEBRITY—*famous and publicly known*
122 HAIKU—*Japan's poetry*
123 FASHION—*jumping into time*
124 ARCHAIC—*jumping out of time*
125 LOAN—*money against time*
126 PENALTY—*money against sin*
127 OCCASIONAL—*from time to time*
128 ELBOW—*shown on person*
129 POSTPONE—*push later*
130 SOCCER—*ball between legs*
131 SPOILED—*stale stale* (*stale = descending in time*)
132 VIOLATION—against law, hence *perpendicular to justice*
133 YEARLY—year in-year out, hence *year* with *in and out arrows*
134 WINDOW—*added to a house sign*
135 AWKWARD TIME—*clumsy time*
136 PREPARE—*work before* (work starts)
137 CLEANUP—*work after* (an event ended)
138 PRINCIPAL—*basic money* (for investment)
139 CAPITALIST—*person* with *capital behind* him/her
140 BET—*money against money*
141 FOOLISH—*path of a fool*
142 OFFEND—*attack feeling*
143 INSULT—*offend offend*
144 OUTRAGE—*insult insult*

145   MEDDLE—make *work awkward* for someone
146   INTERFERE—*meddle meddle*
147   OBSTRUCT—*interfere interfere*
148   CONTEMPORARY—*of parallel time*
149   CONDUCT—*path of behavior*
150   FAITHFUL—*path of believing*
151   SHOPWINDOW—*window of a building*
152   CHESS—*table battle* (i.e., battle at a table)
153   LAWYER—*person soaked in law*
154   JUSTICE—*law law*
155   COURT—*building of justice*
156   UNJUST—*opposite of justice*
157   CRIPPLE—*person with* one good leg, hence one *leg* is *crossed*
158   VETERAN—*person having war behind*
159   VICTIM—*person with knife in*
160   RATIONAL—*follow reason* (reason = brain chooses)
161   FUNERAL—*people follow dead*
162   OLIVE—*tree of oil* (*oil* = *water with friction,* that is dense)
163   OLIVE BRANCH (symbol of peace)—*branch of olive tree*
164   SHALE—*oily stone* (*stone* = *hard on the ground*)
165   VETERINARIAN—*doctor for animal diseases* (*doctor* = *person in front of illness*)
166   SENATOR—*person in front of the Senate building*
167   CONGESSPERSON—*person behind the Senate building*
168   PUP—*"child" dog* (dog = teeth)
169   ROYALTY—people close to king (the crown), hence *people* and *crown*
170   RICKSHAW—*person pulling a wheel*
171   NICKNAME—*not* (*reciprocal*) *name*
172   PSEUDONYM—*name not name*
173   PAGAN—*person with many gods*
174   RUFFIAN—*crude crude person*
175   PARACHUTE—*umbrella in air*
176   SLAVEHOLDER—*person ahead of chains*
177   TITLE—*person under quotation marks*
178   MAJESTY—*king's title*
179   PUSHER—*person pushing drugs*
180   SCUM—*person for waste, refuse*
181   SHAVE—*cut beard*

182 EUTHANASIA—*kill dying*
183 PACIFIST—*person loves peace* (*peace = not war*)
184 SEASICKNESS—*sea* and *illness*
185 SQUARE DANCE—*square* and *dance* (*dance = legs and music*)
186 VERBOSE—*words words*
187 SETTLE—*pay unpaid*
188 TOWN—*house parallel to house*
189 LOUDSPEAKER—*magnifying sound*
190 THANKLESS—*not thankful*
191 SLAUGHTER—*killing cattle*
192 SUGGEST—*jump into brain*
193 RICH AND FAMOUS—*living above globe* (i.e., person living well and known around world)
194 CHILDHOOD—the *time* of *child*
195 ADDRESS—*lines on an envelope*
196 TITLE—*lines on a book*
197 EGG—*added to bird for better recognition*
198 WAR CRIME—*war crime* (*crime = knife in* already *injured*)
199 CAPITAL PUNISHMENT—*kill legally*
200 CONSCRIPT—*must soldier* (*must = no choice*)
201 PORK—*pig after* (slaughter), (*animal after = meat*)
202 AFRAID—*with fear*
203 BATHROOM—*room & bath* (*bath = body in water*)
204 AGONY—*pain pain*
205 INFERNO—*all fire* (as hell is sometimes depicted)
206 VITAMIN—*essential food* (*ingredients*)
207 OVERSEAS—*over sea* (*sea = water water*)
208 MAIN—*central central*
209 LEGAL FEE—*legal money*
210 OVERJOYED—*joy over joy* (joy = smile and be *pleased*)
211 CARCASS—*animal dead body*
212 BULLFIGHT—*person, battle & bull*
213 BORDER—*line between countries*
214 BARRACKS—*military barn*
215 COOL—*cold and not cold*
216 BARTER—*item against item*
217 BARK—*dog sound* (*dog = teeth; sound = music and noise*)
218 IRONY—*meaning* is opposite (*reciprocal*) *meaning*
219 ASSAILANT—*person behind attack*

220   HANDSOME—*face for picture*

221   ANTENNA—*transmission & ground*

222   AVIARY—*building for birds*

223   GOOD-FOR-NOTHING—*person for waste basket*

224   UNSOCIABLE—*avoids people*

225   COCK—*male hen*

226   HOBBLE—*walk awkwardly*

227   COCKTAIL—*mixed drink*

228   PIDGIN—*mixed language* (*language* = *sign between people*)

229   LOGICAL—*parallel to logic* (*logic* = *reason behind reason*)

230   PRUDENT—*avoid danger*

231   CONCEIT—*think of self*

232   SELFISHNESS—*feeling selfish*

233   PRIDE—*brain praise*

234   BOAST—*pride on podium*

235   VANITY—*boast on podium* (that is publicly)

236   NIGHTMARE—*fear and sleep*

237   PHILOLOGY—*science of language* (language = *sign between people*)

238   KEYBOARD—*lot of buttons*

239   BAZAAR—*eastern market*

240   THANKSGIVING—*day of thanks* (in USA the fourth Thursday in November)

241   PAINKILLER—*kill pain*, hence *knife* (kill) *into pain*

242   PAINLESS—*without pain* (*pain* = *friction in body and mind*)

243   RODEO—*horse jumping* (*horse* = *animal indicated with horseshoe*)

244   RISKY—*walk on ice* (*ice* = *solid water*)

245   FIREFIGHTER—*person around fire*

246   UNCONTROLLABLE—*impossible to control*

247   FIREBIRD—*Baltimore oriole* (scientific name *Icterus galbula*)

248   FIRE DOOR—*door against fire*

249   FIRE ESCAPE—*fire exit*

250   FIREPROOF—*safe against fire*

251   FIRE TOWER—*fire tower*

252   BENEDICTION—*God's blessing*

253   SNEER—*face curse*

254   FULL MOON—*moon* (*crescent*) *face*

255   NEW MOON—opposite (*reciprocal*) *to full moon*

256   HALF-MOON—*full moon and no full moon*
257   BEEF—*meat meat (cattle meat)*
258   REMEDY—*medication that improves* health
259   BEHEAD—*cutting head*
260   RESONANCE—*parallel signals*
261   SANITARY—*path of health*
262   INDIGNATION—*anger* with *reason behind*
263   MARRIAGE BROKER—*mixing hearts*
264   STRIFE—*battle of hearts*
265   BIT—*small part*
266   VENGEANCE—*injury against injury*
267   WRESTLE—*body against body*
268   CRISIS—*time of life or death*
269   TILL—*work on land*
270   UNHARMED—*without injury*
271   UNPROTECTED—*without umbrella*
272   NUTRIENT—*food value (value = time & money)*
273   UNTIMELY—at *awkward time*
274   SABBATH—*God's day*
275   RENOVATE—*make new again*
276   RECYCLE—*use again*
277   TOBACCO—*smoke & leaf*
278   NOTARIZE—*official signature (signature = sign path)*
279   MOTHER TONGUE—*mother language*
280   BOOKLET—*small book*
281   VIRGIN TERRITORY—*territory not walked* upon
282   HERMAPHRODITE—*mixed sex*
283   GONORRHEA—*sex inflammation*
284   MOLEST—*sex misuse*
285   ROSTER—*list of people*
286   LITANY—*list list*
287   SEX OFFENDER—*person-sex-guilty*
288   SALVAGE—*opposite (reciprocal) of destroy*
289   EXHIBITION—*pictures on podium*
290   HOP—*jump on one leg* (hence one leg crossed)
291   HOST—*person in the house* (when visitors are coming)
292   SCURVY—*bleeding teeth*
293   AMPLE—*good measure (scale)*
294   VIVISECTION—*cutting animals (cut = scissors)*

295   HERD—*overlapping animals*

296   STABLE—*horse & barn*

297   NITROGLYCERIN—*heavy colorless violent oily liquid,* chemically: $C_3H_5(ONO_2)_3$, used as explosive, until replaced by dynamite, invented by Alfred Nobel, which is based on nitroglycerine but more stable for transportation

298   EDUCATED—*person with many books behind*

299   ERUDITE—*very educated person*

300   ANONYMOUS—*book without author*

301   MARIACHI—*Mexican street music*

302   POLARIS—*polar star*

303   POLEMIC—war *between mouths*

304   CHIMNEY—added to the sign of *house*

305   JAW—*mouth and teeth*

306   BANYAN—*tree spreading around*

307   COLANDER—*pot with many holes*

308   HARVEST MOUSE—*cornfield rodent*

309   OPOSSUM—*marsupial of new continent*

310   NEW CONTINENT—combination of *new* and *continent*

311   OLD CONTINENT—combination of *old* and *continent*

312   STALACTITE—*hanging stone in caves*

313   STALAGMITE—*standing stone in caves*

314   CAVE—*hole in a mountain*

315   SERIAL KILLER—*person behind lot of killing*

316   RIOT—*people against police*

317   REVOLT—*people against government*

318   REVOLUTION—*people against dictatorship*

319   PITCHFORK—*field fork*

320   LADLE—*deep spoon*

321   SCOOP—*wide spoon*

322   PERFUME—*nose love*

323   HEAVY WATER—*water & heavy weight*

324   GLOVES—*cover hands*

325   SMOOTH—*without bump*

326   NATIVE AMERICANS—USA *aborigine people*

327   INUIT—ALASKA *aborigine people*

328   MIKADO—*Japan's emperor*

329   POET—*person behind poem*

330   SAVAGE—*wild person*
331   SCALE—*fish cover*
332   SARDINE—*lot of fish in a box*
333   PAJAMAS—*loose night clothes*
334   TIGHT—*overlapping adjacent*
335   LOOSE—*opposite (reciprocal) of tight*
336   THIMBLE—*thumb cover*
337   STONE AGE—*stone time*
338   BRONZE AGE—*after Stone Age*
339   WHEELCHAIR—*wheel & chair*
340   CAR—*wheel and armchair*
341   SALOON—*gate and lot of drink*
342   TALENT—*natural ability*
343   ABOLISH—*kill law (legal document)*
344   RAM—*male sheep*
345   PARASOL—*umbrella against sun*
346   ROSE—*beautiful flower*
347   ORCHID—*beautiful beautiful flower*
348   PHILATELY—*loving stamps*
349   PERHAPS—*possible and not possible*
350   PERIL—*hanging danger*
351   PRECARIOUS—*unstable danger*
352   PRUDENT—*avoid danger*
353   PROPOSE—*tell an idea*
354   RIGID—*not flexible*
355   REITERATE—*say again*
356   REAPPEAR—*appear again*
357   SELDOM—*not often*
358   SLEEPING MEDICATION—*sleeping medication*
359   SKULL—*head bone*
360   SKIRMISH—*battle not war*
361   PANG—*sharp pain*
362   RUMOR—*jumping talk*
363   SHADE—*under sombrero*
364   RUST—*iron friction*
365   SLAP—*attack face*

We could have continued for a while, but this is enough for testing one's ability to make correct guesses on words not outlined in advance. Readers should take a pause and insert the answers for all the words listed above. After having done this, they should return to the list of the 365 words and review each of the signs to see if they find the proposed solutions acceptable and related sufficiently well to the concept the sign represents. In doing this, one should recall that we are interested in formulation of a *sign language* and that Nobel is neither subject to rigorous mathematical judgments nor does it have to follow all the rules of linguists. After all, every language has its own rules and its own specialties. What we ought to be concerned with is to maintain internal consistency and avoid contradictions within Nobel itself.

Before proceeding to the third part of this book, we will continue with a list of additional words of Nobel. There are two reasons for doing this: first, to impress readers to the great potential of combinatorics, which allows us to come close to three thousand signs starting with only sixty basic signs and some forty arrows, in total, about hundred signs. The second reason is to allow readers before meeting additional signs to become more familiar with signs and simple combinations of signs that occur repeatedly in many different words. As undoubtedly readers have noticed, some signs occur more frequently in various combinations of words as other signs. In the table below, we give an approximate indication on which words are occurring more often than others. The numbers were based on examining a larger collection of words, less than three thousand, which is the total of all numbers shown because several signs appear in more than one word. The table indicates the relative importance of various signs, not according to their meaning but more for facilitating in learning the language of Nobel.

In reviewing this table, observe that some basic signs listed have not yet appeared while other basic signs we included among the sixty that we started and some of the additional conventional signs included later do not appear in this short list of the forty most frequent basic signs of Nobel.

Table 1

PERSON	380	MOUTH	100	HEAVY	60	POSSIBLE	30
HEART	280	MONEY	100	HOOK	60	SEX	30
BODY	180	ANIMAL	90	HOUSE	60	EYE	20
LEGS	140	BUILDING	80	CROWN	40	FOLLOW	20
TEXT	140	BATTLE	70	PICTURE	40	FRICTION	20
TIME	140	DOCUMENT	70	CLOUD	30	MAGNIFYING GLASS	20
WITHOUT	120	HAND	70	HARD	30	POSTER	20
WORK	120	PODIUM	70	ILLEGAL	30	SIGNAL	20
BRAIN	110	SHIELD	70	IMPOSSIBLE	30	SMOKE	20
BOOK	110	SUDDEN	70	PARALLEL	30	PERPENDICULAR	10

There are seven signs that we still have to introduce, which we will in part 3 of the book. Let us also mention that among almost 2,500 words that we have seen so far there are many important words that are missing.

In table 2, we have listed a selection of some two hundred of the most often spoken words in American English merely to give an indication that some often spoken words have not yet been introduced. We excluded from the list of the most common words articles *a, an,* and *the* as there are no articles in Nobel and many other languages, like for example all Slavic languages. In languages that have articles (like besides English, also German and Italian) if one wants to emphasize a specific article one can use instead of "*a*" and "*the*" (or in German *der, die, das* and in Italian, *il, la, lo*) the words *one* and *this/that* respectively. We have separated the words into nouns, verbs, auxiliary verbs, adjectives, adverbs, verbs, prepositions, and pronoun/pronominal adjective, and conjunctions and interjections. We stopped just after the first forty verbs have been encountered, counting separately grammatical forms of the same verb, as has been reported in the source book by Hartwig Dahl, *Word Frequencies of Spoken American English* (A Verbatim Book, Essex CCT, 1979, ISBN 0-930454-07-3). In this way, one can also get some insight into the relative frequency of nouns, verbs, adjectives, etc. The numbers shown have been rounded to the nearest thousand. Several words could be noun and verb, or noun and adjective, etc. A notorious example is the word OK, which can be interjection, adjective, adverb, and even noun. Such words have been indicated by asterisks and listed in corresponding categories if we felt that the different grammatical classifications may have a similar frequency of usage. An example is the word *like*, which can be both a verb and a preposition. On the other hand, the word *mean* is only listed as a noun and not as verb, as we (subjectively) felt that in common usage it is by far more often used as a verb than as a noun.

Table 2

Nouns

MEAN	4.0	THINKING	1.9	LOT	1.0	PART	0.8
SOMETHING	3.9	GUESS	1.7	TWO	1.0	YESTERDAY	0.7
WAY	3.1	BACK	1.4	FEELINGS	0.9	GIRL	0.7
THING	2.9	PEOPLE	1.4	FACT	0.9	POINT	0.7
THINGS	2.9	ANYTHING	1.4	DAY	0.9	COURSE	0.7
SORT	2.8	MOTHER	1.3	FATHER	0.8	SCHOOL	0.7
TIME	2.7	MIND	1.2	REAL	0.8		
FEELING	2.3	NIGHT	1.2	TODAY	0.8		
THOUGHT	2.1	SAYING	1.2	HOME	0.8		
KIND	2.0	DREAM	1.0	WORK	0.8		

Verbs

KNOW	15.3	SEE	2.4	MAKE	1.2	CAME	0.9
LIKE	7.2	CAN	2.4	SAYING	1.2	SUPPOSE	0.8
THINK	6.1	THOUGHT	2.1	WENT	1.1	TALK	0.8
SAID	4.1	GOT	1.8	TALKING	1.1	TELL	0.8
GET	3.3	COULD	1.7	SEEMS	1.0	COULDN'T	0.8
GOING	3.2	CAN'T	1.7	WANTED	0.9	MADE	0.7
SAY	3.1	LAST	1.4	TRYING	09	USED	0.7
FEEL	3.0	COME	1.3	MIGHT	0.9	TOLD	0.7
WANT	2.7	FELT	1.3	GETTING	0.9	LOOK	0.7
GO	2.4	REMEMBER	1.2	TAKE	0.9.	UNDERSTAND	0.7

Auxiliary Verbs

WAS	15.1	WOULD	3.8	THERE'S	1.2	WILL	0.8
IS	8.9	GOING	3.2	HAS	1.2	SHE'S	0.8
DON'T	8.3	WERE	2.8	I'LL	1,1	ISN'T	0.8
I'M	7.2	DIDN'T	2.7	HE'S	1.0	WOULDN'T	0.8
HAVE	6.9	ARE	2.4	WASN'T	1.0	DOES	0.8
IT'S	6.7	BEEN	2.1	I'D	1.0		
BE	6.1	YOU'RE	1.9	DOESN'T	1.0		
DO	5.5	I'VE	1.9	SHOULD	1.0		
HAD	4.3	BEING	1.7	AM	0.9		
THAT'S	3.8	DOING	1.3	HAVING	0.9		

Adjectives

THAT	27.6	WHICH	2.0	SURE	1.0		
THIS	8.8	MUCH	1.7	STILL	0.9		
JUST	8.3	EVEN	1.6	WHOLE	0.8		
ALL	4.2	ANY	1.6	OFF	0.7		
MEAN	4.0	LITTLE	1.5	ANOTHER	0.7		
ONE	2.8	THESE	1.4				
SOME	2.3	GOOD	1.4				
OTHER	2.3	LAST	1.4*				
RIGHT	2.1	SAME	1.0				
KIND	2.0*	FIRST	1.0				

Adverbs

ABOUT	8.3	OUT	3.2	TOO	1.6	ALSO	0.9
SO	6.8	UP	3.2	ALWAYS	1.4	AROUND	0.9
NOT	6.3	NOW	2.6	BACK	1.4	ELSE	0.8
WELL	5.5	WHY	2.3	ANYTHING	1.4	YES	0.8
REALLY	4.8	HOW	2.2	DOWN	1.1	SOMEHOW	0.7
AS	4.8	MORE	2.1	BEFORE	1.1	ANYWAY	0.7
WHEN	4.3	NO	2.1	WHERE	1.1	PROBABLY	0.7
THEN	3.9	HERE	2.0	AGAIN	1.1	AWAY	0.7
THERE	3.7	YEAH	2.0	NEVER	1.1		
VERY	3.5	MAYBE	1.9	ONLY	1.0		

Prepositions and Pronouns / Pronominal Adjectives

TO	29.7	INTO	1.2	I	65.2	YOUR	2.6
OF	20.3	OVER	1.2	YOU	26.6	THEY	2.6
IN	13.0	AFTER	0.8	IT	20.5	HIM	2.3
LIKE	7.2			ME	8.5	THEM	1.9
WITH	5.9			MY	8.2	MYSELF	1.7
FOR	5.2			WHAT	8.1	WHO	1.4
ON	4.8			HE	5.7	ANYTHING	1.4*
AT	4.6			SHE	4.2	HIS	1.3
FROM	1.9			WE	3.4	EVERYTHING	0.7
BY	1.3			HER	3.2		

Conjunctions and Interjections

AND	38.0			AH	1.9		
BUT	9.8			OH	1.3		
OR	6.9			UM	0.9		
BECAUSE	4.8			EH	0.8		
IF	4.5			OK	0.7		
THAN	1.2						
WHETHER	1.0						
THOUGH	0.7						

There are two important messages that follow from table 2: first, there are numerous words occurring often in spoken language (words of high frequency) that we still have not considered. For instance, among nouns: WAY, THING, SORT, GUESS, LOT, etc.; among verbs: SAY, GET, LAST, MAY, etc.; among adjectives: JUST, MUCH, EVEN, SAME, etc.; among adverbs: ABOUT, SO, AS, VERY, etc.; among propositions: ON, AT, BY; among pronouns and pronominal adjectives: IT, MY, WHAT, HER, etc.; and among conjunction and interjections BUT, OR, BECAUSE, IF, etc. Thus, clearly, at this stage we are not ready to use Nobel for everyday communications. In part 3 of this book, we will introduce signs for most, if not all, these important words, but before we advance, we should secure knowledge of most of the words of Nobel so far introduced. A way of doing this is to continue to list words that we can, construct using the basic signs so far discussed, regardless of whether the words are important or not. In fact, we have already met some esoteric words and will meet more that are included so to illustrate usage of the basic signs. Neither do we expect that readers have to learn all the words listed nor is knowledge of all these almost 2,500 words essential for continuing to get comfortable with Nobel. For example, if you are not a bird lover, you may forget about the words ORNITHOLOGY and AVIARY (to be soon shown) as it is unlikely that you will come across them in normal communications with anyone, except an ornithologist or zoo visitors!

So we continue with words that can be constructed using hitherto explained basic signs just to show the potential and the flexibility of Nobel. We have selected *Thorndike + Barnhart Beginning Dictionary* (by E. L. Thorndike and C. L. Barnhart, published by Scott, Foresman and Company, Chicago, 1959), but any dictionary of a similar size could do, and screened words starting with A to see how many words we can construct using basic signs of Nobel. We have been able to depict some 75 percent of words, of which about one-third use signs already considered, while two-thirds will be accounted for in part 3 of the book. For a dictionary that has approximately fifteen thousand words (some of which have several sub-terms not counted separately) this means that we can represent over ten thousand words by Nobel and close to four thousand words with the signs hitherto introduced.

Before continuing, we ought to tell the meaning of the five words of Ojibway and Maori people that we listed before. They are

ALREADY—time has come, hence TIME with LEGS
JUSTICE—BALANCE BALANCE
TWILIGHT—NIGHT is NOT NIGHT
HEEL—PART of a LEG
CRIPPLE—person with broken leg, hence PERSON and CROSSED
    LEG

Ojibway Indians, also spelled Ojibwa or Ojibwe and known as Chippewa Indians, originally inhabited the area from western Lake Erie to North Dakota. We adopted the spelling Ojibway even though Ojibwa is the most widely used, as the former was preferred by the Minnesota Historical Society Press. The language of Ojibway Indians belongs to the Algonquian family of languages, which includes Arapaho, Cheyenne, Blackfoot, Shawnee, Ottawa, and others, known also as Central Algonquian, which is the second most spoken American Indian language (after Athapascan family of languages widely scattered from Alaska to northern Mexico, including Navaho living on reservations in Arizona, New Mexico, and Utah, and Apache of northern Mexico and southwestern United States).

The words JAIGWA, DIBAKONIGEWIN, etc. have been taken from *A Dictionary of the Ojibway Language*, prepared by Slovenian priest Frederic Baraga (1797-1868), who became later the first Roman Catholic bishop of Upper Michigan. Baraga introduced his dictionary with the words "*it is yet very defective and imperfect*"—the very words that we ought to extend to our Nobel *universal language*. But, as indicated in the "Foreword to the Reprint Edition" by John D. Nichols, of the Department of Native Studies of the University of Manitoba in Winnipeg, "Some 150 years later it is not only a classic, but still the largest Ojibway dictionary and the most useful over the range of dialects." Our Nobel *universal dictionary* that is anticipated in the near future (and, in view of my age, will be worked on in a hurry as I have no time to work slowly), which awaits completion and is part of our efforts to "spread the word about Nobel" is not a classic, and if it remains "some 150 years later . . . still the largest" Nobel *dictionary*, it will mean that we have failed.

Now that we have selected words from Maori for illustration, we should also say a few words about that language. Maori is a Polynesian language. It has been said (according to *Webster's Unabridged Dictionary*) that "Maori" means "native, of the usual kind." We used as a source for selection of few words *The Reed Concise Maori Dictionary* compiled by A. W. Reed and revised by Timoti S. Karetu from University of Waikato, sixth edition, published by Reed Publishing, Auckland, New Zealand, 2001. In Maori language, there are only ten consonants:

H, K, M, N, P, R, T, W, NG, WH   and five vowels: A, E, I, O, U.

This, of course is more than Hawaii's language, which has no R, T, NG, and WH but instead has L, as witnessed by the name of the last queen of independent Hawaii, Liliuokalani. Her husband,

John Dominis, incidentally, was half Croatian. His father was a sea captain from the island Rab in the northern Adriatic, and his mother was English. John Dominis died shortly before Queen Liliuokalani was forcibly removed from the throne and imprisoned for seventeen years before she died, while Hawaii was annexed by the USA. President Clinton was the first US president to apologize to the Hawaiian people for the loss of their independence.

W = 2,600

We are ending the second part of the book with some 2,600 words. What is left are two shorter parts of the book. The first will cover half a dozen signs that need some introduction because they are not obvious, which will be introduced in the next section and will also cover grammatical rules of Nobel. The second part will illustrate use of Nobel on one hundred Chinese proverbs.

Should I apologize for bringing in several very rare and very exotic words? I don't think so. Just recall the story of Richard Feynman and ornithology! Rare words come rarely, but they come. But, if you press me to identify the most exotic word that was included, I would have no problems—I think this is the term "leap second." This despite that leap seconds come more often than leap years, which are around every four years, with the exception of those years coming every one hundred years but not every one thousand years. Most people may even not have heard of leap seconds. "Leap second" is "a second added at the end of June or December to a timekeeping system in order to keep measured time synchronized with the movement of the earth around the sun" (as briefly summarized in *Encarta* dictionary). If this is not enough, go to the Internet and search for *leap second.* The exact time is kept by atomic clocks. Since the year 1972, when the leap second was introduced for the first time (both in June and December of 1972), only thirteen years passed without correction. Thus in thirty-six years, since 1972, almost twice as many years had leap second either in June or December. The last leap second was in December 2008, the time this book was near completion, giving to the author one more second to end the book! The cause for adding seconds is slowing down of earth rotation.

PART 3

Signs That Need Some Introduction

$\mathbf{W}$e will introduce here half a dozen new signs that have no apparent connection with the words they represent. We will follow with a set of arrows of novel shape that broaden the already wide spectrum of arrow signs and we will end with a list of additional signs that complete the collection of the basic signs of Nobel.

WITH

We have seen the sign for WITHOUT, shown below, which we adopted from Greek alphabet, the sign that is used in typography to indicate text or words in correcting the proofs that should be deleted before printing. We have taken the beginning of Greek letter theta to represent WITH:

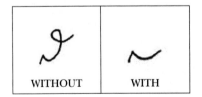

| WITHOUT | WITH |

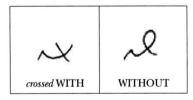

| *crossed* WITH | WITHOUT |

In fact, with a little imagination one can think of the sign WITHOUT as being derived from the sign for WITH (although it is the other way round), which is *crossed* and then drawn in a single move!

The basic sign WITH is used to arrive at signs for to HAVE and to OWN.

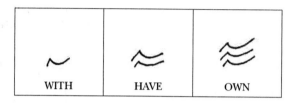

For example, person with a book, person has a book (but does not own it), and person owns a book would look like:

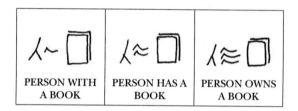

We continue with a list of words that use WITH:

LACK *not have*	OWE *not own*	LOST *have not have*	RENT *own not own*	NOT HAVE *crossed "have"*
NOT OWN *crossed "own"*	FORCEFUL *with force*	POSSIBLE *work with work*	VULNERABLE *possible injury*	TOOL *work with*
AGREE *parallel with*	ANYHOW *agree / don't agree*	USEFUL *with use*	VALUABLE *with value*	STRONG *with muscle*

人 ⌐⊂⊃				
CITIZEN *person with country*				

SUDDEN

We have seen the sign for DANGER, which in fact represents doubling of the sign for SUDDEN. Thus in Nobel, the word DANGER = SUDDEN SUDDEN. When you think of it, this is quite fair characterization of danger, which usually comes very suddenly, and because of that, it is dangerous. We have now to explain the origin of the sign for SUDDEN. When one thinks of what comes suddenly, one can characterize LIGHTNING as sudden phenomena. Lightning in Nobel is represented as "lot of electricity," so we took as the basis for the design of the symbol for SUDDEN the symbol for ELECTRICITY, but have erased the arrowhead. Thus, combining SUDDEN with itself, we obtain:

𝄢	𝄢𝄢	𝄢𝄢𝄢
SUDDEN	**DANGER** *sudden sudden*	**VIOLENCE** *danger danger*

We can now examine words based on SUDDEN.

⦰	⦰	⦰	𝄢	⊕
SPASM *sudden in body*	**CONVULSION** *danger in body*	**EPILEPSY** *violence in body*	**GRADUAL** *not sudden*	**RISK** *potential danger*

DARING *against sudden*	**COURAGE** *against danger*	**HEROISM** *against violence*	**MENACE** *continuous danger*	**EVOLUTION** *gradual gradual*
DARING *with daring*	**COURAGEOUS** *with courage*	**HEROIC** *with heroism*	**BLIZZARD** *dangerous snow*	**AVALANCHE** *violent snow*
TOUCH AND GO *dangerous instability*	**BRAVE** *showing courage*			

Observe how in Nobel one can differentiate between words that are close in meaning, like the words COURAGEOUS and BRAVE. COURAGEOUS is shown as going AGAINST DANGER, and BRAVE is shown as SHOWING COURAGE, hence BRAVE is COURAGEOUS on a PLATFORM. PLATFORM indicates publicity (showing).

HAND

The sign for HAND is based on Roman number five, which can still be seen on some clocks, which appears as capital V and stands for five fingers of a hand. Recall that Roman numbers 1-4 appear as I, II, III, and IIII, which you can take to stand for fingers of your hand. Only later IIII has been written as IV, which one can read as one before five, just as nine is one before ten: IX. In passing, one may recall that Romans did not have zero, and the decimal point did not exist even in the time of Galileo in the first half of the seventeenth century, so in that time, all numbers were integers. In order thus to increase the accuracy of experimental measurements, Galileo had to use very small measurement units so that the measurement numbers are very large, and hence are expressed with many digits. Thus Galileo introduced a unit for measuring distance, called punto, which was about 1 millimeter (to be precise, punto was equal to 0.094 centimeter), and his unit for time was almost as small as 0.01 second, which is the precision with which time is measured in present-day races. Galileo measured time by measuring the weight of the water flowing from a container at the constant rate. His unit for weight was grain, and grain was very close to one gram (to be precise, one grain was 0.945 grams). The unit for time, called tempo, was defined as the weight of 16 grains of running water, which was 1/92 seconds.

Coming back to Roman five, V, all that we did to this old sign is to orient it horizontally, because when the sign is written horizontally it can be readily combined with arrows and other signs. We will illustrate now many such combinations:

APPROVE *OK*	DISAPPROVE *not OK*	ACCEPT *take up*	TAKE *take in*	GIVE *hand out*
HELP *give a hand*	LEAVE *don't take*	SUPPORT *give give*	GREEDY *takes doesn't give*	CHARITABLE *gives doesn't take*
HANDSHAKE *overlapping hands*	REJECT *take down*			

CLOSE

There is no explanation for this sign. As you know by now, it is a rule of Nobel that all pictograms and ideograms of Nobel have some, even if tangible, connection with the words they represent. The sign for CLOSE represents an "exception that confirms the rule"! We have briefly mentioned this and even indicated the sign for ADJACENT as *overlapping* CLOSE. We will now elaborate and introduce signs for closely related concepts to CLOSE.

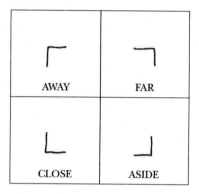

The three concepts ASIDE, FAR, and AWAY have been selected as "opposites" of CLOSE, representing mirror reflections and inversion of the original sign. We can immediately use this relation of the four words in making a number of useful words:

CASH	SAVING	INVESTMENT	TAX
close money	*money aside*	*money far*	*money away*
CENTRAL	TANGENTIAL	PERIPHERAL	IRRELEVANT
close to center	*aside of center*	*far from center*	*away from center*

The same four signs can be combined in an overlapping mode, giving

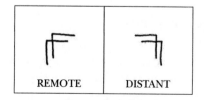

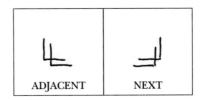

By combining the same signs with the mathematical sign of EQUAL, one obtains

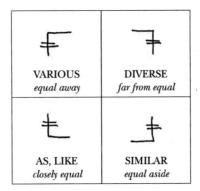

Finally, we can emphasize the vertical side of the sign to give them additional meanings:

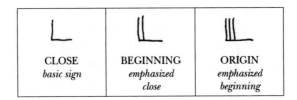

and

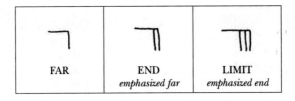

These signs can be combined with themselves and other signs as illustrated below:

SHORT *beginning close to end*	BEYOND *through limit*	START *move beginning*	DELICATE *as flower*	ROBUST *far from delicate*
EXCISE *cut away*	UNLIMITED *without limit*	RELATIVE *close blood*	REPTILE *animal close to the ground*	TAIL *body end*
DISPLACE *push aside*	EXPEL *push far*	OUST *push away*	DISTANT RELATIVE *far blood*	

MOUTH

We have briefly shown the sign for mouth when introducing the sign for language. Here we will elaborate. We depicted the word MOUTH by showing open mouth in profile that is very similar to the picture of Pac-Man in one of earlier computer games in which a "mouth" moves through a labyrinth and, if possible, feeds itself. Of course, mouth appears also in the sign for SMILE and SAD, but this particular shape makes possible combinations of the sign of mouth with various arrows simpler as is shown in the list of words collected below.

MOUTH *basic sign*	SPEAK	QUIET *don't speak*	TACIT *speak & don't*	TELL

PRAISE *speak upward*	**BLAME** *speak downward*	**GLORIFY** *praise praise*	**CONDEMN** *blame blame*	**MUTE** *not speak*
LOUD *above speak*	**SHOUT** *above loud*	**CRY** *above shout*	**WHISPER** *below speak*	**SING** *mouth & music*
CONVERSE *mouth parallel mouth*	**ARGUE** *mouth against mouth*	**VOICE** *mouth & sound*	**SPELL** *speak alphabet*	**LANGUAGE** *signal between mouths*
PHONE *mouth & transmitting*	**CHIN** *lower part of mouth*	**LIPS** *outside mouth*	**TONGUE** *inside mouth*	**BEAK** *bird & mouth*
SNOUT *mouth & pig*	**MESSENGER** *mouth & legs*	**TALKING SIMULTANE- OUSLY** *overlapping mouth*		

THE FINAL SET OF SIGNS AND ARROWS

There are still about two dozen basic signs that we have to introduce in order to complete the list of basic signs of Nobel. We will now list these signs and will briefly comment on some of them. This we will follow with a half dozen arrows that we have not yet introduced, and in this way, we will complete the list of basic signs and basic arrows used in Nobel.

The sign of CROSS has been used to indicate Christian religion, just as the signs of CRESCENT and the STAR OF DAVID were used when referring to ISLAM and JUDAISM, respectively. There are other religions that need to be recognized, including BUDDHISM and

SHINTO, the native religion of Japan, for which we use SWASTIKA and TORI (Shinto gate), respectively (to be shown shortly). Of course, we have not exhausted religions of the world, and Nobel is open to adopt additional religious symbols providing they are chosen to fit with the general requirements of Nobel for novel signs.

The sign for DOCUMENT is depicted as somewhat bent sheet of paper (or parchment as documents used to be placed on). Another sign which has an obvious appearance is the sign for KEY, which also stands for ESSENTIAL. The sign for LINE is shown as straight line. The sign for ROAD is shown as *horizontal* PARALLEL LINES. The sign for PALM, which, although not used often, is needed. We will now first present the above-mentioned signs and will illustrate their use in a selection of combinations.

ATTENTION FLAG	BOMB	CUP	DOCUMENT	ESSENTIAL KEY
LINE	MINE	OPEN BOOK	PALM	ROAD
ROCKET	SEAL	SEQUOIA	STRIPES	VIRUS

Sequoia, (official name: *Sequoia sempervirens*) is the tallest tree in the world, growing up to almost 380 feet (over 115 meters) and living over two thousand years—so it deserves its own recognition in Nobel! Below we show two signs of swastika and a sign for TORI

| SWASTIKA *left* | SWASTIKA *right* | TORI | | |

and additional arrows.

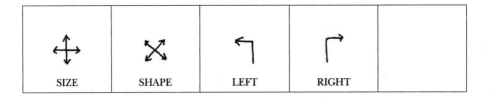

| SIZE | SHAPE | LEFT | RIGHT | |

The signs for SIZE and SHAPE, which we briefly mentioned when describing AMOEBA, a one-celled organism of no definite shape, are very similar, in fact are the same except for orientation. Both size and shape of objects can be different in different directions, but in order to differentiate between them, we took the advantage of graphical writing, which allows different orientations of such signs.

Combinations of Novel Signs

⊓ **ATTENTION**	⊓⊓ **ATTRACTION** *lot of attention*	⊓⊓ **ALARM**	⊓ϟϟ **WARNING** *attention danger*	ϟ⊓ **CAUTION** *sudden attention*
⊓✳ **SEXY** *attention over sex*	⊓⊓✳ **SEX APPEAL** *attraction over sex*	⊓⊓✳ **AIDS** *alarm over sex*		
BOMB	⊕ **ATOMIC BOMB**	⊕⊕ **HYDROGEN BOMB**		
DOCUMENT	**CONSTITUTION** *basic document*	**GRANT** *money document*	**LAW** *justice document*	**RULE** *document with direction*
TREATY *overlapping documents*	**EXCEPTION** *avoids rule*	**REGULARITY** *soaked in rules*	**ABOLISH** *kill law*	**WILL** *"dying" document*

APPLICATION *in-document*	**OFFER** *out-document*			
ESSENTIAL	**NOT ESSENTIAL**	**CAFFEINE** *coffee essential*	**ABSTRACT** *text essential*	**VITAMIN** *food essential*
FLAG	**WIN** *flag over battle*	**LOSE** *not win*	**TIE** *win and not win*	**CLAIM** *push flag*
PRETEND *claim and not claim*				
KEY	**LOCK**	**LOCKED** *under key*	**UNLOCKED** *key above*	**LOCKER** *locked/unlocked*
MASTER KEY *key above key*	**KEYBOARD** *key & alphabet*	**KEYHOLE** *key & hole*	**KEYNOTE** *key idea*	
LINE	**MIDDLE** *vertical line*	**SPINE** *middle of body*	**HALF** *horizontal line*	**BORDER** *line between*
BORDER *line between countries*	**ZONE** *line across country*			

MINE	**LAND MINE** *land & mine*	**SEA MINE** *sea & mine*	**MINEFIELD** *filed & mine*	
OPEN BOOK	**SCHOOL**	**SECONDARY SCHOOL**		
PALM	**COCONUT** *large fruit*	**DATE** *small fruit*		
ROAD	**BOULEVARD** *road with trees*	**MALL** *people road*	**PAVEMENT** *legs road*	**AVENUE** *building & road*
STREET *house & road*	**MARIACHI** *Mexican road music*			
SEAL	**SECRET** *in sealed letter*	**SECRET POLICE**	**SECRET SERVICE** *secret defense*	**PUBLIC KNOWLEDGE** *secret not secret*
SHAPE	**AMOEBA** *cell without shape*			
SIZE	**GREAT** *big in all directions*			

STRIPES	ZEBRA *animal with stripes*	US FLAG *stars & stripes*		
SWASTIKA	BUDDHIST TEMPLE	BUDDHIST	BUDDHIST MONK	BUDDHISM
SWASTIKA	NAZI	NAZISM	NEO-NAZI	

As we have seen, there are two different swastikas. Let us refer to the swastika which is oriented in mathematically *positive* sense (that is, anticlockwise), *positive* swastika. It is a symbol of Buddhism. And let us refer to the swastika, which is oriented in mathematically *negative* sense (that is clockwise), *negative* swastika. One can refer to the two swastikas by less emotional labels, like the left swastika and the right swastika, respectively, but *positive* and *negative* are more descriptive. The *negative* swastika was the symbol of Nazism and stands for Nazi movement, which of course is associated with *negative* activities. By doubling the sign of negative swastika, we obtain the sign for NAZISM. In contrast, *positive* swastika is a symbol of *positive* aspirations of Buddhism, a religion of central and eastern Asia, including India, China and Japan, developing from the teachings of Siddhartha Gautama, known as Buddha (enlightened one), living about five hundred years before Christ. According to Buddha, perfect enlightenment (nirvana) is achieved by mental and moral purification, which can free people from suffering, which is part of the life.

By doubling the sign of swastika, we obtain sign for BUDDHISM, and similarly by doubling the corresponding symbols for other major religions we obtain their signs. Thus by doubling the CRESCENT, we obtain the sign for ISLAM; by doubling the STAR OF

DAVID, we obtain the sign for JUDAISM; and by doubling the CROSS, we obtain the sign for CHRISTIANITY:

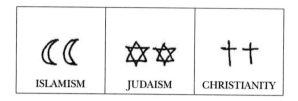

ISLAMISM	JUDAISM	CHRISTIANITY

In the same fashion and in parallel with NAZISM, we can obtain signs for other extreme political systems. Thus, by doubling the sign of HAMMER AND SICKLE, we obtain the sign for COMMUNISM. We need a sign for FASCISM, another extremist movement that was started in the 1920s by Mussolini in Italy, which got its name from "fasces," a bundle of rods bound together, including an axe, which was in Roman times the symbol of magistrates. However, drawing fasces, which became the symbol of Fascists, is somewhat involved, so we decided just to use in Nobel two axes as a sign for FASCISM. Nazism, Communism, and Fascism are more recent scourges of our civilization but by no means exhaust the sources of the misery brought to humanity by extreme ideological systems in more recent time as well as in the past. We may add and end our list with the notorious Inquisition of medieval Roman Catholic Church, which used torture and secret denunciations against its opponents. Among its victims, one finds Galileo Galilei (1564-1642), who spent part of his life in house arrest, for adhering to the heliocentric system of Nicolaus Copernicus (1473-1543) and Johannes Kepler (1571-1630). Even though Galileo had to denounce his views, legend attributed to him the famous statement *e pur si muove* (and yet it moves)—that is, the earth is not in the center of the universe. His contemporary Giordano Bruno (1548-1600), philosopher and, according to the church, heretic, who among other contributions has also interested in relationship of geometry and languages, was burned by the Inquisition. So we may symbolize terrorism of the Inquisition by doubling the sign of torch, to be thus reminded of February 17, 1600, when Giordano Bruno, a martyr of science, was burned at the stake in the center of Rome. After hearing the death sentence, he replied, "Perhaps you, the judges, pronounce this sentence against me with greater fear than I receive it." The sign for INQUISITION will remind us of the price paid by those who resist oppression.

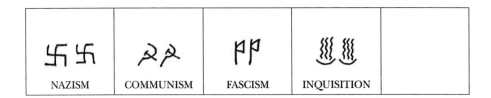

NAZISM	COMMUNISM	FASCISM	INQUISITION	

Doubling symbols in order to obtain signs for religions and political movements is not a novelty in Nobel. We have already seen similar doubling of crossed swords, a symbol for battle, as signs for military and police.

We have seen earlier the signs for SALT and PEPPER represented as the signs for WHITE and BLACK POWDER. The signs for white and black appeared as an EMPTY TRIANGLE and a FULL TRIANGLE. These two signs need some explanation. As many readers know, the color spectrum was for the first time shown when Newton let a sun ray fall on a prism, which dispersed colors as we see them in the sky on a sunny day after a rain in a rainbow. The story is that Newton had some money to buy a ring and get married, but by passing a store, he bought a prism rather than rings and made experiments on light spectra and got married with science rather than with a girl! Be that as it may, we will use triangle as a simplified figure of a prism and will construct signs for colors in this way. The order of colors in a spectrum is RED, ORANGE, YELLOW, GREEN, BLUE and VIOLET, which we will respect and use to get signs for the six colors as follows:

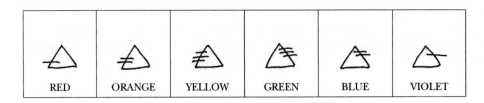

RED	ORANGE	YELLOW	GREEN	BLUE	VIOLET

BLACK and WHITE are then shown as all colors, or FULL TRIANGLE, and no color, or EMPTY TRIANGLE. With the color signs, we can create few additional words:

BLACK	WHITE	PINK	GREY	PENCIL	CHALK
		red & white	*black & white*	*black on white*	*white on black*
UV	IR	PALE	DARK	BROWN	COLOR
beyond violet	*beyond red*	*white and not white*	*black and not black*	*ground color*	*all colors*
RUBY	EMERALD	SAPPHIRE	AMETHYST	AQUA-MARINE	QUARTZ
red jewel	*green jewel*	*not red jewel*	*violet jewel*	*blue jewel*	*transparent stone*

Here UV stands for ULTRAVIOLET rays that darken and, in fact, harm your skin, and IR stands for INFRARED light, the part of spectrum that offers heat. Beyond UV comes x-ray, for which we have an alternative sign of HARD RADIATION, and beyond IR is MICROWAVE, for which we have alternative sign of SOFT RADIATION. The electromagnetic spectrum extends beyond x-rays to gamma rays and beyond microwave to radar and radio waves, which have to be considered separately.

There are number of signs based on SQUARE and many more based on CIRCLE, a number of which we have already seen. Let us first show a few signs based on square, some of which we have already seen:

SQUARE	BOX	SQUARE DANCE	BULLDOG *square face dog*	BULLFROG *square face frog*

GIFT	CORNER *part of square*	SQUARE KNOT		

We could have additional signs for words using "square" as a descriptor. Words like "square meal" for "a filling and nourishing food". But we have to realize that this is an idiom of American (English) language, that is, a "fixed expression with non-literal meaning," and that in other languages may mean nothing or even be a source of confusion. In order to appreciate this, we have to consider literal translations of idioms from other languages into English. You will see that they may convey confusing information. The same to a degree is true of some folk sayings that ought not to be literary translated. Thus for instance, English saying: *Who lives in a glass house should not throw a stone* is equivalent to Croatian saying: *Who has butter over his/her head should not go on sun.* Clearly with English weather, fog and rain, peasants going to the market (to sell butter) need not to worry much about sun. But in the continental part of Croatia, sun can be oppressive in summer, and butter will melt before you reach the market—if not protected.

The sign of circle appears in various combinations, some of which we will list below:

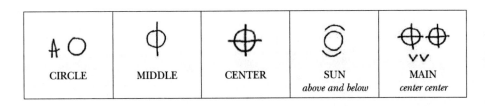

CIRCLE	MIDDLE	CENTER	SUN *above and below*	MAIN *center center*

PETTY *not center center*	CENTRAL *close to center*	TANGENTIAL *aside center*	PERIPHERAL *far from center*	IRRELEVANT *away from center*
IN	OUT	INPUT	OUTPUT	THROUGH

ATOM	CELL	ION	INSIDE	OUTSIDE
FORBIDDEN	VETO	TABOO		

Days, Months, Years

Now that we settled the signs for the base colors of the rainbow, let us show how the days of the week and the months of the year are designated in NOBEL. We start with the days of the week:

DAY *overlapping time*	**MONDAY** *first day after (Sunday)*	**TUESDAY** *second day after (Sunday)*	**WEDNESDAY** *third day after (Sunday)*	**THURSDAY** *third day before (Sunday)*
FRIDAY *second day before (Sunday)*	**SATURDAY** *first day before (Sunday)*	**SUNDAY**	**WEEK** *overlapping days*	**WEEKEND**
HOLIDAY *vertical day*	**HOLIDAY** *horizontal day*	**BEGINNING OF THE WEEK**	**NEXT WEEK** *coming week*	**LAST WEEK** *past week*

As one sees, the second part of the week is counted backward from Saturday. Sunday is shown as being "between" (or a "transition from") Saturday and Monday. Justification for using "vertical" and "horizontal" to indicate the working day and the holiday is in part that on a working day you have to be standing up (and working),

343

hence being "vertical," while on holidays you may stay in your bed or lie on a couch, that is, being "horizontal."

In a similar manner, we can indicate the months of the year using the sign for YEAR, which is depicted as "overlapping seasons." The sign for SEASON is that of a "global time," hence a superposition of a GLOBE (circle with equator line) and the sign for TIME (basic sign).

YEAR	JANUARY	FEBRUARY	MARCH	APRIL
overlapping seasons	*first month I*	*second month I*	*third month I*	*first month II*
MAY	JUNE	JULY	AUGUST	SEPTEMBER
second month II	*third month II*	*first month III*	*second month III*	*third month III*
OCTOBER	NOVEMBER	DECEMBER		
first month IV	*second month IV*	*third month IV*		

The Roman numerals I—IV below each month indicates the quarters of the year. The sign for year has four half-circle sections, which we use to indicate the four quarters (see below), and each quarter is used to count the corresponding months. We included as additional the sign for LEAP YEAR as JUMPING YEAR, as it occurs every four years:

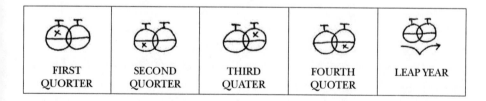

FIRST QUORTER	SECOND QUORTER	THIRD QUATER	FOURTH QUOTER	LEAP YEAR

Finally let us add signs for the twelve constellations that form Zodiac, the signs that play the visible role in Astrology, which unfortunately appears to be more popular subject than it deserves:

ZODIAC	ARIES *fire*	TAURUS *bull*	GEMINI *twins*	CANCER *crab*
LEO *lion*	VIRGO *virgin*	LIBRA *balance*	SCORPIO scorpion	SAGITTARIUS *archer*
CAPRICORN *goat*	AQUARIUS *water & person*	PISCES *fish*		

I Ching

Now that we sank into mysticism, we will continue with the wisdom of the old Chinese tradition as reflected in a classic of religious literature, the sixty-four hexagrams of *I Ching,* one of the world's oldest books. We displayed all the sixty-four hexagrams with their titles.

I CHING	THE ORIGIN	SUCCESS	BIRTH PANGS	REBELLIOUS YOUTH
	1	2	3	4
PATIENCE	CONTENTION	THE ARMY	UNITY	HOLDING BACK THE LESS ABLE
5	6	7	8	9

WALKING CAREFULLY	BENEVOLENCE	OBSTRUCTION	COMPANIONS	MANY POSSESSIONS
10	11	12	13	14
MODESTY	ENTHUSIASM	ACCORDING FOR	DECAY	TO DRAW NEAR
15	16	17	18	19
EXAMINE	BITING THROUGH	TO ADORN	PEELING OR SPLITTING	RETURN
20	21	22	23	24
NOT FALSE	GREAT DOMESTICAT-ING POWERS	TAKING NOURISHMENT	GREAT EXPERIENCE	THE WATERY DEPTH
25	26	27	28	29

TO SHINE BRIGHTLY, TO PART	ALL EMBRACING	CONSTANT	TO HIDE	GREAT STRENGTH
30	31	32	33	34
TO ADVANCE	BRIGHTNESS DIMMED	THE FAMILY	OPPOSITION	OBSTRUCTION
35	36	37	38	39
LET LOOSE	INJURED	INCREASE	NEW OUTCOME	TO MEET
40	41	42	43	44
TO COLLECT	RISING UP	TO SURROUND AND WEAR OUT	THE WELL	CHANGE
45	46	47	48	49

THE COOKING POT	SHOCK	RESTING	GRADUAL DEVELOPMENT	MARRYING THE YOUNGER SISTER
50	51	52	53	54
PROSPERITY	THE TRAVELER	GENTLE AND YIELDING	HAPPINESS	SCATTERED
55	56	57	58	59
LIMITATIONS	INNER CONFIDENCE	MINOR PROBLEMS	ALREADY DONE	NOT YET DONE
60	61	62	63	64

As we have shown, we were able to design Nobel signs for all sixty-four hexagrams, except for the word hexagram itself. But there is no problem here. Hexagram is a *geometrical* object having the shape of a six-pointed star, which consists of two intersecting equilateral triangles of the same size (i.e., congruent) having a common center and parallel sides, and it looks like STAR OF DAVID, the symbol of Judaism. Thus to get the sign for hexagram, we combine the signs for COMPASS (that signifies geometry) and the STAR OF DAVID:

HEXAGRAM

In contrast, a regular hexagon has six sides all of equal size and all angles being equal. It is the shape that bees use in building their hives, and the smallest hexagon is the chemical structure of MOLECULE OF BENZENE C_6H_6:

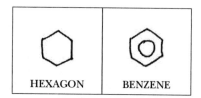

HEXAGON   BENZENE

We have depicted benzene in a way that a doyen of benzenoid chemistry, the late Professor Eric Clar, advocated: regular hexagon with inscribed circle. The circle symbolized *electrons*, which, in benzene and related compounds are delocalized and move around the whole hexagon. In contrast, electrons forming the usual chemical bonds in saturated compounds tend to be formally localized to individual chemical bonds.

Some hexagram titles of I Ching are simple and we have seen the corresponding signs before, but some titles are more challenging. One of the reasons to include these sixty-four hexagrams is just to draw attention to readers that signs can always be constructed but they may not offer the best illustration for the concepts considered. So it is an art to balance the urge to invent a sign or find a suitable combination of signs with the critical evaluation of the quality of the sign, from the point of view of how closely it relates to the concepts involved, how easy it is to reproduce it, and how easy it will be to remember it. Suppose we use 1-3 to grade for the quality of signs, by assigning the grade "3" to indicate that we feel a sign is quite satisfactory, grade "2" if a sign is plausible and acceptable although not as good as the signs having grade "3," and the grade "1" if one feels that the sign is somewhat arbitrary or having decreasing visual and aesthetic qualities. Such signs can even be viewed as a temporary solution, but until we get something better to replace them, they may remain useful. Finally, one should assign the value "0" to signs that one finds unsatisfactory or not good, and one feels that they ought to be discarded.

Readers may now go back to the sixty-four hexagrams and evaluate them individually. The maximal score would be 192, if all hexagrams are evaluated as grade "3." An intermediate grade of 128 would indicates an average of the grades 3, 2, and 1, while a low sum of 64 would result if one is equally unhappy with each of the hexagram signs. The score could go even lower, if one or more signs are found utterly unacceptable and got score "0." Just as instructors at colleges and universities in the United States are evaluated by the students near the end of the course, here readers have an opportunity to evaluate the transcription of *I Ching* into Nobel. Instead of 192, 128, and 64 as boundaries of the "outstanding," "fair," and "mediocre," more realistic numbers could be 150, 100 and 50. Since I, as the author, am not likely to hear your critical examinations and arguments in favor or against, you may share your scores with your friends or your members of family and argue among themselves to convince them in your judgments. But more constructive would be to come up with better solutions for the cases that appear unsatisfactory.

I should add that I am not necessarily satisfied with all the signs that so far are presented in Nobel, but after working on Nobel for close to twenty-five years, there comes a time when perfection has to be sacrificed to expediency. Otherwise, there will be no end in sight. I hope that the future, with possible interest and involvement of others, will bring further improvements to Nobel. I do, however, believe that there is a *core of signs,* to which I refer as *the best of Nobel,* to which I would assign the grade "3," that will survive criticisms and ought to be viewed to represent the spirit of Nobel. Let us list below a fraction of these signs not only to refresh the form of the signs that we have seen before but also as a guidance to readers of Nobel to show how novel signs and combinations of signs of Nobel ought to be shaped. We have mentioned at the very beginning of this book, in the introduction to Nobel, the very desirable features of Nobel:

1. Close association between the sign and what it represents;
2. Simplified forms that are easy to be reproduced;
3. Pictorial forms that are easy to be recognized.

The above three requirements may be viewed as "materialistic" or pragmatic. To this we may now add a "spiritual" component or idealistic component to be incorporated into Nobel when possible, which will elevate the quality of Nobel by associating with Nobel, if we may say so, some literary or poetic content. As illustration, we listed a selection of over 320 out of some 3,000 signs that have appeared in this book that may deserve the label "the best of Nobel" signs. They are shown on the next pages and are described on the pages that follow this short dictionary of the best of Nobel. All the signs shown have been already introduced, and thus this "exhibition" may serve to remind readers of what they by now know or could know.

1-35

ABDICATE	ABORTION	ABOUT	ABSURD	ABUNDANCE
ACCOUNT	ADDICT	ADJACENT	ADVENTURE	ADVERTISE
AIR	ALCOHOLIC	ALL	ALREADY	AMBIGUOUS
AMBITION	AMPUTATION	ANACONDA	APPOINT	APPOINTMENT
ARCHAIC	ARGUE	ARSON	ARTIFICIAL	ATMOSPHERE
ATTRACTIVE	AUSTRALIA	AUSTRIA-HUNGARY	AUTOPSY	AWKWARD
BACK	BEAUTIFUL	BEER	BERMUDA	BEVERAGE

36-70

BEYOND	BIBLE	BICYCLE	BINGO	BIOPSY
BLEEDING	BONE	BOSS	BRANDY	BREEDING
BREWERY	BRIBE	BRILLIANT	BROWSE	BUBBLE
BUDGET	BULLDOG	BUREAUCRACY	CALCULUS	CANCER
CANDID	CANOPY	CERTAIN	CESAREAN	CHALLENGE
CHARACTER	CHOOSY	CHRONOLOGY	CLIMATE	COALITION
COBRA	COLOMBIA	COMMON GRAVE	COMPLETE	CONDOR

71-105

CONFEDERA-TION	CONNECTION	CONSTANT	CONSTELLA-TION	CONSTITU-TION
CONTEMPO-RARY	CONTRADIC-TION	CONVERSA-TION	CONVULSION	CONVOY
CORRESPON-DENCE	COURAGE	COZY	CRAFT	CRITICAL
CROOK	CUBA	DEADLINE	DEEP	DELICATE
DEMOCRACY	DEMOCRATS	DESPITE	DETER	DIARRHEA
DIET	DIGEST	DIPLOMACY	DISCUSS	DISHARMONY
DISTANT	DISTILLERY	DIVERSE	DIVORCE	DNA

106-140

DRUGS	DUPLEX	DURING	ELEGANT	EMBARRASSED
EMOTION	EMPIRE	ENDANGERED	ENEMY	ENOUGH
EROTIC	ESTIMATE	EVENT	EXCEPTION	EXCESSIVE
EXCUSE	EXECUTION	EXIST	EXPECT	EXTINGUISH
EXTRAVAGANT	EXTREME	FACT	FALSE ALARM	FAMILY
FAMOUS	FATE	FEDERATION	FEVER	FICTION
FLAMINGO	FOCUS	FOOTPRINT	FOR	FOREST

141-175

FOX	FREQUENCY	FREQUENTLY	FRESH	FRIEND
FRIGID	FRONT	FRUIT	FRUSTRATED	FUTURE
GALAXY	GAMBLE	GANG	GHOST	GIFT
GLASS	GLUE	GOODBYE	GREAT	GUILTY
HAIKU	HARMONY	HEAT	HEAVEN	HELP
HEMORRHAGE	HESITATE	HIDE	HOLIDAY	HOLIDAY
HONESTY	HONEY	HONEYMOON	HOSTILITY	HUMANITY

176-210

IDENTICAL	IDENTICAL TWINS	IDIOT	IMITATE	IMPEACH
IMPOSSIBLE	INCOMPATIBLE	INCUBATION	INDEED	INDUSTRY
INFECTED	INFECTIOUS	INFLAMMATION	IN SPITE OF	INSTANT
INSTRUCTIONS	IOWA	JOKE	KISS	LANGUAGE
LET	LIE	LIFE	LIVING	LOITER
LOSS	LOYAL	LUGGAGE	LUKEWARM	MAGIC GLUE
MAIN	MAKE LOVE	MARKET	MASK	MASTER

211-245

MAYBE	MEAT	MEETING	MEXICO	MIDDLE AGED
MIDDLE CLASS	MIRACLE	MIRROR	MODERATE	MODERN
MORE	MORE THAN ENOUGH	MOTORBIKE	MULE	MUSCLE
MUST	NATION	NATURAL	NEIGHBOR-HOOD	NEWS
NOBEL PRIZE	NO SMOKING	NOT GUILTY	NOW AND THEN	OBESE
ODDS	OLD	ORDER	PARTY	PAST
PENGUIN	PERMANENT	PHILOSOPHY	PIG	POEM

246-280

POISON	POLITICS	POLYGRAPH	PORNOGRAPHY	PREGNANT
PRETEND	PRETTY	PRIVILEGE	PROFIT	PROMISCUOUS
PROOF	PROSTITUTE	PROTEIN	PUBERTY	QUALITY
QUARREL	RAPE	REASON	RECEPTION	REPUBLICANS
RIPE	ROBUST	RODENT	ROOT	SANDWICH
SATISFIED	SCAR	SEASON	SENSITIVE	SHALLOW
SIMULTANEOUS	SINGLE	SIT	SKELETON	SKY

281-315

SLAVE	SPECULATION	SPEED	STRAIGHT	SUCCESS
SWITZERLAND	TAX	TEENAGER	TEMPORARY	TEMPTATION
TEXAS	TEXTBOOK	THICK	THIN	TIBET
TIMBER	TIME CONFLICT	TOOL	TRADITION	TRAP
TREATY	TRIFLE	TRUST	TWINS	UNIQUE
UNITED NATIONS	UNTANGLE	VACATION	VALUE	VIRGIN
WEATHER	WEED	WELCOME	WIDOW	WILL

316-320

YÏŧ	YYÏŧ	ΔΔ	ŌŌⅡ	⋏ŌŌ
WINE	WINERY	WOOD	WORKDAY	YOUNG

We could continue, but these three hundred twenty signs should suffice for the time. Explanations for the signs illustrated are shown below. Words are grouped in set of 35 for easier inspection and search. We will make comments on very few of these signs only, because most can be understood without discussion.

1-35

ABDICATE = CROWN INTO BASKET
ABORTION = STOP BIRTH
ABOUT = CLOSE AROUND
ABSURD = AGAINST REASON
ABUNDANCE = OVERLAPPING FRUIT
ACCOUNT = MONEY PATH
ADDICT = HOOKED BODY
ADJACENT = OVERLAPPING CLOSE
ADVENTURE = FRICTION ON TRAVEL
ADVERTISE = LOT OF POSTERS
AIR = OVERLAPPING ABOVE THE GROUND
ALCOHOLIC = HOOKED ON GLASS
ALL = INWARD AND OUTWARD
ALREADY = TIME HAS COME
AMBIGUOUS = SMILE AND CRY AT THE SAME TIME
AMBITION = TOO MANY GOALS AHEAD
AMPUTATION = CUTTING PART OF BODY
ANACONDA = EMPEROR SNAKE
APPOINT = AUTHORITY CHOOSES
APPOINTMENT = OFFICIAL TIME
ARCHAIC = JUMPING OUT OF TIME
ARGUE = MOUTH AGAINST MOUTH

ARSON = ILLEGAL FIRE
ARTIFICIAL = OVERLAPPING OVALS
ATMOSPHERE = OVERLAPPING AIR
ATTRACTIVE = LOVELY BODY
AUSTRALIA = DOWN UNDER
AUSTRIA-HUNGARY = DUAL MONARCHY
AUTOPSY = CUTTING DEAD BODY
AWKWARD = CUMBERSOME HEART
BACK = PART OF BODY NOT SEEN
BEAUTIFUL = FOR PICTURE
BEER = GLASS & SMOKE
BERMUDA = COUNTRY, PART OF BERMUDA (DANGEROUS) TRIANGLE
BEVERAGE = COFFEE AND TEA

36-70

BEYOND = THROUGH LIMIT
BIBLE = BASIC BOOK
BICYCLE = LEGS PUSH WHEEL
BINGO = GAMBLE & LOT OF MONEY
BIOPSY = CUTTING DETAIL OF BODY
BLEEDING = LOT OF BLOOD
BONE = HARD INSIDE BODY
BOSS = PERSON ABOVE PERSON
BRANDY = GLASS & FIRE
BREEDING = OVERLAPPING BIRTHS
BREWERY = LOT OF BEAR
BRIBE = ILLEGAL MONEY
BRILLIANT = CUT DIAMOND
BROWSE = JUMP THROUGH BOOK
BUBBLE = AIR UNDER WATER
BUDGET = MONEY FRICTION
BULLDOG = SQUARE FACE DOG
BUREAUCRACY = PEOPLE AROUND DESK
CALCULUS = INFINITE AND INFINITESIMAL
CANCER = UNCONTROLLED CELL DIVISION
CANDID = OPEN HEART (HART ON TABLE)
CANOPY = FOREST TOP
CERTAIN = TOSS APPLE, FOR CERTAIN IT WILL FALL ON THE GROUND

CESAREAN = CUTTING PREGNANT

CHALLENGE = SILVER AHEAD

CHARACTER = HEART PATH

CHOOSY = CHOOSE CHOOSE

CHRONOLOGY = TIME PATH

CLIMATE = WEATHER WEATHER

COALITION = GOVERNMENT AND OPPOSITION

COBRA = KING VIPER

COLOMBIA = COUNTRY OF MOUNTAIN COFFEE

COMMON GRAVE = OVERLAPPING GRAVE

COMPLETE = BODY AND MIND

CONDOR = MOUNTAIN RANGE BIRD

71-105

CONFEDERATION = WEAKLY OVERLAPPING STATES

CONNECTION = OVERLAPPING HOOKS

CONSTANT = CROSSED CHANGE

CONSTELLATION = LOT OF STARS

CONSTITUTION = BASIC DOCUMENT

CONTEMPORARY = TOUCHING TIME

CONTRADICTION = HORIZONTAL AND VERTICAL AT THE SAME TIME

CONVERSATION = PARALLEL TALK (AGREEABLE MOUTHS)

CONVULSION = DANGER INSIDE BODY

CONVOY = LOT OF SHIPS

CORRESPONDENCE = OVERLAPPING LETTERS

COURAGE = WALK AGAINST DANGER

COZY = WARM & COMFORTABLE (COMFORT IS IMPLIED BY ARMCHAIR)

CRAFT = ART AND NO ART

CRITICAL = LIFE OR NO LIFE, THAT IS, A MATTER OF LIFE OR DEATH

CROOK = ILLEGAL PERSON

CUBA = COUNTRY OF (BEST) CIGARS

DEADLINE = BEFORE NOT LATER

DEEP = LEGS UNDER WATER

DELICATE = AS FLOWER

DEMOCRACY = PEOPLE ABOVE GOVERNMENT

DEMOCRATS = WE THE PEOPLE

DESPITE = AGAINST ABOVE AGAINST

DETER = ACT AGAINST

DIARRHEA = TOO MUCH EXCRETION

DIET = FOOD AND NO FOOD

DIGEST = TAKE FOOD & EXCRETE

DIPLOMACY = AVOID BATTLES

DISCUSS = CONVERSE AND ARGUE

DISHARMONY = PERPENDICULAR HEARTS

DISTANT = OVERLAPPING FAR

DISTILLERY = LOT OF BRANDY

DIVERSE = DISTANTLY EQUAL

DIVORCE = CUT MARRIAGE

DNA = MOLECULE OF LIFE

106-140

DRUGS = POISON POISON

DUPLEX = FUSED (TOUCHING) HOUSES

DURING = TIME IN BETWEEN

ELEGANT = NOT CUMBERSOME

EMBARRASSED = COMPLEX HEART

EMOTION = HEART CHOICE

EMPIRE = COUNTRY ABOVE COUNTRY

ENDANGERED = EXTINCT AND NOT EXTINCT

ENEMY = PERSON HATED

ENOUGH = STOP THE SCALE

EROTIC = INSIDE KISS

ESTIMATE = MEASURE AND NOT MEASURE

EVENT = SPACE AND TIME

EXCEPTION = AVOID RULE

EXCESSIVE = BEYOND LIMIT

EXCUSE = PLEASE-THANKS

EXECUTION = LEGAL KILL

EXIST = TOSSED IN TIME

EXPECT = THINK COMING

EXTINGUISH = KILL FIRE

EXTRAVAGANT = WASTING MONEY

EXTREME = TOP AND BOTTOM OF MOUNTAIN

FACT = HOOKED IN THE GROUND (THAT IS, HAVING A FIRM BASIS)

FALSE ALARM = FIRE NOT FIRE

FAMILY = OVERLAP OF MALE AND FEMALE

FAMOUS = ABOVE GLOBE
FATE = TIME CHOOSES
FEDERATION = STRONGLY OVERLAPPING STATES
FEVER = FIRE IN BODY
FICTION = HOOKED IN CLOUDS (THAT IS, NOT HAVING FIRM BASIS)
FLAMINGO = BIRD & FLAME
FOCUS = MERGE INTO BRAIN
FOOTPRINT = PATH BEHIND LEGS
FOR = AGAINST AGAINST
FOREST = LOT OF WOOD

141-175

FOX = ANIMAL WITH DOUBLE FACE
FREQUENCY = RECIPROCAL OF TIME
FREQUENTLY = COMING OFTEN
FRESH = COLD AND NOT COLD
FRIEND = PERSON LIKED
FRIGID = NOT KISSING
FRONT = PART OF BODY WE SEE
FRUIT = OVERLAPPING APPLES
FRUSTRATED = COMPLICATED HEART
FUTURE = TIME AHEAD
GALAXY = LOT OF CONSTELLATIONS
GAMBLE = TOSS COIN
GANG = ILLEGAL TEAM
GHOST = WITHOUT BODY
GIFT = BOX FROM LOVE
GLASS = HARD TRANSPARENT
GLUE = LIQUID WITH HOOK
GOOD BYE = HEART BEHIND LEGS
GREAT = BIG IN ALL DIRECTIONS
GUILTY = JUSTICE & DOWN ARROW
HEAVEN = ABOVE SKY
HAIKU = JAPAN'S POEM
HARMONY = PARALLEL (AGREEING) HEARTS
HEAT = ABOVE FIRE
HELP = GIVE HAND
HEMORRHAGE = LOT OF BLEEDING

HESITATE = GO OR NOT GO
HIDE = SET UNDER COVER
HOLIDAY = HORIZONTAL DAY
HOLIDAY = DAY TO RELAX
HONESTY = STRAIGHT TRUTH
HONEY = SWEET SWEET LIQUID
HONEYMOON = SWEET SWEET TRAVEL
HOSTILITY = LOT OF HATE
HUMANITY = PEOPLE AROUND THE WORLD

176-210

IDENTICAL = COMPLETELY EQUAL
IDENTICAL TWINS = TOUCHING TWINS
IDIOT = FACE AND NO BRAIN
IMITATE = COPY BEHAVIOR
IMPEACH = PUSH AUTHORITY UNDER JUSTICE
IMPOSSIBLE = WORK WITHOUT WORK (ENERGY)
INCOMPATIBLE = FRICTION IN BED
INCUBATION = SMOKE IN BODY
INDEED = TRUE TRUE
INDUSTRY = OVERLAPPING FACTORIES
INFECTED = ILLNESS JUMPING IN
INFECTIOUS = ILLNESS JUMPING OUT
INFLAMMATION = FLAME IN BODY
IN SPITE OF = AGAINST AGAINST
INSTANT = TIME IS NOT TIME
INSTRUCTIONS = OVERLAPPING DIRECTIONS
IOWA = TALL CORN STATE
JOKE = JUMPING LAUGH
KISS = TOUCHING HEARTS
LANGUAGE = SIGN BETWEEN PERSONS
LET = NOT KEEP
LIE = NOT SIT
LIFE = HEARTBEAT
LIVING = HEART BEATING
LOITER = WASTING TIME
LOSS = COST OVER REVENUE
LOYAL = LIKES AUTHORITY

LUGGAGE = OVERLAPPING SUITCASES

LUKEWARM = WARM AND NOT WARM

MAGIC GLUE = GLUE GLUE

MAIN = CENTRAL CENTRAL

MAKE LOVE = NATURAL LOVE

MARKET = FOLDING TABLES

MASK = FACE AND NOT FACE

MASTER = PERSON ABOVE PEOPLE

211-245

MAYBE = WILL OR WILL NOT

MEAT = ANIMAL AFTER (SLAUGHTERED FOR FOOD)

MEETING = PEOPLE AROUND TABLE

MEXICO = COUNTRY OF SOMBRERO

MIDDLE AGED = TIME AHEAD & TIME BEHIND

MIDDLE CLASS = RICH AND POOR AT THE SAME TIME

MIRACLE = WALK OVER WATER

MIRROR = NOT TRANSPARENT (REFLECTING LIGHT)

MODERATE = DRINK NOT DRINK

MODERN = JUMPING IN TIME

MORE = GO SCALE

MORE THAN ENOUGH = SURRENDER SCALE

MOTORBIKE = WHEEL PUSHES LEGS

MULE = HORSE & DONKEY HYBRID

MUSCLE = BODY FORCE

MUST = NO CHOICE

NATION = PEOPLE AROUND COUNTRY

NATURAL = OVERLAPPING BODIES

NEIGHBORHOOD = OVERLAPPING HOUSES

NEWS = OVERLAPPING NEW

NOBEL PRIZE = DECORATION DECORATION

NO SMOKING = SMOKING IS BAD

NOT GUILTY = CROSSED GUILTY

NOW AND THEN = NOW AND NOT NOW

OBESE = HOOKED ON FOOD

ODDS = WINNING AGAINST

OLD = LOT OF TIME BEHIND

ORDER = LOT OF DIRECTION

PARTY = LOVING DRINK

PAST = TIME BEHIND

PENGUIN = BIRD OF ANTARCTIC

PERMANENT = HOOKED IN TIME

PHILOSOPHY = SCIENCE OF EXIST AND NOT EXIST ("TO BE OR NOT TO BE")

PIG = ANIMAL & MUD, MUD IS SHOWN AS WATER OVER GROUND

POEM = TEXT WITH PATTERN

246-280

POISON = NOT MEDICATION

POLITICS = SOAKED IN BATTLES

POLYGRAPH = MEASURE TRUE/FALSE

PORNOGRAPHY = SINFUL KISS

PREGNANT = BODY IN BODY

PRETEND = CLAIM AND NOT CLAIM

PRETTY = CRAWLING BEAUTY

PRIVILEGE = SILVER BEHIND

PROFIT = REVENUE OVER COST

PROOF = STEP BY STEP

PROMISCUOUS = NOT CHOOSY

PROSTITUTE = HOOKER, WOMAN FISHING

PROTEIN = MOLECULE OF LIVING

PUBERTY = GROWING SEX

QUALITY = RATIO OF SIGNAL TO NOISE

QUARREL = BATTLE BETWEEN MOUTHS

RAPE = MAKE HATE (NOT LOVE)

REASON = BRAIN CHOICE

RECEPTION = OFFICIAL PARTY

REPUBLICANS = WE THE PERSONS

RIPE = FRUITS ON PLATE

ROBUST = OPPOSITE TO DELICATE

RODENT = GROWING TEETH

ROOT = PART OF TREE

SANDWICH = BREAD ABOVE AND BELOW

SATISFIED = PLEASED BODY AND MIND

SCAR = INJURY PATH

SEASON = GLOBAL TIME

SENSITIVE = HEART AND BALANCE
SHALLOW = LEGS IN WATER
SIMULTANEOUS = OVERLAPPING TIME
SINGLE = WITHOUT OTHERS
SIT = NOT STAND
SKELETON = OVERLAPPING BONES
SKY = ABOVE ABOVE ABOVE

281-315

SLAVE = PERSON BELOW PEOPLE
SPECULATION = HOOKED IN FOG (THAT IS, IT COULD BE FACT AND IT
       COULD BE FICTION)
SPEED = DISTANCE OVER TIME
STRAIGHT = NOT RIGHT NOT LEFT
SUCCESS = HAVE GOAL BEHIND
SWITZERLAND = ARROW THROUGH APPLE (WILLIAM TELL STORY)
TAX = MONEY AWAY
TEENAGER = CHILD AND ADULT (ADULT IS SHOWN AS NO CHILD)
TEMPORARY = NOT PERMANENT
TEMPTATION = SIN OR NOT TO SIN
TEXAS = STATE OF LONGHORNS
TEXTBOOK = IN-OUT BOOK
THICK = NOT THIN
THIN = ABOVE CLOSE TO BELOW
TIBET = COUNTRY ROOF OF THE WORLD
TIMBER = TREE AFTER (IT HAS BEEN CUT)
TIME CONFLICT = TIME BATTLE TIME
TOOL = WORK WITH
TRADITION = FUTURE FOLLOWS PAST
TRAP = PIT WITH HOOK
TREATY = OVERLAPPING DOCUMENTS
TRIFLE = NOT WORTHY
TRUST = BELIEVE AND CONFIDENCE
TWINS = PREGNANT PREGNANT
UNIQUE = COMPLETELY DIFFERENT
UNITED NATIONS = COUNTRIES AROUND GLOBE
UNTANGLE = CUT KNOT
VACATION = LOVELY TRAVEL

VALUE = TIME AND MONEY
VIRGIN = FEMALE NOT WOMAN
WEATHER = CLOUD OR NO CLOUD
WEED = GRASS WITHOUT USE
WELCOME = HEART AHEAD LEGS
WIDOW = WIFE OF DEAD MARRIAGE
WILL = (AFTER) DEATH DOCUMENT

316-320

WINE = GLASS & FLAME
WINERY = LOT OF WINE
WOOD = LOT OF TREES
WORKDAY = VERTICAL DAY
YOUNG = LOT OF TIME AHEAD

Let us make brief comments of a selection of signs, before we return to signs depicted in *I Ching*. Among the signs shown, there is only one pair of signs that are true synonyms. These are the signs for HOLIDAY, which is depicted as a day of relaxation and as "horizontal" day. This means that on that day, if you wish, you may stay horizontal (in bed), while on workdays, you have to be "vertical." The sign for VIRGIN is shown by crossing the sign for woman. This is meant to suggest that virgin is not yet fully woman just as teenagers are not fully persons. Of course, similarly crossing the sign for man, one obtains sign for young person who is not yet fully man. Perhaps with time, alternative signs would emerge that would replace current signs; time will tell. The signs for PREGNANT and TWINS are obvious, but observe the distinction between the sign for twins and IDENTICAL TWINS, where the two small bodies are touching, which can be understood as they have developed from the same egg.

Perhaps the signs for BOSS, MASTER, and SLAVE need a comment. Boss is a person in charge at work, above the rest, so he/she is person above all other persons under his/her supervision. Master is a title with its roots in medieval times and is a stronger position, a person with higher authority, such as in a school or college, and also ruling over slaves. So we presented it as PERSON ABOVE PEOPLE. The opposite then, SLAVE, is PERSON UNDER PEOPLE.

Let us also comment on UNITED NATIONS. The sign for United Nations in Nobel is COUNTRIES AROUND THE GLOBE, which, if you give it some thought, you may find that it is not only accurate, but also more accurate than the official name of the organization is, United Nations. It all depends on how one defines nation. My little *Merriam-Webster's Notebook Dictionary* has listed two meanings for NATION: (1) people of similar characteristics; (2) community with its own territory and government. Larger dictionaries tend to elaborate and have additional interpretations, but the two simple definitions will suffice. Clearly, United Nations' name and organization adhere to the second definition, which appears to be a practical approach. But one should not overlook that there are many nations, people of similar characteristics, who have a territory but not their own government (yet). They tend to be overlooked not only by United Nations but by other nations that have forgotten their own past when they have been deprived of self-government. Take for illustration Croatia, which oscillated between the two definitions of "nation." Croatia existed in the ninth and tenth centuries as a nation (just look at historical maps of that period); it was a kingdom for close to one hundred years at the time when there was no England, no France, and no Germany. Unfortunately, Croatia lost its freedom for one thousand years, being too close to more powerful countries, Austria and later Hungary, except for the coastal city of Dubrovnik (Ragusa), which kept its independence till came Napoleon, who, a year after crushing Venice, ended the independence of the republic of Dubrovnik. The long period of darkness that followed the loss of independence of Croatia in the eleventh century, however, did not mean that the nation of Croatia did not exist during all that time. The thousand-year dream, as people of Croatia have been referring to their desire for independence, finally became reality in 1991, when Croatia again emerged as an independent state. In Nobel, the sign for country stands in fact for both definitions of a nation. The sign for Croatia, which is BEAUTIFUL COAST, as its Adriatic coast with thousand islands, large and small, does not state whether Croatia is independent country, part of Austria or part of Hungary, or part of Yugoslavia. It merely indicates that there is such a country and such people, just as the sign for Tibet, ROOF OF THE WORLD, indicates that there is such a country and such people, and does not speak of its past, its present time, or its future.

We already commented on "the leap second," but let us return to comment the sign for LEAP YEAR, as JUMPING YEAR. It used to be that a leap year would occur every four years, and this is still correct for the Julian calendar, which has 365 days except every fourth year, 366. Julian calendar is still observed by several Orthodox churches, and interestingly, it has been adopted by computers! This calendar was inaugurated by Roman Emperor Julius Caesar in the year 46 BC. Because the movement of the earth around the sun cannot be simply described by integers, even if corrected every four years by adding a day, in 1582 Pope Gregory XIII approved a revision of the Julian calendar by having a leap year every year divisible by four, with a restriction that centennial years are leap years only if divisible by four hundred. This is the so-called Gregorian calendar that we use today. Thus, every one hundred years, the difference between the Julian calendar and Gregorian calendar increases by one day, except every four hundred years. With this rule, the year 2000 was a leap year in both calendars, leaving thus the difference between the two calendars to fourteen days till 2100, when it will jump to fifteen days.

A comment may be in place to elaborate on the sign for VIRUS. We have seen signs for atom and cell, circle with plus and minus signs, respectively. By connecting two atoms, we obtained a sign for molecule (strictly speaking, for chemists this would be a diatomic molecule, but we took the sign to represent any molecule). By connecting two cells, we obtained a sign for bacteria (strictly speaking, bacteria is the plural of bacterium, i.e., lot of bacterium). A bacterium is a single-cell system, which is why we speak of bacteria. We hardly need a sign for bacterium, because a single bacterium is hardly to cause problems; it is bacteria that cause problems (illness) or are useful (e.g., in fermentation of beer and wine). Combination of two circles, one with positive sign (atom) and one with negative sign (cell) suggests something that has properties of molecules and bacteria—and that is virus. It can form crystals like molecules, and it can cause illness as bacteria, thus the sign for virus appears appropriate, although somewhat abstract.

We have seen the signs CUMBERSOME, COMPLEX, and COMPLICATED. We have also seen two combinations involving these signs:

| AWKWARD | EMBARRASSED | FRUSTRATED |

| BLURRED | MIRAGE | HALLUCINATION |

Here we collected additional illustrations:

| NOVICE | COMPETENT | GENIUS |

| BEGINNER | EXPERT | MASTERMIND |

Observe the distinction between the two sets of signs. In the first group, the arrow is coming out of brain (like in the signs THINK, THOUGHT). Clearly a novice has no good idea of what is going on, but a brain with complex thoughts can only come from a competent person, while finally, complicated thoughts characterize genius, scientists like Albert Einstein, Stephen Hawking, Nikola Tesla; or composers like Johann Sebastian Bach, Wolfgang Amadeus Mozart, Ludwig van Beethoven; or writers like Miguel de Cervantes, William Shakespeare; or artists like Leonardo da Vinci (a scientist, mathematician, engineer, inventor, anatomist, painter, sculptor, architect, botanist, musician, and writer) and Michelangelo Buonarroti (sculptor, painter, architect, and poet).

There is only one small group of signs that we would like to introduce and comment, and they relate to sex or, to be more specific, to sex organs. The reason for adding these signs is to put the matter to rest and to prevent teenagers from speculating or considering construction of alternative signs for these words (that one can find in any sizable dictionary). Here they are:

PENIS	GLANS	TESTICLE
VAGINA	VULVA	UTERUS

Let leave this delicate topic of sex, which is important for propagation of life, and which itself can be cumbersome, complex, and complicated for humans but also other species with the corresponding sign, without contemplating to describe details:

SEX CUMBERSOME	SEX COMPLEX	SEX COMPLICATED

Let us end this section with comments on the signs for the sixty-four hexagrams of *I Ching*:

1. Origin = emphasized beginning; beginning = emphasized close
2. Success = having goal behind

3. Birth = female output; pain = friction in body and soul (mind)
4. Children against elderly people
5. To be parallel (not against) to those against (perpendicular)
6. Claim = push flag; contention = have claim against those not agreeing with
7. Army = lot of military people
8. Unity = merge into union; union = overlapping rings
9. Pulling (back) those not capable
10. Walk alert; alert = be awake awake
11. Benevolence = leaning to kindness; leaning = not vertical
12. Obstruction is shown as having lot of difficulties
13. Companions are people with whom we agree
14. (People) who own much have many possessions
15. Modest is shown as being not proud
16. Enthusiasm is shown as heart over heart (liking something very much)
17. Agree is shown as being parallel with (something)
18. Decay is shown as spreading (disappearing) with time
19. Draw near is the same as pull close
20. To examine something one may use magnifying glass, hence push magnification
21. Biting thorough = complete bite; complete = body and mind
22. Adorn = give decoration; decoration = star
23. Peeling is shown as cutting away the top top part of something
24. Return means to come again
25. False = not true, hence not false is shown as the opposite (reciprocal)
26. Great = big in all directions; power = emphasized force; domestic = roof
27. Taking nourishment is shown as taking food
28. Experience is shown as having lot of work behind
29. The watery depth is shown as depth below water
30. To shine brightly = lot of shine; shine = lot of light; light = part of lightning
31. Embracing is shown as hands close around
32. Constant = not (crossed) change
33. To hide is shown as pushing something under cover

34. Strength (of a person) is shown as muscle; muscle = body force
35. In order to advance, one has to push legs forward
36. Bright = lot of shine; shine = lot of light; dimmed is shown as being overturned
37. Family is made of male and female (person)
38. Opposition = not government (reciprocal)
39. Obstruction means having lot of difficulties
40. Let loose is shown as let let; let = not keep; keep = fence
41. Injured (person, animal) is (person, animal) with injury
42. Increase is shown as moving up the present state (indicated by adding arrow head)
43. New = coming in time; outcome = final result; result = end output
44. To meet somebody, one has to cross paths
45. Collecting is shown as adding and adding, hence summing and summing
46. Rising up is showing ascending against authority
47. To surround (something) is shown as completely encircle (it)
48. The well is shown as water hole; hole is shown as a part of a loop
49. Change = opposing bent arrows (one of the basic signs of Nobel)
50. For = against against; flame = smoke smoke
51. Shock is shown as sudden worsening emotion; emotion = heart choice
52. Relaxing = crossed legs
53. Gradual = not (crossed) sudden; development = grow grow
54. Marriage = overlapping rings; sister = overlapping females; younger = after
55. Prosperity = wealth wealth (touching values); value = time & money
56. Traveler is shown as a person with suitcase
57. Gentle = kind kind
58. Happiness is shown as being very pleased (pleased pleased)
59. If there are a lot of spreading, things will be scattered
60. Limitations = lot of limits; limit = emphasized end; end = emphasized far

61. Confidence = believe and trust; inner confidence = feeling confidence
62. Minor = size below; major = size above
63. Already complete, already = time has come
64. Not already = crossed already

On Grammar of Nobel

Before we continue with illustrations of text written in Nobel, it is time to make some comments on the grammar of Nobel. All those who speak other languages besides their own mother tongue may recall difficulties that grammar introduces in the learning of languages. Some languages have simpler grammar, some more elaborate. Let take Latin language as a standard. Then there are languages with more complicated grammar, and I dare to say that my native Croatian is one of these, but there are languages with simpler grammar, which include German and English. The first hurdle is the so-called declension, the rules that govern how are words modified when conveying the state and the direction of activity involving them. In English the noun remains constant, and the meaning is conveyed with prepositions such as "of," "to," "from," etc., but in Latin (and Slavic languages, with exception of Bulgarian and Macedonian) the noun ending usually also changes. Because different words having different endings, there are plenty of complications that one has to learn if one is to speak correctly. And even if this is not enough, there are situations when different cases have the same ending, but may have different accents! I recall how, soon after coming to England for graduate study, I received an invitation from a certain Dr. Walker, presumably one of the faculty of Cambridge University, for an afternoon drink of tea. He expressed his interest in the Croatian language, which was the reason for contacting me. Upon my arrival, Dr. Walker brought me into a room full of books, journals, and newspapers and suggested that he read sections in Croatian language from one of the best-known epic poem in Croatian literature, considered the pearl of Croatian literature, *The Death of Smail Aga Čengić*. The poem describes the time of the conflicts of Christians with Muslims during the Turkish occupation of Bosnia and was written by Ivan Mažuranić, a governor of Croatia, the founder of the University Library of the University of Zagreb in 1876. I may add that reading poetry in foreign language is more difficult than reading prose, which only indicated that Dr. Walker was not a beginner but a scholar of the Croatian language.

After getting over a few pages, Dr. Walker stopped for a minute and asked me whether a particular word was dative or accusative (the third or the fourth case out of seven cases of Croatian language). I tried with the standard "to whom, to what" against "of whom, what" and was not sure because the ending of the particular word could fit both cases. Just to get rid of the question, I decided that this is more likely to be dative than accusative and so told Dr. Walker. He looked at me suspiciously and then told me that it is not dative but accusative because, he continued, a noun that ends in "a" has ending "u" for both dative and accusative, but in dative, the accent is "short" and in accusative it is "long" (or vice versa, I never even tried to figure this rule out), and he said that the accent shown in the text is "long." I may add that Croatian language when written or printed does not show accents in text. There are in Croatian four accents: up, down, short, and long; and obviously Dr. Walker had a book that was specially printed with accents for foreign-speaking people. I should also add that during eight years of intermediate schooling, I never heard of the rule that Dr. Walker knew about! Well, I may have not been a talent for languages, including the official Croatian, as we who originally came from northern part of Croatian Adriatic coast (and islands) speak a dialect, which is sufficiently different from the official Croatian language that people in the capital of Croatia, Zagreb, have difficulty to understand us. Be that as it may, I was astonished with Dr. Walker and his mastering of Croatian grammar—and a few days later I was even more astonished when, visiting the Philosophical Library of the University of Cambridge, on the board next to the entrance door I saw an announcement listing Dr. Walker as official translator for twenty-six European and other languages.

For sure, I am not alone in complaining about complexities and difficulties of grammars of different languages. Italian mathematician Giuseppe Peano (1858-1932) was interested in promoting Latin as an international language, at the time when Latin was practically a dead language (used still by many Roman Catholic priests and for nomenclature in biology and medicine). Peano decided to simplify grammar of Latin and thus created an artificial language, modified Latin, which he thought may be more acceptable to other users. Thus for example, Peano argued, instead of saying something like "I was yesterday in theater," one could say "I am yesterday in theater" because the word "yesterday" already indicates the past. Artificial languages can afford such simplifications based on simple logic, and for example, Esperanto has only sixteen grammar rules, all which can fit on a single page of a book—not hundreds of pages that grammars of natural languages often require. This is encouraging, and we thus set very simple grammar rules for Nobel that we will briefly outline.

THE PAST—THE PRESENT—AND THE FUTURE

Normally, by writing in Nobel, one expresses the present tense. If one needs to express the past or the future, this is possible in Nobel in two ways. One way is to continue to write in the present but, at the very beginning of the sentence, indicate the past or the future with the respective signs shown below, which have the sign of "time" and down-step and up-step arrows associated with them. The very "down-step arrow" and the "up-step arrow" are the signs what indicate the past and the present, respectively:

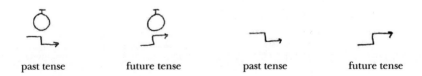

| past tense | future tense | past tense | future tense |

Here are several illustrations of the past and the future tense of selected verbs:

go	went	will go
see	saw	will see
work	worked	will work
listen	listened	will listen
think	thought	will think

We should add that there is yet another way to express future, and that is by using the sign WILL (heart pushes). So the future tense for the five illustrations shown above may also be expressed as

will go	will see	will work	will listen	will think

INFINITIVE

Infinitive is a grammatical form of a verb with no reference to particular person, subject, or tense. In English, it has particularly simple form: the verb is preceded by the word "to." We have adopted the same simple form for Nobel as illustrated below:

to go	to see	to work	to listen	to think

THE PASSIVE FORM

According to the *Encarta World English Dictionary*, "passive" grammatically is defined as

> EXPRESSING ACTION DONE TO THE SUBJECT indicating that the apparent subject of a verb is a person or thing undergoing, not performing, the action of the verb, as in "*We are given work to do.*"

So we need a format of sign that would correspond, for the above illustration, to "are given." We decided in Nobel to depict such passive form with the "past tense" step down arrow to which is superimposed the mathematical sign of *equal.* Thus for the five verbs used for illustration of past and future tense and infinitive, we have

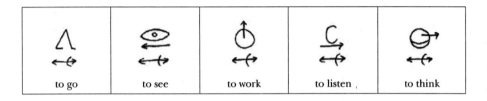

is gone	is seen	is worked	is listened	is thought

Now, if one wants the past tense of passive:

was gone	was seen	was worked	was listened	was thought

All that is needed is to precede the sentence with the sign for the past tense, and in the case of the future passive tense, one precedes the sentence with the sign for the future.

THE CONDITIONAL TENSE

We are now left to design a format for the conditional tense, which, according to *Encarta* dictionary is defined as follows:

> Stating a condition or limitation used to describe a clause, conjunction, verb form or sentence that expresses a condition or limitation.

Thus the conditional tense relates to a situation, which if satisfied would result in certain activities. In other words, they relate to future activities that may or may not occur, which will depend on the conditions posted. We have therefore taken the combination of the *up-step arrow* and the mathematical sign *equal* to stand for conditional tense. Thus, we have

would go	would see	would work	would listen	would think

PRESENT CONTINUOUS

This grammatical tense indicates that an action has started in the past and still continues. In Nobel, this tense is presented as "growing future" or "growing into the future" by simply adding an additional arrowhead to the sign for future.

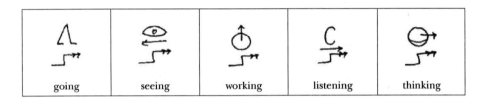

| going | seeing | working | listening | thinking |

PAST PARTICIPLE

This grammatical tense indicates in English an activity that has fully ended and is represented by step-down arrow with additional arrowhead:

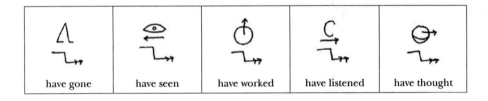

| have gone | have seen | have worked | have listened | have thought |

SUMMARY OF VARIOUS GRAMMATICAL TENSES

In the following cells, we have summarized all grammatical tenses on the verb *to give*, that was used in the *Encarta World English Dictionary* to illustrate the passive voice.

present	past	future	infinite	passive
give	gave	will give	to give	is given
conditional	continuous	past participle	present past	present future
would give	giving	have given	give & given	give & will give

We added two more grammatical tenses at the end for activities that have started in the past and still continue and the activities of the present that will continue.

NOUN-VERB DIFFERENTIATION

There are many words in English (and presumably in other languages) which are the same for the noun and the verb. For example,

gamble	insert	lounge	pass
guess	interview	mold	pattern
halt	judge	monitor	peel
harm	kick	number	pervert
heap	kiss	offer	
hurt	knock	pack	

Sometimes it may be clear from the context whether the sign of Nobel stands for a noun or the verb, but if that is not the case, we need to find a way to clarify the situation. In addition, there are many words that can be either a noun or a verb, but the two have slightly or fully different meanings. Such are the words like

Word	Meaning of the noun	Meaning of the verb
Hurry	Rush	Move quickly
Implement	Tool	Fulfill
Institute	Organization	Establish; start
Keep	Food and shelter	Adhere to; protect; hold
Labor	Job; all workers	Childbirth
Landscape	Natural scenery	Plant gardens and lawns
Light	Light source; brighten	Set fire; brighten
Limit	End point	Restrict
Loom	Weaving machine	Come into sight
Lumber	Building wood	Move heavily

In the case of such words, Nobel just uses a different sign for a noun and for a verb, and thus this kind of overlap of noun-verb configuration does not cause problem. For many signs in Nobel, it may be immediately clear whether they represent a noun or a verb, but this need not be the case when signs can stand for both noun and verb. To avoid such ambiguities, Nobel has two subscript indicators, one in the form of an arrowhead and the other in a form of a chalice or cup (inverted arrowhead). They will be used to make text easy to understand. Some readers may recollect that the two signs also stand for "male" and "female" (and indeed are related to our signs for male and female). We use these signs to indicate nouns (using *cup*) and verbs (*arrowhead*) as illustrated below:

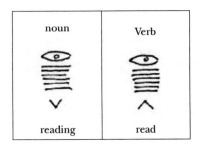

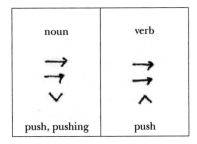

noun	verb
thinking	think
noun	verb
giving	give

noun	verb
speaking	speak
noun	verb
rain	rain

ADVERB-ADJECTIVE DIFFERENTIATION

In a similar manner in which we differentiated nouns and verbs, we can distinguish adverbs and adjectives, the former adding to the description of nouns and the latter to the description of verbs. This we do by doubling the subscript indicators as illustrated below.

adjective	adverb
beautiful	beautifully
adjective	adverb
deep	deeply

adjective	adverb
main	mainly
adjective	adverb
gentle	gently

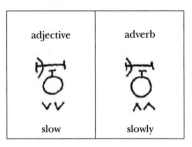

The four subscript indicators, those for nouns, verbs, adjectives, and adverbs, will clarify possible ambiguity when it arrives if a word can have multiple grammatical roles. For example, in English there are words that can be noun, verb, and adjective, like "last," which as a noun stands for "end," as a verb stands for "continue," and as an adverb stands for "most recent, final," and "manifest," which as a noun stands for "cargo list," as a verb stands for "make clear," and as an adverb stands for "obvious." There are also words in English that can be noun, adjective, and adverb, like the word "no," which as noun stands for "denial," as adjective stands for "not any," and as adverb stands for "not at all." By using the subscript indicators, the three cases can be easily distinguished. As if this is not enough, there are words in English that can be noun, adjective, adverb, and pronoun, like the word "none," which as noun and adjective stands for "not any," as adverb stands for "not at all," and as pronoun stands for "no one."

There are words that in addition to being adjectives and adverbs are also prepositions, like "over." Before ending this section on grammar of Nobel, we will list signs for numerous prepositions to make it convenient for readers to locate such signs. As will be seen, many of them involve some convention, and clearly, alternative conventions could be considered.

SINGULAR-PLURAL

As we have seen, very few words in Nobel have distinctive forms for singular and plural, such as person-people, from which one can generate numerous derivatives, like child-children, soldier-soldiers, friend-friends, etc. Clearly one needs a more general rule for forming plural from singular or vice versa. Often, one can, from the text, understand whether one speaks in singular or one refers to plural. In Japanese language, someone told me, there is no difference between the kanji signs for singular and plural, which are inferred from the text. So, as a rule, if it is apparent from the text whether one refers to singular or plural, we would simply do nothing. However, if it is not clear, we will use indicator subscript for an item (#) if the word is singular and will double the sign (# #), which means "many" to indicate plural.

There are words, in English and other languages, which exist only in plural. Such are, for example:

ceramics
dues
fireworks
folks
jeans
overalls

In such situations, clearly, one does not need to use subscript indicator to indicate plural. In addition, there are also words in English, which have different meaning in singular and plural, such as

Word	Meaning of singular	Meaning of plural
Chain	Series of links	Bondage
Cloth	Fabric	Garment
Custom	Usual practice	Import tax
Effect	Result, influence	Belongings

Here again, one does not need to use subscript indicator because the two different meanings will have two different signs. We follow with a few illustrations of singular-plural words:

house	houses	money	monies
tree	trees	flower	flowers
book	books	apple	apples

To make the story about singular-plural complete, we should add that there are words in English (and possibly other languages) that exist only in singular form, like the word "regard" (respect, esteem). Clearly again, in such situations, one does not need to use subscript indicator.

NOUN CASES

We will end this brief review of the grammatical rules of Nobel with illustration of the prefixes to be used in declensions of nouns. They include prepositions and conjunctions.

PREPOSITIONS

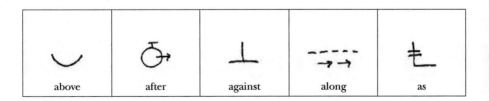

above	after	against	along	as

at	below	between	beyond	but
circa	despite	except	in	inside
into	like	neither	notwithstanding	on
with	without			

CONJUNCTIONS

after	although	but	however	if
inasmuch	neither	notwithstanding	only	or
over	than			

Before we proceed with the next part of the book in which we have collected 35 pages of text to illustrate use of Nobel, we will list signs for words that will enrich our vocabulary and which will make it easier to read the collection of one hundred Chinese proverbs that we selected for illustration of Nobel. This include some words that have been already seen, but appear less frequently, so it will not hurt to see them explained once again. The already-collected set of prepositions and conjunctions shown on previous pages will further help readers when reading given text for the first time. The words are listed in an arbitrary way, but at the end, explanation for the signs is presented in alphabetical order.

UNION *overlapping rings*	**OBSTRUCTION** *many difficulties*	**POSSESSION** *items own*	**MODESTY** *not pride*	**DIM** *brightness collapse*
GREAT *large size*	**MINOR** *size down*	**MAJOR** *size up*	**GREATER** *great great*	**LESS** *small size*
LESSER *less less*	**THOUGH**	**ALTHOUGH**	**EITHER** *this or that*	**ROOT** *part of tree*
ALTERNATIVE *parallel choice*	**SELECTION** *lot of choice*	**FINE** *above good*	**TERRIBLE** *below bad*	**AWFUL** *extremely bad*
THIEF *person with* *long fingers*	**AUTHENTIC** *parallel with* *truth*	**SHOULDER** *part of body*	**FUNCTION** *in-out*	**POLICY** *road of good* *over bad*

FOOTSTEP *leg distance*	**FOOTPRINT** *leg path*	**TRUCE** *war/peace*	**ENORMOUS** *extremely big*	**DIFFICULTY** *heavy heavy*
OUNCE *very small weight*	**REAL** *not fiction*	**FOR** *against against*	**HERE** *close direction*	**THERE** *aside direction*
MODEST *avoids extreme*	**WORKER** *person behind work*	**SHARP** *as blade*	**RESULT** *end outcome*	**SON** *growing father*
WELL *is good*	**NOT WELL** *is bad*	**GAIN** *income above cost*	**TEACH** *push textbook*	**PARDON** *excuse guilty*
ISLAND *land above water*	**LAKE** *water above land*	**CREDIT** *pay later*	**SOW** *female pig*	**PARAGON** *perfect standard*
FATE *time chooses*	**LUCK** *time favor*	**MISFORTUNE** *time curse*	**FORTUNE** *time blessing*	**FORTUNE COOKIE** *cookie & text*
FORTUNATE *coming fortune*	**UNFORTUNATE** *coming misfortune*	**CAVALRY** *horse & military*	**IMPOSSIBLE** *work without work*	**BUSINESS** *emphasized work*
ODDS *win against*	**FREQUENTLY** *coming often*	**DETERMINE** *decide decide*	**EXIST** *in time*	**NICE** *pleasing eye*

CREATE *make from nothing*	**CREATE** *make exist*	**DISCUSS** *converse & argue*	**EVEN** *add against*	**MOREOVER** *add above*
EAT	**FIT** *be parallel*	**NOT FIT** *be perpendicular*	**ACQUAINTANCE** *person known and not*	**BEGGAR** *person asking asking*
CHOOSER *person who is choosy*	**ENCOUNTER** *come face to face*	**PRIVILEGE** *gold behind*	**QUEST** *gold ahead*	**SAILBOAT** *basic sign*
TOO *more than enough*	**EXCESSIVE** *give up give up*	**ADVISE** *give advice*	**MIDDLE AGE** *time ahead & behind*	**TRUISM** *obvious truth*
DECEIVE *push lie*	**DECEIVED** *accept lie*	**DECEIT** *against truth*	**THAN** *basic sign*	

ACQUAINTANCE = *person known and not known*

ADVISE = *give advice.* Give is shown as *hand and out-arrow* while advice is *brain return.*

ALTERNATIVE = *parallel choice*

ALTHOUGH = *basic sign*

AUTHENTIC = *parallel with truth.* Truth is shown as *"equal over heart,"* which is to symbolize placing hand *over heart,* as sometimes people do when swearing to truth.

AWFUL = *extremely bad.* Extreme is shown as the *top* and the *bottom* of a *mountain. Bad* is shown as down bent arrow.

BEGGAR = *person asking asking.* Ask is shown as saying *please.*

BUSINESS = *emphasized work.* Business is *hard work.* "Hard" has been indicated by emphasizing. Work is shown as *lifting ball* against gravity (which is work as lifting anything).

CAVALRY = *horse and military*. Horse is *animal* identified by *horseshoe*. Military is shown as to do with *battle over battle*. Italian (Latin) for horse is *caval*, which is the root of the word cavalry.

CHOOSER = *person who is choosy*. Choosy is shown as considering *many choices*.

CREATE = *make from nothing*. Make is shown in Nobel as *output of work*. Work is shown as lifting ball (weight) against force of gravity. The definition of *work* in physics, in simple language, is to move against force.

CREATE = *make exist*. That something exists means that it is *in time* (as time will exist even when we do not). Thus "exist" is suggested by arrow that is of opposite form from arrow depicting "death" or extinction.

CREDIT = *pay later*. Pay is shown in Nobel as *"money down"* while prepayment is "money up." Later is shown in Nobel as *after after*.

DECEIT = *against truth*. Deceit is being dishonest, not truthful, thus working *against truth*.

DECEIVE = *push lie*

DECEIVED = *accept lie*. Person is deceived when he/she is misled and *accepts lie* for truth.

DETERMINE = *decide decide*. Determine is to decide something conclusively, thus emphasized *decide*. Decide is shown in Nobel as *cutting choice*.

DIFFICULTY = *heavy heavy*. Heavy is shown as an object of *heavy* weight, which is not easy to lift. Difficulty is something that is not easy to understand, easy to do or make or deal with, so is very heavy, or *heavy heavy*.

DIM = *brightness collapse*. Bright is something having a *lot of shine*. Shine is something having *lot of light*. Light is *part of lightning* (electricity). Collapse is shown as *up-down curved arrow*.

DISCUSS = *converse & argue*. Converse is in Nobel shown as *parallel talk* (mouth), argue is in Nobel shown as *perpendicular talk* (mouth), thus discussion, being both, is shown as *tolerant* (parallel&perpendicular) talk. The phrase "agree to disagree" is a sign of tolerance, and in general, tolerant persons agree with (parallel) with disagreements (perpendicular or against stands).

EAT = *into mouth*

EITHER = *this or that. This* in Nobel is shown as *pointing close* and *that* in Nobel is shown as *pointing aside.*

ENCOUNTER = *come face to face* or one may say *come face against face. Against is shown as perpendicular*

ENORMOUS = *extremely big.* Extreme is shown as the *top* and the *bottom* of a *mountain. Big* is mathematical sign.

EVEN = *add against.* The sign *against* suggest something not expected (surprising, unlikely or extreme)

EXCESSIVE = *give up give up.* Stop the scale means *enough,* more than enough is to *surrender,* and excessive is to *surrender surrender.*

EXIST = *in time.* Recall Descartes: Cogito ergo sum! That something exists means that it is happening *in time.* Thus, "exist" is suggested by arrow entering time. The arrow is of opposite form from arrow depicting "death" or extinction.

FATE = *time chooses.* Outcome that *time* brings, that one cannot *choose*

FINE = *above good.* Good is good enough, but fine is better, so it is *above good* on an informal scale of good-bad.

FIT = *be parallel.* To agree is in Nobel to be *parallel with,* to fit is to *be parallel.* "To be" is shown by overlapping sign *equal* and *time.*

FOOTPRINT = *leg path*

FOOTSTEP = *leg distance*

FOR = *against against.* Recall an old adage: Enemy of your enemy is your friend, thus being *against* of someone who is *against* amounts to being *for.*

FORTUNATE = *coming luck*

FORTUNE = *time blessing*

FORTUNE COOKIES = *cookie & text.* These are Chinese pastry cookies wrapped around a written message, predicting someone's fortune, served in Chinese restaurants.

FREQUENTLY = *coming often.* Coming is indicted by *legs.* Often is shown as *again again.* Again is shown as *time returning.*

FUNCTION = *in-out.* In mathematics, function is defined as a process in which given a number (symbolized by *in*), you get only one answer; hence you put number in and you get a number out.

GAIN = *income above cost.* Income is money coming in, and cost is money going out. In business, the difference, the *money coming in above the money spent* is gain or profit.

GREAT = *large size.* Large is shown as mathematical sign *big,* while size is shown as expanding in *all directions.*

GREATER = *great great,* that is, *greater* than *great*

HERE = *at close direction*

IMPOSSIBLE = *work without work.* According to laws of thermodynamics, work is not possible without energy, which is capacity to do work. Thermodynamics is part of physics, which is concerned with the exchange of work into heat and heat into work (more precisely dealing with conversion of energy from one form to another and how this depends or affects temperature, pressure, volume, mechanical movements and work). The first law of thermodynamics states that energy cannot be created or destroyed, thus it is not possible to create work without using outside energy.

ISLAND = *land above water.* Land is shown in Nobel by emphasizing (doubling) the sign for *ground.*

LAKE = *water above land.* Land is shown in Nobel by emphasizing (doubling) the sign for *ground.*

LESS = *small size.* Small is shown as *not big* (crossed big) mathematical sign, while size is shown as expanding in *all directions.*

LESSER = *less less,* that is, *less* than less

LUCK = *time favor,* good fortune, favorable outcome that seems to happen unexpectedly and accidentally without apparent logical background

MAJOR = *size up*

MIDDLE AGE = *time ahead & behind.* This is in analogy with middle-aged person, a person who had time behind and has time ahead. Behind and ahead are suggested by placing *time* (the sign of watch) *behind and ahead of legs.*

MINOR = *size down*

MISFORTUNE = *time curse*

MODEST = *avoids extreme.* Avoid is shown by an arrow that bends away along it path, as it avoids some obstacle. Extreme are shown as the *top* and the *bottom* of a *mountain.*

MODESTY = *not pride.* Pride is shown by fusing signs for *brain* and *praise,* which is brain (person) that praises self. "Not" is shown as reciprocal.

MOREOVER = *add above.* Add above suggests *in addition.*

NICE = *pleasing eye*

NOT FIT = *be perpendicular.* To fit is in Nobel shown as to be *parallel.* Hence, not fit is to *be perpendicular.*

NOT WELL = *is bad.* "Is" is shown as *equal,* "bad" is shown as *down bent arrow.*

OBSTRUCTION = *many difficulties.* Difficulties is shown as heavy, heavy. Obstruction is then heavy, heavy, heavy.

ODDS = *win against.* Odds are calculated by considering the *ratio* of *winning* against *loosing*

OUNCE = *very small weight.* Until recently, the United States and Yemen were the only two countries in the whole world that do not use metric system, but of recently, Yemen went metric. So we have to comment on nonmetric units for readers who have abandoned various nonmetric systems long ago, and may not have been exposed to English and American nonmetric systems, which are similar but different. In medieval times in Europe, cities had their own systems of measure and on entrance of cities, there were customs offices using their own standards. Later this extended to larger regions, but still units for measure were regional, rather than international. Current efforts to standardize units involve the International Standards Organization. The International System of Units is internationally accepted system of measures for scientific work (United States being also part of this). The basic units are meter for length; kilogram for mass (weight); second for time; kelvin for temperature, mole for amount of substance; ampere for electric current; tesla for magnetism; and candela for luminous intensity. In order to distinguish metric system from nonmetric system used in USA (and formerly in England), Nobel places crown *above* signs for metric units and places crown *below* signs for nonmetric units. The sign of *crown* indicates an "official" status of the measure units. Ounce, which is one-sixteenth of a pound (which is approximately half a kilogram) is shown as very small weight of nonmetric system.

PARAGON = *perfect standard.* Paragon is the very best example of something. "The very best" is represented by *perfect,* which is *exact exact.* Exact is shown in Nobel as emphasized equal, that is, *equal equal.* The "example of something" is shown as *standard,* an *item on podium.* Etymology of the word paragon goes to medieval French for touchstone, the stone used to test the purity of gold, which comes from Greek *parakonan,* which stands for *to sharpen, whet* and whetstone (stone used to sharpen blade of tool). Briefly, paragon is a single word for "the best of the best." Few languages have such a single word for the best of the best, Slovenian is one and Croatian coastal dialect is another, have the same word *žlahti*, which does not exist in the official Croatian language, except that the word survived only as a name for one of the best white wines from coastal island Krk, called Žlahtina. Most people drinking this wine will find it very good, but not understanding the label, which for them does not mean anything, will not realize that this is not only the best white wine form that region, but best of the best wines!

PARDON = *excuse guilty*. Excuse is shown in Nobel as superposition of *please* and *thanks*, because when excusing one says first *please* (excuse me) and then *thanks*.

POLICY = *road of good over bad*. Policy is a plan for course of action adopted by an individual, group, organization or government, and usually implies prudence, that is, good sense in managing practical matters. Prudence is depicted in Nobel as adopting good over bad, shown as *path of good over bad*, while policy becomes a *road of good over bad*.

POSSESSION = *items own*. "Own" is shown as emphasized have, that is, as *have have*. "Have" is shown as emphasized with, that is *with with*.

PRIVILEGE = *gold behind*. Advantage is shown in Nobel as having *difficulty behind*, benefit is shown in Nobel as having *silver behind*, and privilege is handsome advantage and benefit, hence having *gold behind* (which indirectly suggest having money behind).

QUEST = *gold ahead*. Challenge is shown in Nobel as *silver ahead*. Quest, being more than challenge, involving searching and possibly adventure, is then shown as *gold ahead*.

REAL = *not fiction*. Fiction is shown in Nobel as being *hooked in a cloud* and should be contrasted to the sign for *fact*, as something hooked to the *ground*, that is, having *base*. One can hook something to the ground, but nothing can be hooked to clouds, suggesting such things are fictitious. *Real* is opposite (reciprocal) to fiction, that is *not fiction*.

RESULT = *end outcome.* Result is the product of particular action, condition or event, hence is the end output or *end outcome.* End is shown as emphasized *far,* just as beginning is shown as emphasized *close.*

ROOT = part of tree *below tree* under the ground. Hence the positioning of the sign below at the stem of tree sign.

SAILBOAT = *basic sign.* Sail was added to the sign for boat.

SELECTION = *lot of choice.* This is shown as *choice over choice* in order to differentiate this sign from the sign for choosy, a person who is considering lot of choices (one after another, so they are drawn sequentially). In order to be *choosy* one has to have *selection.*

SHARP = *as blade.* "As" is shown as *equal close,* while "blade" is shown by emphasizing one edge of a *knife.*

SHOULDER = *upper part of body*

SON = *growing father.* Indeed, one day, son will become father, so *son* in Nobel is shown as *growing* into *father.* "Growing" is shown by *adding arrowhead* to the sign for father, just as *child* is shown as *growing person* and *baby as growing child.*

SOW = *female pig.* Pig is shown in Nobel as *animal of mud,* in view that it likes to rest in mud. Mud is shown as *water over ground.*

TEACH = *push textbook.* Textbook is book characterized by in-out arrows, as one uses it more than once. Actually, the more one uses it, the better student one becomes. The in-out arrows stand in analogy to the sign for *digest* that relates to food that goes in-out of a body. So, to teach someone, one has to see that student *digests* the book used in a course.

TERRIBLE = *below bad.* Bad is bad enough, terrible is worse, so it is indicated on an arbitrary scale of good-bad as *below bad,* just as very cold weather would be indicated as below freezing.

THAN = *basic sign*

THERE = *at aside direction*

THIEF = *person with long fingers.* This is a figurative speech. Person with skilful fingers can take things while others do not notice, so it appears as if he operates from a distance, having *long fingers.* In Croatia, and possibly some other countries, people refer to thieves as people with *long fingers.*

THOUGH = *basic sign*

TOO = *more than enough.* Enough is shown as *stop the scale.* More than enough is shown by adding *"more"* (go scale).

TRUCE = *war/peace.* Truce is a temporary interruption of hostility, so it is neither *war* (lot of battles), nor *peace* (no battles).

TRUISM = *obvious truth.* Obvious is something that *all see.*

UNFORTUNATE = *coming misfortune*

UNION = *three overlapping rings.* Overlapping rings in Nobel symbolize marriage, which is a special kind of a *union,* union between two persons, husband and wife. By generalizing and adding a third overlapping ring, one obtains a symbol of a more general kind of *union.* This design of three overlapping rings is known as the Borromean rings as they form the coat of arms of the aristocratic Italian family Borromeo. The three rings when considered together cannot be separated, but if one removes any one ring, the remaining two are not interlocked. The picture of Borromean rings is shown below.

WELL = *is good.* "Is" is shown as *equal,* "good" is shown as *up bent arrow.*

WORKER = *person behind work.* This sign is self-evident. Person *in front of* work is foreman.

Borromean rings

In explanation of the above ninety signs, we have mentioned several additional signs, which are listed below.

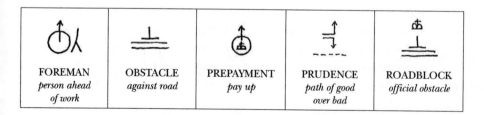

FOREMAN	OBSTACLE	PREPAYMENT	PRUDENCE	ROADBLOCK
person ahead of work	*against road*	*pay up*	*path of good over bad*	*official obstacle*

TUBER *part of root*	VERY COLD *below cold*	VERY HOT *above hot*		

Although we will be adding a few more words before reaching the end of the book, now is the time for the final word count. We have reached

$$W = 3,000$$

Isn't this amazing that we have, with relative ease, arrived at an impressive vocabulary of 3,000 words?

We are ready now for reading text in Nobel, which is illustrated in the next section of the book on one hundred Chinese proverbs.

PART 4

Illustration of Nobel

Selection of
Chinese Proverbs

In this section of the book, we will illustrate use of Nobel by "translating" some text from English into Nobel. This is to be the first public demonstration of Nobel, in a way, a historic event. For quite some time, I was pondering what text to select for this very honorable situation. One of the thoughts was to take the initial verses of the Bible, which itself is a historic book. So I did prepare some twenty pages of the translation, but decided that this may not be the best choice in view of the religious context of the Bible, which would put Judaism and Christianity in somewhat privileged position. One could compensate this by including a translation of number of pages from Koran, then another selection from the holy book of Buddhism, and so on. That may show some fairness, except for atheists, who would be left out. So I realized that the best is to keep religion out—in the spirit of the forefathers of these United States, who decided that there is no official religion and that state and religion be treated separately.

Next thought was to consider the document on the human rights, which is politically correct, and even those politicians (dictators) who are not practicing it do not dare publicly to denounce them. However, looking at the document, I realized that while it deserves to be translated into Nobel, and one day I hope to find time for that, the text is not easy to read, it lacks narrative.

An alternative would be to select some classic piece from fine literature, but that is easy to say and almost impossible to accomplish—not because there are not fine compositions, but because there are too many fine pieces to select from. I could select something from Croatian literature that goes back to the poet of the free town of Dubrovnik, Ivan Gundulić (1589-1638), who wrote, among others, a hymn to freedom, who is considered the patron of Croatian literature. Or I could select something from his predecessor, the writer Marin Držić (1508-1567), also from Dubrovnik, who is viewed as father of Croatian literature and whose comedy *Dundo Maroje* is still occasionally performed in Croatian theaters. This would be a good choice to add to the celebration of the five hundred years since the birth of Marin Držić and thus contribute to the festivity as Croatia announced year 2008 as the year of Marin Držić. The five hundredth anniversaries do not come often, because most of the Europe was at that time in darkness, with of course the exception of Italy, the birthplace of the Renaissance. We may mention that not long ago, the five hundredth anniversary of the use of mathematical sign + (for addition) was observed.

While the choice of some writing of Marin Držić or Ivan Gundulić, which are outstanding and have their own merit, would be a welcome promotion of the cultural heritage of the small country Croatia (of which many have hardly heard in view of its unfortunate history and lost identity since the beginning of the eleventh century, since when it was ruled by Hungarians, Austrians, Austro-Hungarians, and eventually Serbians under the mask of Yugoslavia), there are a multitude of outstanding literary contributions of those before Marin Držić or Ivan Gundulić, and of greater fame, like Italian poet Dante Alighieri (1265-1321) of *The Divine Comedy*, and Francesco Petrarca (Petrarch) (1304-1374), Italian lyric and scholar, and there are multitudes of outstanding literary contributions of those after Marin Držić or Ivan Gundulić, like Miguel de Cervantes (1547-1616) of one of the most famous novels, *Don Quixote*, who greatly influence literature to follow. If we are to consider more recent literature, then the choices exponentially grow, and for every good choice, there are hundred equally good, if not better.

A way out of this nightmare is to turn to folk literature and folk wisdom. There are many folk stories that have been transmitted through generations and eventually saved for posterity with the emergence of the print. By examining a special journal that was printing text in Glagolytic script, which was widely used and died around the tenth century in Bulgaria, Ukraine, Moravia (part of Czech country), but barely survived in Croatia till the nineteenth century and is cherished by a few, including myself, even these days; I came unexpectedly across one lovely short Ukrainian folk narrative. It is a story of a dying young son, waiting to be taken by Death (a ghostly skeleton holding a scythe), who has been approaching. Father wanted to sacrifice himself instead, and when Death agreed, he changed his mind. The sister followed the same and also changed her mind. Then the mother met Death and promised to give herself instead of Death taking her son, which was accepted. Mother then asked Death just once again to see her boy and was permitted to return to the house, but when she returned, Death was walking away, and the boy recovered. This would be an excellent story worthy of inauguration of Nobel, except that I misplaced the text and could not find it. I will, however, when I recover the text, go ahead with transcription of this text into Nobel.

While I should apologize for the incident, I am also very happy that I come across an outstanding alternative. During frequent visiting of bookstores on an occasion of visiting Half Price Bookstore (either in Houston or Des Moines, I do not recall now exactly) I came across the book *Dictionary of 1000 Chinese Proverbs* (edited by Marjorie Lin and Schalk Leonard, published by Hippocrene Books, Inc, New York, at the price of $3.98). This book is one of the Hippocrene Bilingual Proverbs Series, which includes African proverbs; American proverbs; Arabic proverbs; dictionary of one thousand Dutch proverbs; dictionary of one thousand French proverbs; dictionary of one thousand German proverbs; dictionary of one thousand Italian proverbs; Irish proverbs; dictionary of one thousand Jewish proverbs; dictionary of one thousand Polish proverbs; dictionary of one thousand Russian proverbs; comprehensive bilingual dictionary of Russian proverbs (5,335 proverbs); Scottish proverbs; dictionary of one thousand Spanish proverbs; Spanish proverbs, idioms, and slang; and international dictionary of proverbs.

I felt fortunate and blessed to come across the *Dictionary of 1000 Chinese Proverbs,* which I selected to transcribe in Nobel. First, with excerpts from this book, we give the honor of introducing Nobel script to common people, to humanity at large. Moreover, we honor Chinese folk, people of long history of universal script. In fact, in the second part of the *Dictionary of 1000 Chinese Proverbs,* those one thousand proverbs are all written in Chinese characters (thus book being bilingual English-Chinese). We have thus resolved our tantalizing problem of selecting the first written text in Nobel, and on the following 35 pages, we extracted one hundred Chinese proverbs out of those one thousand. We hope that readers will have double pleasure: reading Nobel script and reading a selection of Chinese proverbs.

Love me little, loved me long.

LOVE	ME *person self*	LITTLE not *big*	LOVE	ME *person self*
LONG *part of distance*				

In times of peace, do not forget danger.

DURING	PEACE not *war*	DO NOT crossed *do*	FORGET not *remember*	DANGER basic sign

The well-fed don't know how the starving suffer.

PEOPLE	HAVING	LOT OF FOOD	DON'T KNOW	HOW
STARVING *hungry hungry*	SUFFER not *pleasure*			

Good has its reward, and evil has its cost.

GOOD	HAS	ITS	REWARD *income above income*	EVIL
HAS *with with*	COST *money depart*			

Eloquence is silver, silence is golden.

ELOQUENCE *flying mouth*	IS *equal*	SILVER basic sign	SILENCE *not speak*	IS *equal*
GOLD *silver silver*				

Health is not valued until illness comes.

HEALTH crossed *illness*	HAS NO crossed *has*	VALUE *time & money*	TILL	ILLNESS *friction in body*
COME *crawling legs*				

Wealth attracts thieves, as beauty attracts evil.

WEALTH *lot of value*	ATTRACTS *lot of attention*	THIEVES *people with long hands*	BEAUTY *all beautiful*	ATTRACTS *lot of attention*
EVIL *overlapping bad*				

Better to drink the weak tea of a friend than the sweet wine of an enemy.

BETTER	TO DRINK *water in mouth*	WEAK *not strong*	TEA *not coffee*	OF
A FRIEND *person loved*	THAN	THE SWEET *good taste*	WINE *wineglass*	OF

ENEMY *person hated*				

Practice makes perfect.

PRACTICE *work again* *work again*	**MAKE** *work output*	**PERFECT** *accurate* *accurate*		

Honesty is the best policy.

HONESTY *straight truth*	**IS** *equal*	**THE BEST**	**POLICY** *good over bed*	

You can't please all of the people all the time.

YOU	**CAN'T**	**PLEASE** *crawling pleased*	**ALL OF**	**PEOPLE**
ALL OF	**TIME** basic sign			

The lesson you learn when you are taken advantage of puts you at an advantage.

LESSON *part of textbook*	YOU	LEARN *crawling in brain*	WHEN	YOU
ARE TAKEN	ADVANTAGE *burden behind*	OF *from from*	PUTS basic sign	YOU
AT	ADVANTAGE *burden behind*			

Don't wash your dirty laundry in public.

DON'T *do not*	WASH *in water in & out*	YOUR *belongs to you*	DIRTY with spots	LAUNDRY *fabric*
IN PUBLIC *on podium*				

Small boats shouldn't carry large load.

SMALL *not large*	BOAT *basic sign*	SHOULDN'T *must not*	CARRY *basic sign*	LARGE *basic sign*

LOAD *heavy toss*				

Clever people may be victims of their own cleverness.

CLEVER *brain up*	**PEOPLE** *basic sign*	**MAY BE**	**VICTIMS** *injured person*	**OF** *from from*
THEIR *belongs to them*	**OWN** *self*	**CLEVERNESS** *clever clever*		

You can't appreciate the weight until you shoulder the load;
you can't appreciate the length of the road until you travel it.

YOU	**CAN'T** *can not*	**APPRECIATE** *understand effort*	**WEIGHT**	**UNTIL**
YOU	**SHOULDER** *carry*	**LOAD**		
YOU	**CAN'T** *can not*	**APPRECIATE** *understand effort*	**LENGTH** *distance from-to*	**OF**

THE ROAD	UNTIL	YOU	TRAVEL	IT

The load carried by another does not seem so heavy.

LOAD	CARRIED	BY	ANOTHER *some other*	DOES NOT
APPEAR *under eye*	HEAVY			

A single ant hole may lead to the collapse of an enormous dyke.

SINGLE *without others*	ANT	HOLE *part of a loop*	MAY *need not*	LEAD
TO	COLLAPSE	OF	ENORMOUS *extremely large*	DYKE

You win by not gambling.

YOU	WIN	BY	NOT	GAMBLING *tossing coin*

You can never really fathom the mind of another.

YOU	CAN *with potential*	NEVER *not before not after*	REALLY *not fiction*	MEASURE *use scale*
MIND *basic sign*	OF	ANOTHER *some other*		

If you don't do bad deeds, you will not harm yourself.

IF	YOU	DON'T DO	BAD	DEEDS *output of doing*
YOU	WILL NOT	HARM *knife in body*	YOURSELF	

Selfishness is the root of all evil.

SELFISHNESS	IS	ROOT *part of tree*	OF ALL	EVIL *overlapping bad*

When the prince breaks the law, he should be punished like everyone else.

WHEN	PRINCE *not a king*	JUMP OVER	LAW *justice document*	HE
SHOULD	TAKE	PUNISHMENT *not luxury*	LIKE	EVERYONE *all persons*

A walk after a meal makes for a long life.

WALK	AFTER	MEAL *time of food*	MAKES	FOR *against against*
LONG *shown on distance sign*	LIFE *heart signal*			

Do not swallow your food without chewing, and do not speak without thinking.

DO NOT	SWALLOW	YOUR *belongs to you*	FOOD	WITHOUT
CHEWING	AND	DO NOT	SPEAK	WITHOUT THINKING

Every one hundred miles you'll find different customs.

EVERY	ONE HUNDRED	MILE *official long distance*	YOU WILL	FIND
DIFFERENT	CUSTOMS *people around common*			

Every dog has his day.

EVERY	DOG	HAS	HIS	DAY

Where there's a smoke, there's fire.

WHERE	EXIST	SMOKE	THERE	EXIST
FIRE				

Great wealth is a gift from heaven, moderate wealth results from frugality.

GREAT *big size*	WEALTH *lot of value*	IS	GIFT	FROM
HEAVEN *above sky*	MODERATE *avoid extreme*	WEALTH *lot of value*	RESULTS *end output*	FROM
FRUGALITY *controlled spending*				

A tiger father will not produce a dog son.

TIGER *big cat*	FATHER	WILL NOT	PRODUCE	DOG
SON *growing father*				

A pardon produces good fortune.

PARDON *excuse excuse*	PRODUCES	GOOD	FORTUNE *future wealth*	

An ounce of tolerance, an ounce of good fortune.

OUNCE	OF	TOLERANCE	OUNCE	OF
GOOD	FORTUNE			

Like father, like son.

LIKE *close equal*	FATHER	LIKE	SON *growing father*	

If you don't kill the root, the problem will return.

IF	YOU	DO NOT	KILL *knife in heart*	ROOT *part of tree*
DIFFICULTIES	WILL RETURN			

Constant effort yields certain success.

CONTINUOUS *follow follow*	EFFORT	PRODUCES *push output*	CERTAIN *toss apple*	SUCCESS *goal is behind*

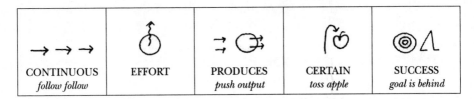

A workman must first sharpen his tool if he is to do his work well.

WORKMAN person behind work	MUST no choice	FIRST number 1	SHARPEN refine blade	HIS belongs to him
TOOL work with	IF	HE	WILL DO	HIS
WORK basic sign	WELL			

The cock that loves a fight grows no feathers

COCK male hen	THAT	LOVES	FIGHT part of battle	GROWS NO
FEATHERS bird detail				

The arrow once released cannot be retrieved.
What is done cannot be undone.

ARROW basic sign	AFTER	LET not keep (fence)	TO FLY	IS

IMPOSSIBLE *work without work*	PULL	BACK *direction back*		
WHAT	IS DONE	CAN NOT	BE	UNDONE

A day of reading is a day of gain; a day without reading is ten days of loss.

DAY *overlapping time*	OF	READING *eye above text*	IS	DAY *overlapping time*
OF	GAIN *revenue above cost*	DAY *overlapping time*	WITHOUT *basic sign*	READING *eye above text*
IS *equal*	10	DAY *overlapping time*	OF	LOSS *cost over revenue*

Monkcy see, monkey do.

MONKEY *brain and no brain*	SEE *eye and in-arrow*	MONKEY *brain and no brain*	DO *basic sign*	

A barking dog seldom bites.

| DOG
teeth | PUSHING | SOUND
music & noise | SELDOM
not often | BITE
part of an apple |

You cannot teach an old dog new trick.

YOU	CANNOT	TEACH *push textbook*	OLD	DOG *teeth*
NEW	TRICKS *uncommon ability*			

No man is an island.

PERSON	IS NOT	ISLAND *land above sea*		

As you sow, so shall you reap.

| AS | YOU | SOW
field input | SO | YOU |

WILL REAP				

Ghosts exist only for those who believe in them.

GHOST *without body*	EXIST	ONLY	FOR	PEOPLE
BELIEVING	GHOST	EXIST		

Time passes quickly—don't waste it.

TIME	FLYING	FAST	DO NOT	WASTE TIME

Ponder your faults and you will avert mistake.

THINK ABOUT	YOUR *belongs to you*	FAULTS	AND	YOU
WILL AVOID	MISFORTUNE			

It is mistake to make mistake and not correct it.

IT	IS	MISTAKE	TO MAKE	MISTAKE
AND	NOT	CORRECT *eliminate error*	IT	

The sea cannot be measured by basket.
Great minds cannot be fathomed by ordinary men.

SEA	CANNOT	BE	MEASURED *use scale*	BY
BASKET				

YOU	CANNOT	MEASURE	GREAT	MIND
BY	COMMON *overlapping parts*	MIND		

A true man does not fight against impossible odds.

TRUE	PERSON	DOES NOT	FIGHT *part of battle*	AGAINST
IMPOSSIBLE	ODDS *win against*			

A true man takes responsibility for his actions.

TRUE	PERSON	TAKES	RESPONSIBILITY *deserving trust*	AGAINST
HIS/HER	ACTIONS			

Without the bitter cold of winter how can one enjoy the fragrance of the plum blossom?

WITHOUT	BITTER	COLD	WINTER *snow season*	HOW
CAN	PERSON	ENJOY *touching pleasure*	FRAGRANCE *sweet air*	OF

FRUIT	BLOSSOM *tree flower*			

If the family lives in harmony, all affairs will prosper.

IF	FAMILY	LIVES	WITH	HARMONY
ALL	BUSINESS	WILL GO	WELL *good*	

Even a small stream can tip a boat.

EVEN	SMALL	STREAM	CAN	OVERTURN
BOAT				

If you want to cross a river, you must first build a bridge.

IF	YOU	WANT	CROSS	RIVER

YOU	MUST *no choice*	FIRST *number one*	BUILD	BRIDGE *basic sign*

Even a vicious tiger will not eat its offspring.

EVEN *all against*	VICIOUS *dangerous* *aggressive*	TIGER *big cat*	WILL NOT	EAT
ITS	CHILDREN			

A glut of food is tasteless; a glut of words is worthless.

GLUT	OF	FOOD	IS	WITHOUT TASTE
GLUT	OF	WORD	IS	WITHOUT VALUE

Square words won't fit into a round ear.

SQUARE	WORDS	WON'T	FIT	INTO
ROUND	EAR			

Pretty flowers are not necessarily fragrant.

PRETTY	FLOWERS	NEED NOT	GIVE	BEAUTIFUL
SMELL				

Too much talk harms a person, and too much food harms the body.

BEYOND	ENOUGH	OF	TALK	WILL INJURE
PERSON	AND	BEYOND	ENOUGH	OF

FOOD	WILL INJURE	BODY		

He who knows when enough is enough will
not encounter misfortune.

PERSON	WHO	KNOWS	WHEN	ENOUGH
IS	ENOUGH	WILL NOT	ENCOUNTER	MISFORTUNE

You can cover up fire, but you could not hide smoke.

YOU	CAN *have potential*	COVER	FIRE	BUT
YOU	COULDN'T	HIDE	SMOKE	

Too much heat destroys the food.

TOO MUCH	HEAT *above fire*	DESTROY	FOOD	

Forging iron requires great heat;
making friends requires sincerity.

MAKING	IRON	NEEDS	GREAT	HEAT
MAKING	FRIENDS	NEEDS	FRANKNESS	

A single spark can start a prairie fire.

SINGLE *without others*	SPARK *flame flake*	CAN	START	PRAIRIE
FIRE				

A strong memory is not as good as a marginally written record.

STRONG *with force*	MEMORY *brain & anchor*	IS NOT	AS	GOOD
AS	WORDS	ASIDE	MARGIN	

Beggars can't be choosers.

BEGGARS	CAN'T	BE	CHOOSERS	

Hoist your sail when the wind is fair.

PULL UP	YOUR	SAIL	WHEN	WIND
IS	FAIR *pleasing eye*			

Disharmony within the home leads to attack from without.

DISHARMONY	INSIDE HOME	IS PATH	TO	ATTACK

FROM	OUTSIDE HOME			

When the neighbor's house is on fire, you put yourself in danger if you don't help extinguish it.

WHEN	NEIGHBOR	HOUSE	IS	ON FIRE
YOU	ARE	IN	DANGER	IF
YOU	DON'T	HELP	EXTINGUISH *kill fire*	IT

The grass is greener on the other side of a fence.

GRASS	IS	GREENER *more green*	ON	OTHER SIDE
OF	FENCE			

Those who don't get their feet wet don't catch fish.

PEOPLE	WHO	DON'T	GET	THEIR
FEET	WET	DON'T	CATCH	FISH

With casual acquaintance, engage not in deep conversation.

WITH	PEOPLE	YOU KNOW & DON'T KNOW	DON'T	TAKE
PART	IN	DEEP	CONVERSATION	

It cost nothing to ask for advice.

COST	NOTHING *empty*	TO	ASK *speak question*	FOR
ADVICE				

Good times don't last long.

GOOD	TIME	DON'T	LAST	LONG

When in Rome do as Romans.

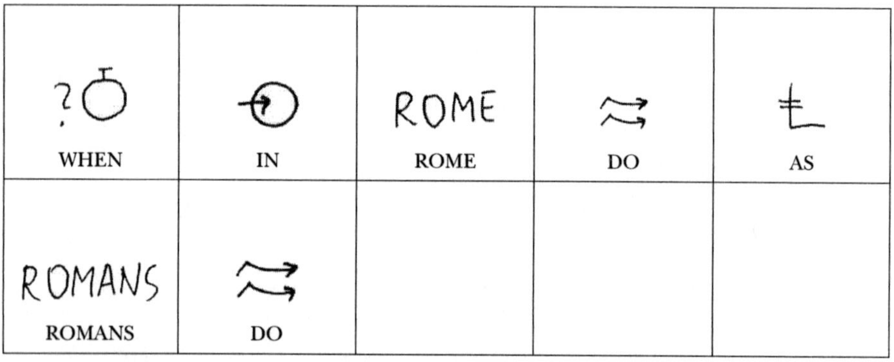

WHEN	IN	ROME	DO	AS
?Ö	⊕	ROME	≋	Ŧ
ROMANS	≋			
ROMANS	DO			

In wine there is truth. (In vino veritas.)

INSIDE WINE	EXIST	TRUTH		
∂Y	Ⓟ	♡		

Wine can make you succeed or make you fail.

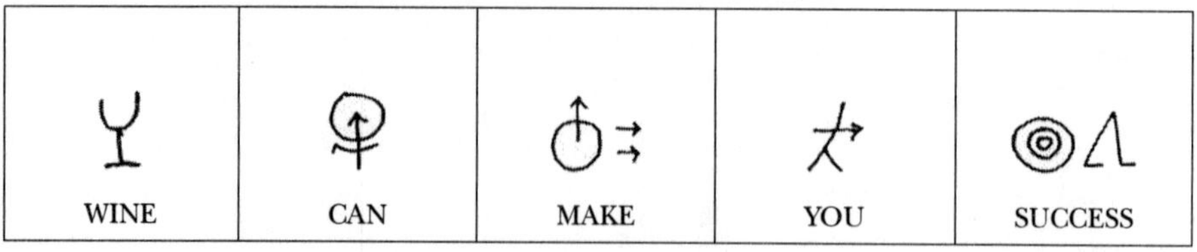

WINE	CAN	MAKE	YOU	SUCCESS
Y	Ⓟ	Ö⇉	�	◎Λ

OR	MAKE	YOU	FAIL	

The good mouth doesn't curse and the good hand doesn't fight.

GOOD	MOUTH	DOESN'T	CURSE	AND
GOOD	HAND	DOESN'T	FIGHT *part of battle*	

He who has not tasted bitter knows not sweet.

HE	WHO	DID NOT	TASTE BITTER	DOES NOT KNOW
SWEET				

Happiness is helping others.

HAPPINESS	IS	HELPING	OTHERS	

It is impolite not to give after receiving.

IT	IS	IMPOLITE	NOT	TO GIVE
AFTER	RECEIVING			

One is never too old to learn.

PERSON	IS	NEVER	TOO	OLD
TO LEARN				

Old men shouldn't marry young wives.

OLD *lot of time behind*	MALE	PEOPLE	SHOULDN'T	MARRY
YOUNG *lot of time ahead*	WIVES			

Excessive joy leads to sorrow.

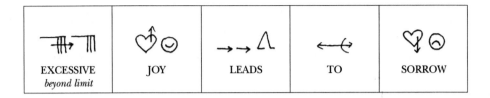

EXCESSIVE *beyond limit*	JOY	LEADS	TO	SORROW

Truth is more powerful than force.

TRUTH	IS	MORE	POWERFUL *with power*	THAN
FORCE				

Excessive politeness conceals deceit.

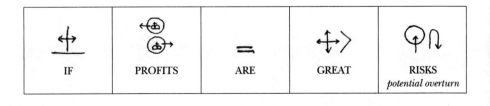

EXCESSIVE	POLITENESS	COVERS	DECEIT	

If profits are great, the risks are great.

IF	PROFITS	ARE	GREAT	RISKS *potential overturn*

ARE	GREAT			

Truth is not determined by the volume of the voice.

TRUTH	IS NOT	DETERMINED	BY	QUANTITY
OF	VOICE *mouth sound*			

A single tree does not a forest make.

SINGLE *without others*	TREE	DOES NOT	MAKE	FOREST

Get along with your neighbors and keep in contact
with distant friends.

GO PARALLEL	WITH	YOUR	NEIGHBORS	AND

BE	IN	CONNECTION	WITH	DISTANT
FRIENDS				

The one who creates the mess should untangle it.

PERSON	WHO	MAKE	MESS	SHOULD *potential need*
UNTANGLE *cut knot*	IT			

A long journey will not deter one with high aspirations.

LONG	JOURNEY *lot of travel*	WILL NOT	DETER *act against*	PERSON
WITH	HIGH	ASPIRATION		

You won't get lost if you frequently ask directions.

YOU	WILL NOT	BE	LOST	IF
YOU	FREQUENTLY	ASK	FOR	DIRECTIONS

If a man makes no provision for the distant future, he will certainly encounter difficulties in the near future.

IF	PERSON	DOES NOT	MAKE	PLAN *think all*
FOR	DISTANT	FUTURE *time ahead*	HE/SHE	WILL
CERTAINLY *for certain*	ENCOUNTER *come face to face*	DIFFICULTIES	IN	NEAR
FUTURE				

One benefits more from taking a trip than reading about it.

PERSON	WILL	BENEFIT	MORE	FROM

TAKING	TRIP	THAN	READING	ABOUT IT

Let sleeping dogs lie.

LET	SLEEPING	DOGS	BE	HORIZONTAL

You can't expect the horse to run fast if you don't let it graze.

YOU	CAN NOT	EXPECT *think coming*	HORSE	TO RUN
FAST	IF	YOU DO NOT	LET	IT
GRAZE				

Walk slowly and you won't fall down;
act carefully and you won't make mistake.

WALK	SLOW	AND	YOU	WILL NOT
FALL DOWN	ACT	WITH	GREAT	ATTENTION
AND	YOU	WILL NOT	MAKE	MISTAKE

Let us end with a brief reminder that this is just one-tenth of the Chinese proverbs that we selected in somewhat arbitrary manner from the mentioned book. But the editors of the book, Marjorie Lin and Schalk Leonard, had a more difficult task in gathering this folklore in the first place. It is fitting to end this exposition of Chinese proverbs by a short paragraph from the introductory part of the book in which the editors explain their selection process for proverbs:

> Significance, as the central criterion of selection, includes frequency of use, but also refers to the tendency of the proverb to express traditional Chinese wisdom, beliefs, values, and aspirations. In this volume may be found proverbs that express Taoist and Buddhist truths, Confucian rules of prosperity, admonishments from the elderly, exhortations from parents, and advice from teachers. The reader may discover, after a generous perusal of the Chinese proverbs contained herein, certain unique and traditional features of Chinese life and thought. Among those features one may note a strong preference

for the particular over the general and the concrete over the abstract, frequent use of symbolism, respect for the wisdom of the ancients, an emphasis on the study and learning, a tendency toward caution and frugality, strong esteem for hierarchy, reliance on individual ethics, and a search for truth through study of nature.

PART 5

Challenges Ahead

Picture is worth thousand words.
In thousand languages
Picture is worth million words.

Recent book *One Thousand Languages*, edited by Peter K. Austin (University of California Press, Berkeley and Los Angeles, 2008) outlines briefly living, endangered, and lost languages all over the globe. Today eleven languages have over one hundred million speakers each:

Chinese	1,055 million	Arabic	205 million
English	760 million	Portuguese	191 million
Hindi	490 million	French	128 million
Spanish	417 million	German	128 million
Russian	277 million	Japanese	122 million
Bengali	230 million		

These 11 languages account for more than half of the humanity. According to this book, there are an estimated 6,900 languages spoken in the world, of which 275 languages cover 96 percent of world population. How can humanity efficiently communicate when even within similar languages there are dialects or variations that are not mutually understood? Just start with Chinese, which has been counted here as one language, which has two major distinct variations, in the north Mandarin, and in the south Cantonese. They are sufficiently different that speakers of these regions do not understand one another. Yet Chinese writings (characters), not only make it possible for them to communicate, but allow people of Japan, who speak a language of quite different family, and who adopted Chinese characters for writing, to have a fair idea what written Chinese messages tell.

Nobel is a language that has the same capabilities, that of being universal, equally accessible to speakers of all languages, including some five thousand, if not six thousand, which are dying and spoken by less than a million speakers, half of which are spoken by less than ten thousand. An advantage of Nobel, which is *in statu nascendi* (Latin for "in the state of being born"), is that it has some simplicity (or elegance) in its structure, which is also reflected in the fact that learning more of Nobel strengthens one's familiarity with the language and does not burden memory, as is the case with learning Chinese characters, at least for people having limited exposure to such writings.

Another advantage of Nobel is its great pictographic content, not at the level of Egyptian hieroglyphics, but having enough of self-recognized elements, that will make it possible for people five thousand years and even twenty thousand years after us to unlock our messages. One may say that we have been lucky to come across Rosetta stone, written in hieroglyphic, demotic (simplified glyphs), and classical Greek, which made possible understanding of hieroglyphic writings. The languages of today are not to be around in the same form, and people of future times will not understand present languages, just as we cannot understand languages of two thousand years ago. An illustration is Etruscan language, which still is not known to us. Etruscan was known to Romans as witnessed by the fact that Emperor Claudius, who reigned two thousand years ago, was the last known scholar of Etruscan in the ancient world. Etruscan language has its own alphabet (based on Greek but modified somehow), and there are numerous written remains, though most are short and, according to a comment in the book *One Thousand Languages*, hardly any of which was bilingual. In fact, the longest Etruscan text, with some 1,200 words, was discovered on wrappings of a mummy, which is in the Ethnographic Museum in Zagreb, Croatia, for some 150 years. The mummy was bought by a Croatian minor official who, after working in Royal Chancellery in Budapest, retired and traveled several countries, including

Egypt, where he bought the mummy as a souvenir. After he died, his family donated the mummy to the Museum in Zagreb. For fifty years, it was not known to what language the inscription on the mummy belonged; finally, after the mummy was sent to Vienna, an expert for Coptic languages identified the script as Etruscan. Now comes an interesting question: Why would a mummy in Egypt be wrapped in folded paper (a book) in Etruscan language? It appears that Romans, who after Greeks ruled Egypt, adopted some customs of Egypt, including mummification of dead. This apparently created demand for cloths for wrapping mummies, which were not available in sufficient quantities and extended demand for other material, paper included. Thus some local community took advantage of good price for paper and sold their Etruscan book (for which they had no need), which thus ended as wrapping of the mummy in Zagreb.

In summary, if we are to leave a message for those coming five thousand years after, not to mention twenty thousand years, the time that our nuclear waste will still be around, hidden in salt mines and other locations, and still dangerous to life, we better also construct new Rosetta stones, which could have hieroglyphic-like signs as they tend to be detailed picture symbols for those words that can be so depicted, Nobel for the actual text, and English—and all this better be all carved in stone—as stone seems to be the material that can withstand time. So a Nobel Rosetta stone is one of the challenges of the future. If the same text used for Nobel Rosetta stone is applied to other leading languages of the world, perhaps future generations will be able to better understand the lack of understanding between the people of today, particularly the ruling people of today. As an alternative to a Nobel Rosetta stone would be multilingual dictionaries, hoping that some may survive the vulnerability of "soft" materials like paper and remain preserved for a long time.

One of the oldest multilingual dictionaries is the five-language dictionary of Faust Vrančić (1551-1617), also known as Fausto Veranzio: *Dictionarium quinque nobilissimarum Europeae linguarum: Latinae, Italicae, Germanicae, Dalmaticae et Hungaricae* (Dictionary of five noble European languages: Latin, Italian, German, Dalmatian, and Hungarian) published in Venice in 1595, with five thousand entries for each language. The term "Dalmatian" stands here for

Croatian Čakavian dialect spoken in Istria, along the northern Adriatic coast, and on most of the Adriatic islands (as well as in Croatian pockets in Austria, Hungary, and Slovakia). The dictionary has been reprinted in Zagreb in 1971. Perhaps it is time to expand this dictionary by including English, French, Spanish, Russian, and Nobel—and stay with its original vocabulary of five thousand words? Not counting Latin (dead) and Nobel (just born), such ten-language dictionary would cover 1,785 million people, which is 10 million more than China (with Mandarin and Cantonese) and India (with Hindi and Bengali), the two most populous countries in the world together. In time to come, Nobel can easily count for additional 1,785 million people, if not more!

But we live today and have other challenges to meet, including when speaking of Nobel, further development of the vocabulary, so that one can meet common needs of our time. Although we passed three thousand words, there are a number of common words that we are still missing—and they are missing because we do not yet have suitable *simple* signs for such. Just to mention a few, consider items of clothes: shirt, jacket, coat, skirt, underwear, socks, scarf, and such. We have seen very few clothing items, e.g., *hat* (basic sign) and *gloves* (hand cover). We could easily add few by taking advantage of the word "cover."

GOWN	SUIT	OVERCOAT	T-SHIRT	SHIRT
body cover	*gown cover*	*suit cover*	*chest cover*	*T-shirt cover*

JACKET	UNDERPANTS	PANTS	OVERALLS	SKIRT
shirt cover	*belly cover*	*underpants cover*	*pants cover*	*not pants*

We could continue, but this suffices to illustrate the spirit of the search for "missing words." Observe that even if the proposed signs are still too general, there is definite logic in the structure

of such words (that is, arrangement of signs forming words).
We have already seen *logic* in several other groups of signs. For
example,

HUMANITY *people around globe*	ADMINIS- TRATION *people around government*	BUREAUCRACY *people around desk*	INTELLI- GENTSIA *people around book*	

and signs like

DOCTOR *ahead of sick*	CAPTAIN *ahead of ship*	INSTRUCTOR *ahead of textbook*	CATTLEMAN *ahead of cattle*	WARDEN *ahead of prison*
NURSE *behind sick*	SAILOR *behind ship*	STUDENT *behind textbook*	COWBOY *behind cattle*	PRISONER *behind prison*

To this we may add, by taking advantage of the two-dimensional
nature of graphical language, which allows placing the same signs
in different orientations, a few illustrations:

LOVE	RICH	BARRIER	WAR	MASSACRE
ENTHUSIASM	CAPITAL	BARRICADE	MILITARY	BLOODSHED

DAY	CONSTEL-LATION	TELESCOPE	WOOD	ORDER
SIMULTA-NEOUS	DECORATION	MICROSCOPE	OLD GROWTH	INSTRUCTION

We could continue with additional illustrations but rather than repeating already presented words or words not shown, which could be constructed, let us show how we can use such opportunities of the two-dimensional nature of graphical language for *novel* words, words that are of *recent time* or *recent interest*, and which one will not find in dictionaries. One such term is "same-sex marriage." Of course, we have sign for *marriage*, sign for *sex*, and sign for *same* and these can be combined to construct sign for same-sex marriage. But there are some hidden *linguistic* problems with the word *marriage*, which, in different languages, only relates to "union of male and female." For illustration, in Croatian language, there are two words that correspond to marriage, one related to female and one to male. Thus, if liberally translated, in Croatian language, for a man *marriage* is "getting woman," and for a woman *marriage* is "giving self." The very words for wedding, marry, get married in Croatian are based on the root "woman"—thus two man cannot "get married," because the word implies woman, though two women could (linguistically speaking)! It is conceivable that in some languages, the etymology of words makes it possible for a man to get married and a female not, or as in English, anyone can get marriage, because the word is asexual. Be that as it may, it seems better if we could have different signs for traditional marriage and same-sex marriage, and yet try to avoid to have signs that would involve visibly different components and thus perpetuate discrimination. Here we take advantage of the two-dimensional nature of graphic language, and we advocate for traditional marriage and the same-sex marriage the signs shown below, respectively:

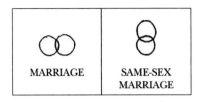

The traditional marriage is shown as *horizontal* marriage and the same-sex marriage is shown as *vertical* marriage. In a way, one can view the two signs as synonyms, two words with the same or similar meaning. Among those three thousand words that we have so far covered, we have seen numerous synonyms, which we have described rather briefly, but because synonyms involve some arbitrary decisions and challenges, we will end this book by an overview of problems and challenges involved in design of synonyms.

Synonyms in Nobel

At the very beginning, after introduction of the first sixty basic signs, we have outlined construction of antonyms, opposites. There are three routes in Nobel for construction of opposites: *inversion* of sign, *crossing* of sign, and constructing the *reciprocal* of a sign. The inversion and crossing are, however, limited to a few signs for which such modifications do not cause confusion, while the third approach has been widely used, and used not only for opposites, but for words that are closely associated with each other. So there are no difficulties in constructing antonyms in Nobel.

In contrast, the situation with construction of signs of synonyms is more complex and lacks any simple rules. There are a few exceptions, the words which are true synonyms and stand for identical concepts or objects. Such is the case with snake—serpent in English, but in Nobel the sign for snake stands for nonvenomous serpent, which is modified for viper by inverting the head-tail positions. The triplet mountain lion—cougar—puma are synonyms and one sign would suffice, but we left two signs for this case: mountain lion is shown as mountain & king animal, and cougar is shown as mountain & big cat. There are but rather few additional synonyms that are represented by two signs, like holiday = day to relax, and holiday = horizontal day (day in which if you wish you can stay in bed—be horizontal). Similarly, vacation is shown in two different ways: vacation = travel we love, and vacation = lot of relaxation; and an old person is shown as person having lot of time behind and as a shrinking person. So one has a choice to use one or the other, or even both, if they apply, because the signs, though relating to the same, like vacation, there are different forms of vacation, and some may like to travel, some may like to lie down in a shade.

We continue with illustrations of several synonyms:

TIME CONFLICT	CONTEMPO-RARY	FRESH	CHALLENGE	GOOD-LOOK-ING
TIME CONFLICT	CONTEMPO-RARY	FRESH	CHALLENGE	GOOD-LOOK-ING

The above signs are fairly transparent and hardly need comment. Why do we need two signs, if one can do? Well, most synonyms refer to similar and not quite identical situations, and this is the case with the sign shown above, except perhaps for the sign for *time conflict*. Consider *good-looking* signs. One refers to a person but the other is more general and applied to anything else that is good-looking. Similarly the sign of *fresh* involving ascending arrow, which bears some relationship with the sign for *new*, involving ordinary arrow entering into time, is OK to use if you speak of fresh fruits, fresh fish, or fresh bread, and in general of fresh food, but if you speak of fresh weather then cold—no cold sign would be appropriate. The same can be said about the sign for *challenge*, which can be physical or mental, and one can discriminate them using the alternative signs.

Some brief comment can be added relating to the elements of arbitrariness in words of similar meaning. Consider, for example, already mentioned love-enthusiasm, barrier-barricade, constellation-decoration, order-instructions, and so on. One could have assigned the same words to the "horizontal" and "vertical" combinations in just the opposite way, and in most cases, both alternatives would be equally legitimate. This is also the case even when different signs are used, as illustrated below:

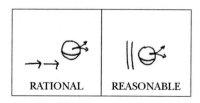

| RATIONAL | REASONABLE |

We have selected *rational* to be shown as *following reason* and *reasonable* as being *parallel with reason,* that is, *agree with reason.* But as said, the other way round could equally suffice.

A real challenge in designing signs are not the strict synonyms, but words that have similar or related meaning, such as, to give but one illustration: atrocious, wicked, cruel, savage, brutal, ruthless, terrible, horrible, dreadful, awful, vile, wretched, contemptible. Among the thirteen words listed above, one can find that six have been included in our list of three thousand words of Nobel considered in this book, while six were not (atrocious, brutal, ruthless, horrible, dreadful, and wretched). The word *contemptible* has also not been included, but the word contempt has been; so we covered in this case half of the words listed under *atrocious* in *The Clear and Simple Thesaurus Dictionary* by H. Wittels and J. Greisman and edited by W. Morris (published by Scholastic Inc., New York 1998). Just to refresh our memories, here are the signs for the selection of the words:

WICKED	CRUEL	SAVAGE	TERRIBLE	TERRIBLE
AWFUL	VILE			

And here are challenges awaiting resolution:

ATROCIOUS	BRUTAL	RUTHLESS	HORRIBLE	DREADFUL
WRETCHED	CONTEMPTIBLE			

Clearly, in order to arrive at signs for such synonyms one has to know the language so well to feel the difference between the synonyms. According to *Encarta* dictionary, one finds the following:

Atrocious   (1)   appallingly bad
               (2)   extremely evil or cruel
               (3)   so ugly in taste or appearance as to elicit revulsion

Brutal   (1) extremely ruthless or cruel
             (2) unrelentingly harsh and severe

Ruthless   (1) having or showing no pity or mercy

Horrible   (1)   very bad, very unpleasant, or caused by anxiety or fear about something bad
              (2)   sufficiently frightening, distressing or shocking as to provoke horror
              (3)   inspiring awe

Wretched   (1)   feeling very unhappy or ill
              (2)   in a state of great hardship, deprivation, and hopelessness and arousing sympathy in others
              (3)   seriously inadequate or of very low quality
              (4)   provoking irritation of anger

As one can see, except for *ruthless*, all other words have three to four different meanings. In addition, *atrocious* and *brutal* overlap in one of their several usages, being described as extremely cruel. Finally, in one of its meanings, *horrible* is described circularly, using the word *horror*, something that mathematicians would frown upon.

We will try to come up with some answers, but there are still some hidden difficulties that need to be considered. Let us return to the already-mentioned doublet for *atrocious* and *brutal* characterized as *extremely cruel*. We have in Nobel signs for extreme (top and the bottom of a mountain) and cruel (without heart), but we cannot combine the two, because in Nobel cruel is shown as *without heart* and if a person is without heart—we cannot have "extremely without heart," just as dead person cannot be more dead than he already is.

We follow with signs for the set of synonyms that we propose:

ATROCIOUS	BRUTAL	RUTHLESS	HORRIBLE	DREADFUL
extremely evil	*extremely ruthless*	*without mercy*	*complete fear*	*extremely unpleasant*
WRETCHED	CONTEMPTIBLE			
extremely unhappy	*have contempt*			

Observe that even though we have not listed the above seven words in our list of some 3,000 Nobel signs, if you would come across these signs, you would read them just as the subtitles in italics show. Thus, if you would come across the first of these seven signs, you would read it as EXTREMELY EVIL, and if you know English sufficiently well, you yourself will recognize the message as ATROCIOUS. What this means is that by learning some 3,000 words you have in fact learned at least double that number! Hence, you may claim knowing not 3,000 but 6,000 words of Nobel. This may appear a preposterous claim, but we will demonstrate that this is the case. For this, we selected words starting with letter *S*, which is the letter in English with the largest number of words. There are 335 words starting with letter *S* in this book. On the following pages, we will list another 335 words starting with *S*, all of which one should be able to understand without elaborations.

SACCHARIN	SACRIFICE	SADISM	SAGA	SAINT
SAKE	SALMONELLA	SALT	SALUTE	SALVAGE
SANATORIUM	SAND	SANDBAG	SANDPIPER	SANDSTONE
SANDSTORM	SANITARY	SANITIZE	SAP	SARCOMA
SARI	SATELLITE	SATIATE	SATISFACTORY	SATISFIED
SAUCER	SAUDI ARABIA	SAVANNA	SAW	SAWDUST
SAWMILL	SAY	SAYING	SCAFFOLD	SCAFFOLD

SCALP	SCALPEL	SCAN	SCAN	SCANDAL
SCANT	SCAPEGOAT	SCARF	SCATTER	SCAVENGER
SCENE	SCENERY	SCENIC	SCENT	SCHEME
SCHIZO-PHRENIA	SCHOLAR	SCHOLARSHIP	SCHOOL	SCHOOL YEAR
SCIENTIST	SCLEROSIS	SCOUT	SCRAMBLE	SCRIBBLE
SCRUTINIZE	SCUM	SCUM	SCURVY	SEA BATTLE
SEA FOOD	SEA HORSE	SEAL	SEAMAN	SEAMEN
SEA MINE	SEAMSTRESS	SEAPORT	SEA RESORT	SEASCAPE

SEA SNAKE	SEA URCHIN	SEA WALL	SEA WARD	SEA WEED
SECEDE	SECLUDED	SECONDARY SCHOOL	SECRET	SECRET POLICE
SECRET SERVICE	SECT	SECULAR	SECURE	SEDIMENT
SEDUCE	SEEDLING	SEEDCAKE	SEEK	SEGREGATE
SEGREGATION	SEISMOGRAPH	SEISMOGRAPH	SEIZE	SELECT
SELECTION	SELF-CON-FIDENCE	SELF-CON-TRADICTION	SELF CONTROL	SELF DECIEVING
SELF-DEFENSE	SELF-GLORI-FICATION	SELF-HARMING	SELF-IMPOR-TANCE	SELF-IM-PROVEMENT
SELF-INTEREST	SELF-JUSTI-FICATION	SELFLESS	SELF-LOVE	SELF-MUTILA-TION

464 MILAN RANDIĆ

SELF-PROMO-TION	SELF-PRO-PELLED	SELF-PROTEC-TION	SELF-PUB-LISHED	SELF-RESTRAINT
SELF-SERVICE	SELF-SUFFI-CIENT	SELF-SUPPORT-ING	SELF-TALK	SELF-TAUGHT
SELF-WILL	SEMANTICS	SEMAPHORE	SEMEN	SEMESTER
SEMIAUTO-MATIC	SEMICIRCLE	SEMI-CONDUC-TOR	SEMINARY	SEMIPRE-CIOUS STONE
SENATE	SENATE	SENATOR	SENILE	SENSATIONAL
SENSE	SENSELESS	SENSIBLE	SENSITIVE	SENSITIZE
SENSUAL	SENTENCE	SENTIMENT	SENTIMENTAL	SENTINEL
SENTRY	SEPARABLE	SEPARATE	SEPARATED	SEPARATION

SEPARATIST	SEPSIS	SEPTIC	SEQUEL	SEQUESTER
SERAPH	SERENADE	SERENE	SERF	SERIOCOMIC
SERPENTINE	SERUM	SERVANT	SERVICE	SERVICEMAN
SEVER	SEWAGE	SEWER	SEX APPEAL	SEX EQUALITY
SEX OFFENDER	SEXUAL	SEXUAL INTERCOURSE	SEXY	SHACK
SHACKLES	SHADE	SHAGGY	SHAKY	SHAMBLE
SHAME	SHAMROCK	SHANTY	SHARE	SHARPEN
SHARP-EYED	SHARP-TONGUED	SHARP-WITTED	SHATTER	SHEAR

SHEATH	SHELF	SHELTER	SHEPHERD	SHERBET
SHIFT	SHILLING	SHIN	SHINGLE	SHIPPING
SHIPYARD	SHIPLOAD	SHIPWRECK	SHIT	SHIVER
SHOAL	SHOCK	SHOE	SHOOTINGSTAR	SHORT
SHORTCOMING	SHORTHORN	SHORT LIST	SHORTLY	SHORT SIGHT
SHORT-SIGHTED	SHORT TEMPER	SHOT	SHOW	SHOWDOWN
SHOWER	SHRAPNEL	SHRED	SHREW	SHREW
SHRINK	SHROUD	SHRUB	SHRUG	SHUFFLE

SHUFFLE	SHUT	SHUTTER	SICKLE	SIDE
SIDE BY SIDE	SIDE DISH	SIDEWALK	SIEGE	SIERRA
SIESTA	SIGHT	SIGHT SEEING	SIGN	SIGNALIZE
SIGNIFICANT	SIGN POST	SILHOUETTE	SILLY	SILO
SIMMER	SIMPLE	SIMPLE	SIMPLIFY	SINCE
SINCERE	SINGER	SINGLE-HANDED	SINISTER	SIP
SIREN	SISSY	SISTER-IN-LAW	SIZABLE	SIZZLE
SKI LIFT	SKILL	SKILLED	SKINNED	SKINHEAD

SKINNY	SKIP	SKIPPER	SKYLIGHT	SLAB
SLANDER	SLASH	SLATE	SLEEPLESS	SLEET
SLIM	SLIT	SLOGAN	SLOWDOWN	SLUM
SLUMBER	SLUMBEROUS	SLUSH	SMACK	SMACK
SMALLPOX	SMITH	SMUGGLE	SNACK	SNAP
SNARE	SNATCH	SNIFF	SNORE	SNOWBALL
SNOW GOOSE	SNOW POWDER	SOAPSTONE	SOBER	SOCIAL
SOFT WATER	SOJOURN	SOLAR ECLIPSE	SOLAR YEAR	SOLITARY

SOLITUDE	SOLO	SOLSTICE	SON-IN-LAW	SOOT
SORROW	SPARK	SPARROW	SPECTACLE	SPECTATOR
SPEED BUMP	SPEED ZONE	SPELEOLOGY	SPLINTER	SPOKESMAN
STAG	STAGGER	STALEMATE	STALL	STANDOFF

We arrived at 335 new words without even exhausting letter *S*, there being still words starting with *St, Su, Sv, Sw,* and *Sy.* There is no word in English that starts with *Sx,* and there is also no word in English starting with *Sz* if we exclude foreign cities (like Szeged in Hungary and Szczecin in Poland) and immigrants coming from foreign countries, like Leo Szilard (1898-1664), Hungarian-born US biophysicist, one of early advocates of peaceful use of atomic energy, mentioned in *Encarta* dictionary at my disposal. This ought to support our supposition that rather than having opportunity to become acquainted with a vocabulary of over 3,000 words of Nobel, more likely is that one will be in a position to make sense of messages using double that many signs.

Who needs three thousand or six thousand signs? Why have we not selected a smaller vocabulary, such as eight hundred words of the Basic English of C. K. Ogden, or one thousand words of *Essential English* of C. E. Eckersley? Well, once we reach three thousand or six thousand, or even twenty thousand, we could consider construction of Basic Nobel of eight hundred words, or Essential Nobel of one thousand words, or Fundamental Nobel (to parallel currently nonexistent Fundamental English) based on judicious selection of two thousand signs, by enlarging vocabularies of C. K. Ogden and C. E. Eckersley. And I am confident that some such versions with limited vocabulary will emerge sooner or later, as most of us can live happily without knowing anything about ornithology or leap second. Italian mathematician Giuseppe Peano (1858-1932) in 1903 announced his work on an international auxiliary language called *Latino sine flexione.* It uses Latin vocabulary with simplified grammar and without irregular and anomalous language forms as much as possible, to make this language easier to learn. I mentioned Peano also to point out that he prepared a dictionary of ten thousand words of this simplified Latin, which I took as an indicator that a vocabulary of ten thousand to twenty thousand may suffice for initial development of a new language.

Let us return to the question: Who needs three thousand or six thousand signs? Well, if one is to consider translating shorter or longer text from English to Nobel, it is better to have available larger vocabulary than being stuck with words for which no translation (or transcription) is available. Or, if one is considering writing one's own diary in Nobel, as I am contemplating, again it is better to have more words than less. To facilitate such exercises for those readers who have time and patience, at the end of this book is compiled an Index of Words, which will make it easy to find an adequate Nobel sign for an English word. Next to each word in the index is indicated the page the first time the sign appeared (and where it has been most likely explained).

Now why should someone wish to write a personal diary in Nobel and not in English? Roman emperor Marcus Aurelius (121-180) has written a book (in Greek) to himself, a book not to be published. This is not a diary, as it is not listing chronologically events of interest, but is more about reflections on self, others, words, and nature around. One may say that this is a *private* book. Only later, the book was discovered and is now available to anyone speaking languages in which the book has been translated. I have the Croatian translation, and I am contemplating, as one option, to translate this book, or more likely, parts of the book, in Nobel. Providing a permission for the translation will be given, this will be important for two reasons: (1) Translation of the book will allow for further development, improvement and possible revision of Nobel, and may even help in identifying fundamental words (those two thousand words that are most useful in practical communication); (2) It will make this excellent book of Emperor Marcus Aurelius (in Latin, Imperator Caesar Marcus Aurelius Antoninus Augustus), the last of five good emperors of Rome, available to speakers of one thousand languages. But let us try to answer the question raised: Now why should someone wish to write a personal diary in Nobel and not in English, or his/her native language? Besides having pleasure to face challenges from time to time, when struggling to find or even invent the most suitable sign for missing words, a diary written in Nobel has some advantage of preserving privacy of your own thoughts at least for a while, for the time that your neighbors are Nobel-illiterate!

Why the book of Marcus Aurelius? I can again think of two reasons: The first reason is that even though one could select almost any book of one's preference for translation, there is an "honor" of the *first translation* in Nobel. We have a selection of Chinese proverbs to honor Chinese four thousand years of writing. The book of Marcus Aurelius, emperor and philosopher, deserves our attention. He was the last of the so-called five good emperors, demonstrating that power need not corrupt, and that it is possible, though exceedingly rare, that world rulers throughout history, have wisdom beside power. The second reason is that Marcus Aurelius, by bringing grape from southern Italy to hilly area of Danube near the border of Croatia and Serbia, has left a gift for posterity, the excellent vine of Fruška Gora (mountain), which we still today, two thousand years later, continue to enjoy. So he deserves to be remembered!

Let us end with comments on translations of text from one language to another—a task which is far from straightforward. Translations are in general considered to be necessarily deficient, involving unsuspected and suspected hurdles. A recent book of Umberto Eco, *The Search for the Perfect Language* elaborates on this theme. Let us only add here that computer-based language translations are still not adequate, even if progress were made. Perhaps here Nobel can be of some interest and help, and play a role of a metalanguage, an intermediate language between two languages? Just a thought.

Finally, let us comment on a single sign that illustrates that language is not mathematics. There are the two signs for SCAN that we have just shown. The word *scan*, according to *Encarta World English Dictionary*, as a verb, has nine different interpretations, and additional two as a noun. We selected the first two (presumably the most common) meaning of this word as a verb, which are as follows:

1. EXAMINE SOMETHING IN DETAIL, to subject something to thorough examination
2. LOOK THROUGH SOMETHING QUICKLY, to look through or read something quickly

So, there is a contradictory message. It is up to the reader to decide which meaning applies in which situation. Be that as it may, similar contradictory meanings of words possibly occur in other languages. Consider the Croatian word *blago*, which has four meanings, two of which are in contradiction as has been the case with English SCAN. Here are the four meanings and comments that may explain the contradiction:

1. TREASURE
2. CATTLE
3. GENTLE
4. WILD BEHAVIOR

In medieval times, having cattle was like having treasure, so the two became synonyms. And if you are gentle with cattle, you may get better yield. There was some report that playing classical music while milking cows gives more milk—if that was the case, it would provide an illustration of gentle behavior. The last and contradictory meaning comes with using the word to describe wild behavior, lack of manners, which is the case with cattle and with wild youth, to which such offensive description are sometimes directed.

Looking to the Future

It has been pointed out at the beginning of the book, in the foreword, that it is difficult and even almost impossible to speculate on the future of chances of an artificial language to be widely accepted. Despite being optimistic, it would be unwise to enter such speculation. There is no doubt that there will be group of enthusiasts as well as skeptics, some of whom will be experts in language affairs and some of whom may be familiar with language issues. Let them debate the issue on the future of Nobel, which is neither constructed for expert linguists nor for university professors, but their views may contribute to further improvement of the graphical language Nobel. Nobel is constructed for "common" people, which of course, includes university professors, language students, and graduate students interested in languages in general and artificial languages in particular. But on the other side of the spectrum are people who may wish to communicate or to be informed about things around, in environments in which they are not able to understand messages. There is one group that we have not mentioned, the illiterate people, or effectively illiterate, who can benefit from some familiarity with Nobel. And this is not so small a group of people even in some developed countries, including the USA. Thus, Nobel offers an opportunity to local authorities to pass written messages to people who have been, not necessarily by their fault or their choice, deprived of possibility to learn to read and write. If one is too skeptical to accept this possibility as viable, just recall that cavemen, who left numerous petroglyphs over all continents of the globe, as well as people who did not have written language, like Native Americans and most of the people of Polynesia, were definitely illiterate, yet their pictograms and drawings passed some messages of the past to the present. In fact, the picture writing of the American Indians is, one can say, a bridge between static signs, such as most petroglyphs of the past or traffic signs of today, and the dynamic signs of pictographic language, which can express history of what has been happening. For example, the picture writing of the Ojibway (Native Americans of northern Minnesota) had over one hundred signs expressing various specific activities, such as "I want to see you," "I lied to my son," "the spirit has given me power to see," "I hear spirit speaking to me," and so on. For more, see *Picture-Writing of the American Indians*, by Garrick Mallery (Dover: New York, 1972). If such "half-languages" were able to pass to us some of messages of the past, surely a full graphical language, like Nobel, will make it possible for messages written today in Nobel to convey present-day messages to readers of the *distant* future, regardless of their tongue. This particular potential of Nobel should not be overlooked, even though there are many possible uses of Nobel in our own time.

Let us comment on some inherent *flexibility* of Nobel, which allows the same message to be written in slightly different but equally understandable forms and, in this way, does not demand that one remember details of some signs, but only their central message. Language is not mathematics, and hence some signs are not necessarily always to be taken very rigidly and duplicated very exactly—though cases in which similar combinations carry different content ought to be respected, if the messages are to be properly understood. Let us show a few illustrations of the flexibility of using Nobel:

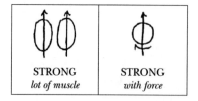

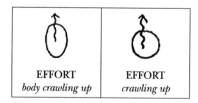

Strong, particularly if we speak of people (and some animals) relates to strong *muscles*, muscles giving strength to the body.

Strong persons can exert force, hence are *with force*. But there could be a *strong wind*, or one talks about *strong material*, in which case a sign "with force" would be more appropriate. We have not exhausted possibilities, as one can consider a *strong argument* or one can have a *strong drink*. Here again "with force" may be better choice than "with muscle" but even better could be some other synonym signifying strength, such as powerful, vigorous, forceful, potent, mighty, and hardy. The situation is similar with EFFORT, because the word can relate to human body involved in achieving a result, or can be used to indicate mental effort, mental activity, for which the alternative sign would be more appropriate.

SELFISHNESS	SELFISHNESS
feeling	*selfish selfish*

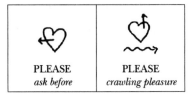

PLEASE	PLEASE
ask before	*crawling pleasure*

There is hardly difference between the two expressions of selfishness in Nobel; both imply some duration, not a temporary disposition. By doubling a sign in Nobel, one always arrives at concepts that indicate "lot of" the same. There is some difference between *please*, when asking for something, and *please*, as when having pleasure of something, which the two signs clearly differentiate.

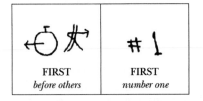

FIRST	FIRST
before others	*number one*

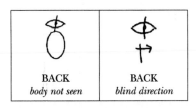

BACK	BACK
body not seen	*blind direction*

In the case of FIRST, again we have signs with similar but also possibly slightly different usage. If one speaks of accomplishment of people, the first variant is proper, but if one speaks of quality (e.g., the prime rib or the first class on trains, hotels, etc.) the second variant is the obvious choice. In fact, one can have in a single sentence both possibilities, like

> Nobel is not the first graphical language (before others), but it has potential to become the first (number one) by the number of followers.

Observe that we said "has potential" thus cutting down on possibility to be accused of speculating on the future of Nobel. BACK in English is relating to *things behind* (e.g., back home, back in old times) and the *part of the body* which is behind and which we cannot see. In some languages, there are two different words for the two different uses of the English word *back*, which is the reason for maintaining two different signs for *back*.

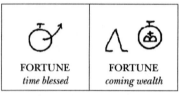

FORTUNE	FORTUNE
time blessed	*coming wealth*

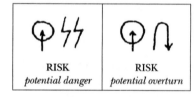

RISK	RISK
potential danger	*potential overturn*

These two sets of signs hardly need comment, being self-explanatory. Recall the sign for FATE = *time chooses,* because fate is outside one's control. In the case of *fortune,* time has chosen "blessing."

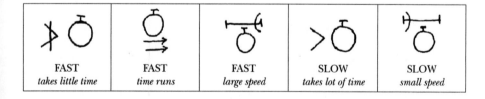

FAST	FAST	FAST	SLOW	SLOW
takes little time	*time runs*	*large speed*	*takes lot of time*	*small speed*

This set of signs is also easily understood. If something takes little amount of time, it has been accomplished fast; if time runs, it again means fast actions, and if something has been completed at high speed (which is shown as passing long distance over time), it implies fast action. *Slow* has been shown as opposite combinations. We could have added also a combination "time does not run" by crossing the arrows indicating "running" as a third option for indicating a slow process.

| SWEET | SWEET | SWEET | BITTER | BITTER |

The sign of HEART basically stands for something we like, and most people, children in particular, like sweet food, chocolate and cookies—thus the sign of heart has an added interpretation indicating something sweet (which includes also one's sweetheart). Opposite of sweet, BITTER, is then shown as reciprocal. By adding sweet and bitter, we obtain the sign for taste, which can vary from sweet to bitter. When the fraction sweet/bitter sign is used for taste, then one can point to numerator (the upper part) and, by marking it, indicate sweet taste, or one can point to denominator (the lower part) and, by marking it, indicate bitter taste. As indicator, one can use the small arrow or the equal sign, both have been used in various combinations of signs of Nobel.

| SCANDAL | SCANDAL | SALVAGE | SALVAGE |
| *sin in public* | *event makes people angry* | *not destroy* | *recover* |

The above illustrations show combinations that send the same message, but one variant is simpler than the other, which is likely that it may prevail, because it will be reproduced readily. "In public" is represented by podium, because if one does something on podium, more people will see it!

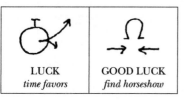

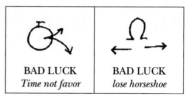

The first sign for LUCK is shown as a preference given by fate. The second sign for luck, or GOOD LUCK, originates possibly in medieval time, when finding a horseshoe was perceived as good luck, and probably was good luck, because in those times horseshoes were not easy to come by. Horseshoes today are not expensive, but they are also in much less demand, so they are not easy to be found—thus we can let "finding a horseshoe" to continue to symbolize good luck. The signs for BAD LUCK are just the opposite of LUCK and GOOD LUCK signs.

Let us end this small gallery of words having alternative signs for the same word:

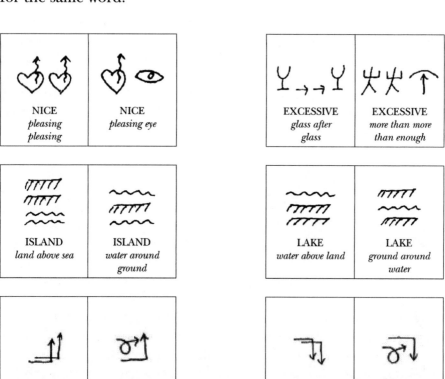

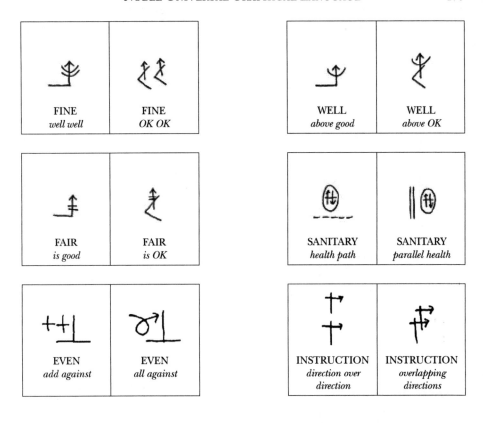

FINE	FINE
well well	*OK OK*

WELL	WELL
above good	*above OK*

FAIR	FAIR
is good	*is OK*

SANITARY	SANITARY
health path	*parallel health*

EVEN	EVEN
add against	*all against*

INSTRUCTION	INSTRUCTION
direction over direction	*overlapping directions*

The last sign, the instruction sign, is shown in two variants, as overlap of directions and as doubling (lot of) instructions—both appear acceptable and illustrate some flexibility in writing Nobel. While in all above cases the selection of sign is left to the user, one should observe different meaning of combinations of the same sign elements when differently positioned. For example, "powder *in* sea" refers to salt, which is extracted from sea, while "powder *aside* sea" stands for sand and sandy beaches.

It appears that in some early Chinese writings when there was need for a sign that a writer did not know or the sign may have not yet been constructed, it was invented at that time. So the same may occur with "early" writings of Nobel, which a writer may introduce his/her own sign for a word not encountered up to that time. This may create duplicates for some signs as those shown above, but with time, better constructions are likely to survive and enrich the vocabulary of Nobel.

To those who came to the end of this introduction to graphical "universal language" Nobel, we congratulate you for understanding, patience, and stamina—and hope that that experience was not traumatic but educational and in part entertaining, even if possible skepticism of some to the future of Nobel may have not fully dissipated. If learning Nobel took some time away from other pleasures of life—it may have also brought to readers a pleasure of enjoyment that they know a new language and have thus joined the growing community of bilingual and multilingual people around the world.

flag of Nobel

The past of Nobel was in my hands, the future of Nobel is in the hands of readers. To the future of Nobel, we can exclaim,

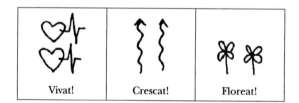

| Vivat! | Crescat! | Floreat! |

The End

Epilogue and Acknowledgments

Work on Nobel, which started some twenty-five years ago, was for a number of years made secretly. One of my first "victims" to whom I dared to show illustrations of Nobel was the young eight-year-old son of my friend in Waterloo, Canada, Professor Milan Pintar. On a few occasions, the boy would guess correctly the meaning of a sign before I had time to explain it. As I continued to outline Nobel to additional young people, like the eight-year-old grandson of a college professor, A. T. Balaban, and two daughters, six and eight years old, of a relative, Silva Karmelić, in my hometown of Rijeka, I found that youngsters were interested and excited about Nobel—which I take to be very a good sign based on the old adage, "On younger, world rest." But Nobel suits any age. The son of a colleague, Anton-Jan Klasinc, who is a teacher in a private high school in Zagreb, introduced Nobel to his class. I tried on a few occasions to contact him while visiting Zagreb to hear his experience but have so far failed to meet him. I did not expose my colleagues in the scientific community to Nobel, except for a few, which include Professor Doug Klein from Texas A&M University at Galveston, with whom I have worked on several joint research projects; Professor Robert G. Parr from the University of North Carolina (formerly at the Johns Hopkins University, where I spent six months with him), the leading authority in theoretical chemistry in the USA and outside the USA; and Professor Per Olov Löwdin, who was six months a professor at Uppsala University in Sweden and six months at the University of Florida in Gainesville, Florida, an outstanding scientist who was delighted to hear about Nobel. For me, these early contacts were important as an encouragement to continue with the project, which some may have viewed as being on the border of sanity and insanity.

With time, I became encouraged and made a few public demonstrations of Nobel. I attended a smaller international meeting of the Language Origin Society (the international society for the study of the origins and evolution of language) in Northern Illinois University, De Kalb, Illinois, in 1991, where I presented elementary outline of Nobel. In 1996, Jeff Long, senior research scientist in the Notational Engineering Laboratory of George Washington University, Washington, D.C., organized a conference, NOTATE'96, at which I presented a talk, "Nobel—Universal Pictographic Language," and also prepared a manuscript for the proceedings, which it appears has never been published, which I believe was well received. The next year I attended the session NOTATE'97 as a part of the Semiotic Society of America annual meeting in Louisville, Kentucky, for which I prepared a talk entitled "Synonyms and Antonyms in Nobel—A Pictographic Sign Language." After my presentation, Professor Farouk Y. Seif, from the Center for Creative Change, Antioch University, Seattle, Washington, who is a registered architect, artist, and design consultant, approached me and expressed interest in Nobel. It was he, or possibly someone else, who joined a brief discussion that mentioned that my approach to construction of Nobel is of interest from linguistic position in trying to express so many different signs by a set of very limited number of signs. Recall now C. E. Eckersley and C. K. Ogden, who based their approach of simplified English on one thousand or eight hundred words, respectively, while here we speak of less than two hundred signs, if modifications of a dozen signs are counted separately as different signs.

I have also presented seminars on Nobel, one in the Department of Mathematics and Computer Science at Drake University and one at the National Institute of Chemistry, Ljubljana, Slovenia, of which recently I became honorary fellow. Meanwhile, I had a few direct inputs from a few individuals worth mentioning. During my six months' stay at Cornell University, where I was on a sabbatical leave, I joined the group of Professor Roald Hoffmann, who actually was at the same time on sabbatical in Sweden but would visit Ithaca occasionally. One late evening, around 10:00 PM, unexpectedly he came (from Sweden) to his office while in the room of his secretary where I was spreading my pages of Nobel. Glancing at these, Roald Hoffmann (Nobel laureate in chemistry 1981) pointed out that I could consider using calligraphic pen for drawing pictograms, which on few occasions I did. I was working at that time to complete a dictionary of Nobel, a project which is still underway. At one stage, I sent him a copy of the dictionary. In an accompanying letter, I mentioned to Roald, in view of his having published books of poetry, "This is not poetry." To this, to my surprise, Roald replied that there are some elements of poetry in Nobel. He in particular mentioned the word "complete," which is a superposition of "body" and "mind" as being an example.

My encounter with an outstanding literature giant was through mail. Sometime in the late 1990s, I got e-mail from a lady in Germany, Margit Galli, who "finally found me" and asked for some information on Nobel, as she was working on a dissertation on languages. I sent her some material and asked how she had found about me and Nobel, in view of the fact that nothing had been published about Nobel. She sent me a chapter of a book of Umberto Eco (b. 1932), Italian writer, known worldwide for his books, in particular *The Name of the Rose* and *Foucault's Pendulum,* and perhaps less known for his critical essays on literature, aesthetics, and semiotics (the study of signs and symbols, their origin and meaning). The book, entitled *The Search for the Perfect Language,* first appeared in Italian in 1993 and was translated into German in 1997. In this chapter, on less than a half page, Umberto Eco had mentioned Nobel. He outlined two signs of Nobel in his book, one of which was the sign for "abdicate," which is represented in Nobel as "throw crown into a basket." I came across this combination recalling how in 1936 King Edward VIII of Great Britain, who married Mrs. Simpson, an American divorcée, was forced to abdicate, to "throw crown into a basket." The book *The Search for the Perfect Language* was translated into Croatian in 2004 and is also available in English.

When preparing this epilogue, and after meeting and communicating with several persons, I was concerned of misquoting some people. So I wrote some letters to be sure who made what comment. I was glad that I correctly identified Margit Galli, as confirmed by her more recent letter (of November 11, 2007):

Dear Mr. Randic,

Yes, I am the Margit Galli who once inquired about your symbolic language "Nobel". At that time I was graduating at the Hochschule Pforzheim with a work on visual communication. Meanwhile I moved into graphic design, professionally, but I was very pleased to learn about the progress you made with your book. Thank you for remembering me and for sending me this e-mail.

Yours sincerely,
Margit Galli

Speaking of semiotics, I learned though the Internet that Giordano Bruno, who was burned alive in the year 1600 in Rome as a heretic, that Giordano Bruno, whom the *Encyclopedia Britannica* describes as "*Italian representative of late Renaissance thought, whose teaching and writing, encompassing philosophy, cosmology, theology, mathematics and creative literature, constantly brought him into collision with orthodox opinion and lead him to heretics death . . .*" was a forerunner of semiotics. In 1998 in a report by Ronald A. T. Judy, "Some notes on the status of Global English in Tunisia," one can find the following:

> We need only recall the numerous antecedent attempts at achieving an artificial language of global extension, such as Milan Randic's Nobel or even Father Marin Mersenne's rumor of des Vallees's nouvelle langue, or of efforts to return to the "original" language of humanity, such as the Christian Kabbalism of Raymond Lull (Ars Magna) or Giordano Bruno (Ars Combintoria), to understand that when we speak today about English as global, we intend something altogether different from a perfect "original" language. That is to say, English as a global language is, in fact, not the consequence of a project for linguistic perfection . . . .

To be mentioned in a company of such outstanding dignitaries as mathematician Marin Mersenne (1588-1648), who is best known today for the so-called Mersenne prime numbers (which are of the form 2P-1 and for p=4253 was the first prime number having more than one thousand digits), Raymond or Ramon Lull (1232-1315), pioneer of early attempt to use logical means to produce knowledge, and the historic figure of Giordano Bruno (1548-1600) is an extraordinary compliment that one cannot even dream of. While I remain eternally indebted and honored for the compliment given, I am equally astounded to find a reference to Nobel, which at that time and until this book came out, existed mostly only in my thoughts and my notes.

Occasionally, I would outline elements of Nobel to people met at random. In all these encounters, people expressed interest and appeared friendly toward Nobel. I may add two more ladies that I met accidentally, one in Duluth, Minnesota, and one in Ljubljana, Slovenia, who mentioned potential use of Nobel. The lady from Duluth, Rhonda Peterson, was a professional nurse, and in particular was involved in caring for stroke and post-operative patients. She is a coauthor of a medical book written with her doctor on the topic of recovery of trauma and recovery of brain-damaged patients. She indicated that Nobel can perhaps be helpful for teaching patients that temporarily lost knowledge of writing and communication. The lady from Ljubljana, Nataša Plausteiner, was by profession a translator at conferences where she would after a speaker say a few sentences that translate into another language. These people developed a kind of their own abbreviations for some words that would often repeat, something that one could loosely refer to as abbreviation of stenography—so that they can reproduce longer sections of one's presentation.

I should also mention that most of the people whom I, in more recent years, exposed to Nobel, expressed some interest, so I became somewhat bold and on a few occasions at the end of my professional seminars on theoretical and mathematical chemistry, I would show one or two transparencies of Nobel. On the occasion of celebration of the twenty-fifth anniversary of one of my research publications outlining construction of an early successful mathematical descriptor for molecules, which was organized as a special symposium held in Washington, D.C., during the annual meeting of the American Chemical Society, I mentioned Nobel and showed a table in which were depicted a set of signs involving hooks and overlapping hooks leading to signs for hook-connection-network; fact-information-knowledge;

fiction-imagination-fantasy; and speculation-hypothesis-theory. I thought this illustration involving words relevant to science to be appropriate for a scientific meeting. Professor L. H. Hall, who was one of the organizers of the meeting, asked for a copy of the transparency—and I was happy to oblige and gave him the original transparency. Professor Jure Zupan, from the National Institute of Chemistry in Ljubljana, Slovenia, and one-time Minister for Science and Higher Education of Slovenia, made a number of useful comments pointing to a need for grammar rules, which only more recently I gave attention to. Mrs. Tatjana Lorković, a librarian of the University of Iowa, and currently librarian at Yale University, was one of a few people who suggested a particular sign for Nobel, which I adopted. After showing her the sign for "life," heart with signal suggesting "beating of alive heart," she suggested a sign of a heart with a "flat" line to be a sign for death. I took this suggestion to represent "clinical death," the last phase of a life, when a heart stops beating. Finally, I should add the patience of Dr. Jan Galik, from Košice, Slovakia, a postdoctoral visitor in the neurophysiology laboratory of my wife, who edited the letter *A* of the English-Nobel dictionary by painstakingly copying all graphic materials for each letter individually so that I can revise the material any time and any sign individually, without necessity to redraw pictures of signs afresh. Todd Mountjoy, Library Director, University of Wisconsin—Fond du Lac has also expressed interest in Nobel and was in communication with me.

I should add also contributions that I received from different people over many years and from whom I learned more about artificial languages, universal languages and graphical languages. For example, Professor Hideyuki Narumi, from Hokkaido University, Sapporo, Japan, sent me a book on Tompa graphical language. Professor Mike Marty, dean of the college of liberal arts and sciences sent me a book by Elmer Joseph Hankes, *A Universal Second Language* (preliminary edition, The Hankes Foundation, Minneapolis, Minnesota, 1992). Editors of the *Journal of Universal Language*, published by the Institute for Universal Language, Sejong Institution, Seoul, Korea, sent me few complimentary issues of the Journal.

I have to add that occasionally one would come across some skeptical opinions or lack of interest. I have been disappointed that on the occasion of Eighty-sixth Congress of Esperanto, which was held in Zagreb, July 21-28, 2001, I had prepared about one hundred pages of the dictionary of Esperanto-Nobel and thought of making a short presentation, but never got any response from organizers. It is possible that they never received my correspondence, but it is also possible that they ignored it.

Finally, I wish to thank Professor Vjera Krstelj from the Faculty of Naval Architecture and Engineering of the University of Zagreb, my youngest sister, for initiative and encouragement to terminate writing of this book and search for a publisher, and Professor Tomaž Pisanski, from the Department of Mathematics, University of Ljubljana, Ljubljana, Slovenia, for engaging his daughter, a linguist, to make an independent evaluation of the material for this book.

There is no end in improving Nobel, as illustrated by a comment of my cardiologist Dr. Wayne Miller, from the famous Mayo Clinic in Rochester, MN, who visited me when I was making final corrections for this book. After showing him less than hundred combinations of sign, which included signs for BLOOD before I was able to continue he made signs for BLEEDING and HEMORRHAGE. I had the same sign for bleeding but I thought that hemorrhage is synonym for bleeding and interpreted the current sign for hemorrhage to stand for hemophilia, serious hereditary bleeding sickness. In this exchange I learned that hemorrhage is a condition of heavy bleeding and is not synonym for bleeding and Nobel was enriched with a sign for hemorrhage and novel sign for hemophilia as BLEEDING SICKNESS. This only shows that it is never too late to improve and enrich the vocabulary of Nobel.

I would also like to thank Dr. Dejan Plavšić, from the Institute Rudjer Bošković in Zagreb, Croatia, for detecting some inaccuracies in the text that have been corrected. Last but not least the author would like to express thanks to Judith Cruz, Caryl Grecia, and Carla Cobar of Xlibris copyediting service for outstanding work on polishing my English, correcting mistakes and improving presentation of material.

I am ending with expressing great appreciation to Hippocrene Books, Inc., New York, publisher of the *Dictionary of 1000 Chinese Proverbs* (edited by Marjorie Lin and Schalk Leonard), from which I selected one hundred proverbs to illustrate Nobel. Here is their letter granting permission:

From: Hippocrene Books
To: 'milan randic'
Sent: Monday, December 10, 2007 8:54 AM
Subject: RE: Proposal for a Book

Dear Mr. Randic,

Many apologies for the delay in responding to you on this issue, Hippocrene has undergone a few changes in the past months, including the departure of the staff member that would typically handle copyright matters. Unfortunately, your request joined a long backlog and only recently emerged at the top.

After a review of your request by our editorial board, the following decision was made: Hippocrene Books grants permission to Milan Randic to reproduce approximately 100 proverbs from *Dictionary of 1,000 Chinese Proverbs*, edited by Marjorie Lin and Schalk Leonard (Hippocrene Books, 1998) in his book, Nobel, Universal Language.

This permission is granted free of charge, but we request that you cite the source of the proverbs in your publication.

We thank you for your patience and wish you success in your publishing endeavor.

Regards,
Hippocrene Books
171 Madison Avenue, Suite 1602
New York, New York 10016
212-685-4371
fax 212-779-9338
hippocrene.books@verizon.net

The financial contribution for publishing of this book was made by the Ministry of Science, Higher Education and Sports of the Republic of Croatia through the understanding and enthusiastic support for Nobel by Professor Dražen Vikić-Topić, Treasurer of the International Academy of Mathematical Chemistry and the State Secretary for Science and Higher Education of the Republic of Croatia.

Word Index

W

Index

Edwards Brothers,Inc!
Thorofare, NJ 08086
10 June, 2010
BA2010161